AF722824

LIBRARY OF NEW TESTAMENT STUDIES

594

Formerly The Journal For The Study Of The New Testament Supplement Series

Editor
Chris Keith

Editorial Board
Dale C. Allison, John M.G. Barclay, Lynn H. Cohick, R. Alan Culpepper, Craig A. Evans, Robert Fowler, Simon J. Gathercole, Juan Hernandez, John S. Kloppenborg, Michael Labahn, Love L. Sechrest, Robert Wall, Steve Walton, Catrin H. Williams

BIBLE AND BEDLAM

Madness, Sanism, and New Testament Interpretation

Louise J. Lawrence

t&tclark

LONDON • NEW YORK • OXFORD • NEW DELHI • SYDNEY

T&T CLARK
Bloomsbury Publishing Plc
50 Bedford Square, London, WC1B 3DP, UK
1385 Broadway, New York, NY 10018, USA

BLOOMSBURY, T&T CLARK and the T&T Clark logo are trademarks of
Bloomsbury Publishing Plc

First published in Great Britain 2018

Copyright © Louise J. Lawrence, 2018

Louise J. Lawrence has asserted her right under the Copyright,
Designs and Patents Act, 1988, to be identified as Author of this work.

For legal purposes the Acknowledgements in the Preface on pp. vi–vii constitute an extension of this copyright page.

All rights reserved. No part of this publication may be reproduced or transmitted in any form or by any means, electronic or mechanical, including photocopying, recording, or any information storage or retrieval system, without prior permission in writing from the publishers.

Bloomsbury Publishing Plc does not have any control over, or responsibility for, any third-party websites referred to or in this book. All internet addresses given in this book were correct at the time of going to press. The author and publisher regret any inconvenience caused if addresses have changed or sites have ceased to exist, but can accept no responsibility for any such changes.

A catalogue record for this book is available from the British Library.

A catalog record for this book is available from the Library of Congress.

ISBN: HB: 978-0-5676-5753-4
ePDF: 978-0-5676-5754-1
eBook: 978-0-5676-8433-2

Series: Library of New Testament Studies, ISSN 2513–8790, volume 594

Typeset by Newgen KnowledgeWorks Pvt. Ltd., Chennai, India
Printed and bound in Great Britain

To find out more about our authors and books visit www.bloomsbury.com
and sign up for our newsletters.

JKM Library
1100 East 55th Street
Chicago, IL 60615

CONTENTS

PREFACE

In 1991, a young British woman committed suicide in a Californian apartment. Her husband was also found dead in an adjacent room. The complex circumstances of the event garnered controversy, legal proceedings and significant press attention. The woman's psychiatric history (and brief incarceration) soon became a key lens through which her identity was reported and inscribed within the media. She was stigmatized as a deviant – one who is perceived to transgress normative boundaries – with a chaotic sexual history, a period of illegal residency and various anarchic, dangerous and risk-taking behaviours projected onto her character. As such, her story can be numbered among the annals of madness, which have all too easily, from biblical times onwards, associated mental distress with 'moral insanity' and deviations from accepted patterns of social behaviour. This book has, in many ways, been inspired by her story and others like it. For behind the sensationalized and stigmatizing spectacles of madness, more complex personal accounts and experiences often lie. Moreover, for every flattened 'mad' character, there are others who recall their rounded lives far more richly, and who loved them as a sibling, a child or a friend.

Writing this book has incurred many debts. I am appreciative of the University of Exeter for granting me internal research leave to write a substantial part of this manuscript, and for funding a trip to Wellcome Collection's 'Bedlam: The Asylum and Beyond' exhibition in 2016. I am also grateful for the continued support of my brilliant colleagues in the Department of Theology and Religion at The University of Exeter. Professor David Horrell read and commented on draft chapters at various stages of completion with his usual incisive and discerning eye, and, as always, offered encouragement and friendship (and lots of coffee) throughout. Professor Morwenna Ludlow, Dr. Susannah Cornwall and Dr. Helen John have also provided really helpful feedback on drafts of this book for which I am very grateful. The students on my 'Deviant Bodies: Disability Studies and the New Testament' module have also thoughtfully engaged with the issues this project seeks to address and, through our work together, have shaped my thinking in various ways. Thanks also to my dad who has, once again, selflessly and painstakingly proofread the entire manuscript.

I am also indebted to the Bridge Collective and Hearing Voices Network in Exeter for letting me conduct research sessions with participants there. Being able to listen to 'voices of experience' and bridge, in some small way, a gap between the academy and advocacy – so central to the tenets of mad studies – was invaluable. I also valued the feedback from the University of Cambridge's New Testament Research Seminar, when I delivered a version of Chapter 4 to them in 2016 and the participants of the Luke-Acts seminar at SBL annual meeting in Boston in 2017, when I delivered a version of Chapter 3 of this book.

Finally, and most importantly, my heartfelt thanks go to my family. Nana and Papa – your support, care and love, as always, have been unstinting and awe-inspiring – thank you so much for looking after us all. You truly are the best mum and dad in the whole wide world! Dan and Andrew – my cherished and beloved 'boys' – thank you so much for sharing your life, love and laughter with me, and for keeping me 'sane' even after long hours in the little room. While sometimes it can feel like our busy lives mirror the proverbial Bedlam, if the term 'asylum' can be reclaimed as a sanctuary, then I am so pleased to be sharing our madhouse with you two (. . . and a couple of dozen dinosaurs)!

INTRODUCTION: BIBLE AND BEDLAM

The Wellcome Collection's 2016 exhibition entitled 'Bedlam: The Asylum and Beyond'[1] set out to illustrate and interrogate notions of madness and its treatment through the cameo lens of the oldest psychiatric institution in Western Europe[2] – Bethlem Hospital in London – from which the colloquial term 'Bedlam' is derived. The exhibition traced different historical moments of this institution and the shifting sociocultural estimations of madness that these inevitably reflect. Bedlam has, of course, long served in popular imagination as an iconic emblem of society's 'segregative response to insanity'.[3] Confining 'the mad' within its walls for centuries, it has also frequently been correlated with madness itself, functioning in popular imagination as a byword 'for the chaos, pandemonium, and loss of control, barbarism, animality and atavism, that madness [is] held to represent'.[4] Bedlam's mythical notoriety is not completely unjustified. As a facility of social control, all number of characters found themselves within its walls: these included street people, outspoken wives and critics of public officials. Under the direction of the infamous John Munro in the late eighteenth century Bedlam's inmates were exhibited en masse as spectacles for the general public's sardonic amusement.[5] As

1. Details available online at: https://wellcomecollection.org/bedlam.

2. Guest curator Mike Jay states that 'its story is the perfect focus … to explore how medicine, art and culture define mental illness, and the big questions it raises about the individual and society'. *Bedlam: The Asylum and Beyond* (2016). Available online at: https://wellcomecollection.org/press/bedlam-asylum-and-beyond-opens-wellcome-collection.

3. Simon Cross, 'Bedlam in Mind: Seeing and Reading Historical Images of Madness', *European Journal of Cultural Studies* 15(1) (2012), 19–34, 19.

4. Jonathan Andrews, 'Bedlam Revisited: A History of Bethlem Hospital 1634–1770', PhD thesis, Queen Mary, London University (1991). Available online at: https://qmro.qmul.ac.uk/xmlui/bitstream/handle/123456789/1365/ANDREWSBedlamRevisited1991.pdf?sequence=1, 1.

5. Steve Rudd, 'Bedlam: A Madhouse by Any Other Name Is Still a Jail!' (no date). Available online at: http://www.bible.ca/psychiatry/psychiatry-history-bedlam-bethlem-bethlehem.htm.

such, many claimed Bedlam acted as a reflection of societal problems, its 'inmates a didactic spectacle of the dangers of excess'.[6]

Can, however, Bedlam (variously conceived of as a physical and/or ideological space) also evoke visions of alternative futures for madness, in which the boundaries between 'sanity' and 'insanity' are deconstructed and damaging mythologies concerning 'different' human experiences are challenged? Mike Jay and Bárbara Rodríguez Muñoz, the co-curators of the Wellcome exhibition, think that it can. However, in order to do so, certain 'transgressions of the archive'[7] need to be instigated. Namely, revisiting and recasting the past by listening to the contemporary voices of those who have variously been maligned, mentalized[8] and muted in medical, social and cultural arenas on account of their presumed madness, mental state and/or social deviance. Such themes are graphically implied in the performance installation *Asylum* (2014) by Czech artist Eva Koťátková, which fronts the entire exhibition.[9] This piece, stimulated by dialogues with patients in psychiatric facilities in Prague, features a table-height plinth buttressing a series of objects, including 'cages, photographs, drawings, diagrams [and] miniature architectural elements'.[10] Live heads and arms interact with the objects through holes in the platform, thereby animating the construction. These dramatize the associations between those bodies and minds deemed 'other' and the oppressive social structures which frequently besiege and censor them. Koťátková seeks to expose the ways such bodies often become segregated and handicapped by their circumstances but can also at times subversively protest against their situation by 'develop[ing] alternative means to communicate', represented in this exhibit through objects, props and devices that 'build parallel identities'[11] and which challenge the repressive structures surrounding them.

6. Andrews, 'Bedlam', 2.

7. 'Transgress the archive' was a turn of phrase used within questions by Dr. Gregory Cuéllar, a plenary speaker at a University of Exeter conference entitled 'Ethnicity/Race/Religion: Identities, Ideologies, and Intersections in Biblical Texts and Interpretation' (9–11 August 2016). Cuéllar was talking about recovering muted racialized voices.

8. 'The mentalized (the "mentally ill person", the "schizophrenic", the "depressive", the "anxious", the "obsessive", the "addictive personality").' See Erick Fabris, 'Experiences Labelled Psychotic: A Settler's Autoethnography beyond Psychosic Narrative', PhD thesis, University of Toronto (2012). Available online at: https://tspace.library.utoronto.ca/bitstream/1807/33990/1/Fabris_Erick_P_201211_PhD_thesis.pdf, xxxix.

9. 'The surreal nature of the piece conveys the frequently dissociative impact of mental illness. This effect is accentuated by actors, who animate the work with parts of their body, highlighting themes of incompleteness and disintegration, restraint and protection.' Howard Ryland, 'New Wellcome Exhibition Invites You into Bedlam' (2016). Available online at: http://londonist.com/2016/09/bedlam-the-inside-story.

10. Mark Rappolt, 'Eva Koťátková', *Art Review Asia* (2016). Available online at: http://artreview.com/features/april_2016_feature_eva_kotatkova/, no pages.

11. Cited in gallery advert, *Eva Koťátková* International Studio & Curatorial Program (ISCP), New York, 2 February–8 April 2016. Available online at: http://www.e-flux.com/announcements/eva-kotatkova-error.

This book will likewise attempt to construct hybrid exhibits that transgress the normative archives of Western biblical scholarship with regard to madness.[12] It will, for the first time, expose and challenge latent 'sanism' (prejudice against individuals who are diagnosed or perceived as mentally ill) and the 'normativity' which grounds prejudice against perceived 'disordered' embodiments and/or minds within the discipline.[13] My aim is *not* to undertake a historical enquiry into madness in the first-century contexts from which New Testament writings emerge, nor indeed to gaze voyeuristically on the performances of madness by specific biblical characters, but rather to interrogate and expose the ways in which contemporary biblical interpretations can be positioned within broader Western cultural narratives, politics, ideologies and dynamics surrounding sanity,

12. There are very few comparative titles. Much energy has been devoted to historical analyses of demon possession, exorcism and perceived madness in the ancient world and New Testament: Graham Twelftree, *Jesus the Miracle Worker: A Historical and Theological Study* (Downers Grove, IL: Intervarsity Press, 1999); John Christopher Thomas, *The Devil, Disease and Deliverance: Origins of Illness in New Testament Thought* (Sheffield: Sheffield Academic Press, 1998); Eric Sorensen, *Possession and Exorcism in the New Testament and Early Christianity* (Tubingen: Mohr Siebeck, 2002). Some limited interface with medical anthropology and biblical studies has been initiated: John Pilch, *Healing in the New Testament: Insights from Medical Anthropology* (Minneapolis: Fortress Press, 2000). Likewise, disability studies have increasingly impacted biblical studies. See Hector Avalos, Sarah Melcher and Jeremy Schipper (eds), *This Abled Body: Rethinking Disabilities in Biblical Studies* (Atlanta: Society of Biblical Literature, 2007); Candida Moss and Jeremy Schipper (eds), *Disability Studies and Biblical Literature* (New York: Palgrave Macmillan, 2011); and Saul Olyan, *Disability in the Hebrew Bible: Interpreting Mental and Physical Differences* (Cambridge: Cambridge University Press, 2008). However, for the most part, this interface has concentrated on physical disability, or if broaching mental disability at all tends to focus solely on the social stigma associated with such conditions, rather than refiguring characters in light of voices from experience. Literature outside biblical studies has broached theological appropriations of mental disabilities and accessibility issues for churches. See Amos Yong, *Theology and Down Syndrome: Reimagining Disability in Late Modernity* (Waco: Baylor University Press, 2007); Stanley Hauerwas, 'Community and Diversity: The Tyranny of Normality', in John Swinton (ed.), *Critical Reflections on Stanley Hauerwas' Theology of Disability* (New York: Haworth Pastoral Press, 2004), 37–43. No works to my knowledge have concentrated on sanism or Mad-positive readings of biblical texts. The nearest book methodologically to the one proposed here is my own previous work which focused on refiguring sensory-disabled characters (blind/deaf/untouchables) in light of sensory anthropology and disability studies. See Louise Lawrence, *Sense and Stigma in the Gospels: Depictions of Sensory-Disabled Characters* (Oxford: Oxford University Press, 2013). In a rather different vein, Simon Mainwaring's important contextual Bible studies among those perceived to have 'poor mental health' will be discussed more fully in Chapter 5. See Simon Mainwaring, *Mark, Mutuality and Mental Health* (Atlanta: SBL Press, 2014).

13. Lynn Tang, *Recovery, Mental Health and Inequality* (London: Routledge, 2017), 5.

insanity and mental illness.[14] I aim to question under what structures and power conditions certain individuals are defined as mad, irrational or insane and to ask whose interests such labelling serves.

More specific goals are threefold: first, to probe and critically question the exclusion and stereotyping of certain biblical characters and scholars perceived as 'mad'. I contend the discipline has, at times, uncritically absorbed medical models (which view mental illness as a functional or biological defect in need of diagnosis and treatment). The discipline has also perpetuated (often damaging) social/cultural assumptions surrounding such conditions, for example, violence, extremity, chaos, genius or creativity, and often communicated in psy-medical terms (psychosis, schizophrenia, asociality) and psy-legal terms (insanity, incapacity) and so on.[15] Second, I will initiate creative exchanges between biblical texts, interpretations and contemporary voices from 'mad' studies and sources (autobiographies, memoirs, etc.), which are designed to critically disturb, disrupt and displace commonly projected (and often pejorative) assumptions surrounding 'madness'. Voices of those subject to diagnostic labelling such as autism, schizophrenia and/or psychosis are among those juxtaposed here with selected biblical interpretations and texts. I propose that these exegetical experiments,

14. James Crossley espouses a similar broad cultural stance in his interrogation of neoliberal contexts (both scholarly and 'not-so-scholarly') in relation to the study of the historical Jesus. He writes that 'they are all part of an interconnected cultural context and removing scholarship from this context would only serve to imply that scholarship is somehow beyond the apparent trivialities of contemporary culture and protected from the dirtiness of the outside world ... This is why the emphasis could be placed on the greatest historical critic of our age, an obscure article in an evangelical journal or a rant on a blog: they all provide insight into our cultural contexts, irrespective of how good or bad they are'. James Crossley, *Jesus in an Age of Neoliberalism: Quests, Scholarship and Ideology* (Durham: Acumen Press, 2012), 9.

15. Brenda LeFrançois et al., 'Glossary of Terms, Madness', in Brenda LeFrançois et al. (eds), *Mad Matters* (Ontario: Canadian Scholars Press, 2013), 334–40, 337. Joel Gold and Ian Gold note that 'words that begin with psych (from the Greek psyche, meaning "mind" or "soul") have proliferated in our language. A number refer to the scientific study of a facet of mental life. Psychopathology is the study of abnormal or disordered psychology. Psychiatry in contrast, refers more narrowly to the medical profession concerned with psychopathology – its investigation as well as its treatment – and it itself distinguished from the profession of clinical psychology in that its practitioners are physicians and can prescribe medications. Clinical psychologists, psychiatrists and clinical social workers may practice one form or another of psychotherapy – the treatment of mental disorder by psychological rather than physical means. Psychoanalysis refers to a particular movement in psychiatry based on Sigmund Freud and his disciples... Psychosis is distinct from psychopathy, a mental disorder characterised by anti-social behaviour, callousness, and impulsivity among other features'. Joel Gold and Ian Gold, *Suspicious Minds: How Culture Shapes Madness* (New York: Free Press, 2015), xxv.

which draw on the experiences of post-1970 survivors/consumers/ex-patients and neurodiverse and mad-identified groups, can function as communicative spaces where 'norms' of madness can be renegotiated. Such perspectives resist biomedical models that frame 'madness' as pathology, deficit or mental disorder and instead constructively forefront lived experience in all its diversity. Third, I will seek to highlight the widespread ideological 'gatekeeping' – 'protection' and 'policing' of madness in both Western history and scholarship – with regard to the celebrated biblical figures of Jesus and Paul.

This book is by no means comprehensive: it constitutes the opening of a conversation, rather than a final word. It also necessarily spends much time scoping out research landscapes and themes familiar within mad studies, but largely absent hitherto from considerations in biblical studies. Ultimately, I hope that perspectives presented here will question and destabilize some widely held (and often unacknowledged) assumptions concerning madness in the field in which I primarily work.

Defining Madness

It is essential at the outset to provide some orientation to the intentional employment of the term 'madness' in this book. 'Madness' is a word which is notoriously hard to concretely define. The terminology of 'madness' evokes a variety of vivid and controlling images and associations[16] and, as such, has been employed within a variety of discourses. Here, I use it primarily to denote the following social, cultural and discursively constructed nexus of ideas: (a) madness as deviance, (b) madness as protest and (c) madness as resistance to biomedical/psychiatric or pathological models.

Madness as Deviance

Madness has frequently been used as a deviance label to represent the binary antithesis of more normative viewpoints, values or positions and often furnishes casual (and derogatory) slurs ('mad', 'mental', 'psycho', 'crazy') of those deemed 'other'. While accounts of the causes and treatments of perceived 'madness' have diverged significantly throughout recorded history and cross-culturally, the social stigma and deviance commonly associated with such labelling is widely attested. As Elvira Sanchez-Blake and Laura Kanost reveal, 'From the ship of fools and mythic allegories to asylums and politics of marginalization, relations of power and exclusion have intersected in the definitions of madness and social control.'[17]

16. Mike Jay, *This Way Madness Lies: The Asylum and Beyond* (Wellcome Collection, Thames and Hudson, 2016), 12.

17. Elvira Sanchez-Blake and Laura Kanost, *Latin American Women and the Literature of Madness: Narratives at the Crossroads of Gender, Politics and the Mind* (North Carolina: McFarland and Co, 2015), 3.

Louis Sass, building on Michel Foucault's influential work in the area, notes how the 'civilized' have frequently been pitted against the 'mad'. The former are assumed to be cultured, competent, rational, self-controlled and, by means of these traits, able to exist harmoniously with others of a similar status. In contrast, the latter are viewed as 'asocial and irrational … refusing (or being unable) to cooperate with others, to organize behaviour, or to adapt to prevailing norms'.[18]

The above is reflected in the construction of madness as deviance in biblical literatures, where the concept of madness is variously employed to denote malevolence, something perceived as contrary to normative conduct, or as a label intended to discredit opponents. Thus, Deuteronomy pictures madness as a punishment exacted on those that do not submit to divine will: 'you shall be continually abused and crushed, and driven mad (שׁגע) by the sight that your eyes shall see' (Deut. 28:33–34). Madness is also frequently pitted against wisdom. Qoheleth declares that 'I applied my mind to know wisdom and to know madness (שׁגע) and folly' (Eccl. 1:17; see also 7:25). Moreover, evil is associated with 'madness (שׁגע) in their hearts' (Eccl. 9:3). Madness is also a performance contrary to normate behaviour as exemplified by David's temporary enactment of madness: 'he pretended to be mad when in their presence' (1 Sam. 21:13) by scratching doors and dribbling because of his fear of Achish. In John's Gospel, the Jews denounce Jesus and his words as deviant through reference to his presumed insanity: 'He has a demon and is out of his mind (μαίνεται). Why listen to him?' (Jn 10:20). Paul is also aware, in his first letter to the Corinthians, of how charismatic congregational behaviour could be perceived as abnormal to outsiders: 'If therefore the whole church comes together and all speak in tongues, and outsiders or unbelievers enter, will they not say that you are out of your mind (μαίνεται)?' (1 Cor. 14:23). Saul Olyan attests that Hebrew Bible terminology used to classify what he identifies as 'mentally disturbed persons' and their distinguishing actions are 'derogatory in nature'. He also illustrates how these disparaging undertones are reproduced in English translations of Hebrew terms: 'e.g. *mešugga* as "madman"; *petî* as "simple minded"' and so on.[19]

Madness as Protest

Madness has also been understood as political dissent, resistance and revolt against a normative patriarchal or colonial status quo. In this sense, 'madness' can be

18. Louis Sass, 'Civilized Madness: Schizophrenia, Self-Consciousness and the Modern Mind', *History of the Human Sciences* 7 (1994), 83–120, 83. David Mitchell and Sharon Snyder's thesis that disability commonly serves within literature as a representation of cultural 'otherness' or as an anti-type of social norms – so-called narrative prosthetics – also resonates with madness as representative of deviance. David Mitchell and Sharon Snyder, *Narrative Prosthetics: Disability and the Dependencies of Discourse* (Michigan: University of Michigan Press, 2000).

19. Saul Olyan, *Disability in the Hebrew Bible: Interpreting Mental and Physical Differences* (Cambridge: Cambridge University Press, 2008), 63.

understood as a feminist and/or postcolonial vehicle of subversion; a purposeful 'performance rather than a manifestation of mental illness in order to protect those who speak and act out against tyranny'.[20] Paul Hollenbach, for example, has conceptualized the shrieks and bodily performances of the demoniac, Legion (Mk 5:1–20), as protests against the colonizing imperial power. Exiled from society, bound and chained among the tombs and writhing around scratching himself, Hollenbach claims Legion's madness allowed him to embody 'what he could not do as sane, namely, express his total hostility to the Romans'.[21]

Madness as Resistance to Biomedical/Psychiatric or Pathological Models

Crucially for the present project, 'madness' is *not* a term or idiom employed within biomedical models,[22] or used within psy-disciplines, which prefer the language of 'mental illness', 'disorder' and/or 'disease'.[23] The biomedical model has been largely dominant (and dominating) in Western culture. The post-1970 era has witnessed three revised publications of the American Psychiatric Association's *Diagnostic and Statistical Manual of Mental Disorders* (*DSM-III* [1980], *DSM-IV* [2000] and *DSM-5* [2013]),[24] a reference work which has become known as the 'Bible of Psychiatry'.[25] These editions have sought to catalogue and describe 'mental

20. Robert Colson, 'The Performance of Madness as Resistance in Nuruddin Farah's Close Sesame', *Ariel: A Review of International English Literature* 46(4) (2015), 1–35, 1.

21. Paul W. Hollenbach, 'Jesus, Demoniacs, and Public Authorities: A Socio-historical Study', *Journal of the American Academy of Religion* 49(4) (1981), 567–88, 581. Postcolonial readings of the performance on Legion also touch upon this theme. See Richard Horsley, *Jesus and the Powers: Conflict, Covenant and the Hope of the Poor* (Minneapolis: Augsburg Fortress, 2011), 128. Christian Strecker contends that possession as performance often enacts behaviour which culture views as 'demonic'. See Christian Strecker, 'Jesus and the Demoniacs', in Wolfgang Stegemann, Bruce Malina and Gerd Theissen (eds), *The Social Setting of Jesus and the Gospels* (Minneapolis: Fortress Press, 2002), 117–34, 122.

22. Anna Harpin and Juliet Foster, 'Introduction: Locating Madness and Performance', in Anna Harpin and Juliet Foster (eds), *Performance, Madness and Psychiatry: Isolated Acts* (Basingstoke: Palgrave Macmillan, 2014), 1–18, 4.

23. Annina Yla-Kapee, 'Telling Madness: Narrative, Diagnosis, Power and Literary Theory', PhD thesis, University of Tampere (2014). Available online at: https://tampub.uta.fi/bitstream/handle/10024/96148/978-951-44-9557-1.pdf?sequence=1, 28. As I am dealing in part with ancient literary evidence, long predating such psy-centric understandings of mental disorders, the use of 'madness' also signifies a certain 'agnosticism' of my data-set with regard to medical models.

24. American Psychiatric Association, *Diagnostic and Statistical Manual of Mental Disorders*, 3rd, 4th and 5th edns (Washington: American Psychological Press, 1980; 2000; 2013).

25. 'A cultural icon', 'the object of undue worship'. See Mark Green, 'DSM-5: Rewriting the Bible', *Progress in Neurology and Psychiatry* (2013), 24–6, 24.

disorders' and have variously been revised in light of changing scientific, social and cultural perceptions. The post-1970 era has also, however, seen the emergence of the survivors/consumer/ex-patients movements. These, inspired by civil rights movements, sought to 'talk back' to the mental health system and defiantly employ the term 'madness' to challenge psy-centric narrations of their experience.[26] Mad perspectives seek variously to expose and reject the discriminatory practices of sanism, which – akin to racism or sexism – is based on the regular suppression of those individuals who have endured 'mental health' diagnoses (real, metaphorical or ideological) or treatment.[27] Such prejudices are often manifested in cultural associations of madness with violence, irrationality and social deviance. Akin to the politicized position of 'queer' (once a derogatory term, which has since been subversively retrieved to expose and critique heteronormativity), 'Mad-identified'[28] cultural positions denote politicized strategies of resistance against oppressive medical and cultural systems. Terminology of 'madness' in this perspective thus signifies, in Anna Harpin and Juliet Foster's words, a 'bid to operate outside the reductive terminology of health and illness in order that we may begin to recalibrate the notion of madness to encompass more than solely "ill" (that is to say bad) phenomena'.[29] This is not, of course, to dismiss or reject the distress endured by individuals; rather, it is to accept and confirm these experiences as part of a broad range of authentic human experiences. It is a bid to reinstate dignity and respect to those identities which have been constructed purely as deficient or negative: denigrated, reduced, pathologized and degraded within various medical, historical, institutional and cultural contexts.[30]

Methodologically, some orientation to the terrains I intend to 'infringe' within this project, namely, 'Mad Studies' and 'Space, Embodiment and Performance', are

26. See Stephanie LeBlanc and Anne Kinsella, 'Toward Epistemic Justice: A Critically Reflexive Examination of "Sanism" and Implications for Knowledge Generation', *Studies in Social Justice* 10(1) (2016), 59–78.

27. C. Kalinowski and P. Risser, *Identifying and Overcoming Mentalism* (InforMed Health Publishing & Training, 2005). Available online at: http://www.newmediaexplorer.org/sepp/Mentalism.pdf, 1.

28. The capitalization of 'Mad' here (akin to the capitalizing of Deaf) expresses a claim to a cultural identity, as opposed to a pathologized identity. Deaf culture sees itself as a minority language group, rather than as the medical model would claim, a people who cannot hear. Similarly, Mad-identified groups embrace their own particular and diverse experiences of the world and do not accept the flattened pathologization of those experiences as 'disorder', 'mental illness' and so on. See Richard Ingram, 'From Mad Movement to Mad Studies'. Available online at: http://www.academia.edu/15986428/From_the_Mad_movement_to_Mad_studies.

29. Harpin and Foster, 'Introduction', 4.

30. Brenda LeFrançois, Robert Menzies and Geoffrey Reaume, 'Introducing Mad Studies', in LeFrançois et al. (eds), *Mad Matters* (Ontario: Canadian Scholars Press, 2013), 1–22, 10.

also necessary by way of introduction. For 'transgressions of archives' inevitably also entail transgressions of disciplinary boundaries and contexts.

Mad Studies

Mad studies is a multidisciplinary and multivocal endeavour that has emerged over the past few decades, and is rooted within social movements of the 1970s surrounding 'Mad' identity politics, Mad pride and advocacy. It intentionally crosses scholarly and activist divides. Grass-roots movements (primarily across Canada, the United States and the United Kingdom) which have included the c/s/x community – an acronym for consumer, survivor, ex-patient, 'all of which signify particular identity politics or relations to the psychiatric system'[31] – have collectively inspired 'knowledge production and political action devoted to the critique and transcendence of psy-centred ways of thinking, behaving, relating, and being'.[32] Advocacy groups, including MindFreedom International (founded in 1986), lobby for 'equal opportunity of mental and emotional well being for all'.[33] The Icarus Project, a largely online community (founded in 2003), has likewise campaigned for self-determination, respect, responsibility, social justice and overcoming of stigma.[34]

Theoretically, mad studies builds upon the legacy of Michel Foucault's *Folie et déraison: histoire de la folie à l'âge classique* (1961),[35] a celebrated treatise on sanity's hostilities towards and exclusions of madness, and the triumph of reason in the Enlightenment age. It constructs and deploys counter-knowledge as a tactic for challenging regimes of truth surrounding madness. Mad studies and M/mad-positive academics[36] conceive of their role as 'negative workers', a term created by the nonconformist psychiatrist Franco Basaglia to portray the advantaged individuals who 'collude with the powerless to identify their needs against the interests of the bourgeois institutions, the university, the hospital, the factory'.[37] Methodologically, mad studies attempts to garner 'counter-knowledge and subjugated knowledge as a strategy for contesting regimes of truth about mental illness and psych-sciences'.[38] It is not primarily about 'studying the mad' (an individual's inner essence) but,

31. LeFrançois et al., 'Glossary, c/s/x', in LeFrançois et al. (eds), *Mad*, 335.

32. LeFrançois et al. (eds), 'Introduction', 13.

33. http://www.mindfreedom.org/who-we-are.

34. http://theicarusproject.net/mission-vision-principles/Values.

35. The complete original version was only published in English in 2006 as Michel Foucault, *History of Madness*, trans. Jonathan Murphy and Jean Khalfa (London: Routledge, 2006).

36. Mad-positive academics are not necessarily mad-identified individuals (with lived experience of certain conditions) but rather those who take seriously and advocate on behalf of mad advocacy ideals.

37. Franco Basaglia cited in N. Schper-Hughes, *Death without Weeping: The Violence of Everyday Life in Brazil* (Berkeley: University of California Press, 1992), 541.

38. LeFrançois et al., 'Introduction', 14.

rather, about exposing the systems of oppression and processes by which some individuals are labelled as such. Mel Starkman estimates that while in times past madness could variously be viewed as 'inexplicable, divine visitation, to be tolerated, pitied and sometimes even honoured', with the dawning of the age of reason 'it needed to be *explained* and could not be'.[39] More recently, with the advent of the biomedical model of psychiatry and its associated pathologizing discourses, a system which colonizes and names madness as 'other' has again attracted widespread currency in the West. Assuming dominance since the eighteenth-century enlightenment, the biomedical model more broadly informs and fosters 'the psychiatrization of experience and social problems'[40] in which those perceived as ill are contained, treated and attempted to be cured by medical professionals. As a result, in Kimberly White and Ryan Pike's estimation, 'In translating madness, a vastly diverse and arguably unquantifiable condition, into the modern definitive vernacular of illness and disease, we simultaneously erase the subjects of mental illness, namely, the mentally ill, from society, from culture, and from humanity.'[41] Some commonalities between mad studies and the social model of disability studies have legitimately been drawn, as both respectively challenge medical models which view the individual body or mind as a problem which needs to be cured and/or normalized. Both the social model of disability and mad studies show how environments, activities and common cultural assumptions surrounding bodily or mental difference are themselves disabling. Within disability studies, however, it is also true to say that there is still a marked absence of consideration of mental illness/disability, and critics have lamented the fact that disability studies seems only tooled to deal with the physical or sensory.[42] Illustrating this discrepancy, Stuart Murray notes how in David Mitchell and Sharon Snyder's magnum opus, *Narrative Prosthesis: Disability and the Dependencies of Discourse* (2000), there are more index references to 'Nazism' than to 'cognitive' or 'consciousness'. Likewise, their second volume, *Cultural Locations of Disability* (2006), stresses at the outset the need for more prominence to be given to neurological diversity. However, ultimately, in Murray's opinion this second volume had 'little to say about cognitive exceptionality generally and [only] a single paragraph on autism in a book of some

39. Mel Starkman, 'The Movement', in LeFrançois et al. (eds), *Mad*, 27–37, 27; original italicization.

40. 'The psychiatric system has also extended its administrative empire to include violent, criminal and dangerous behaviour through the use of an increasing range of labels like "personality disorder", "dangerous personality disorder" and "narcissistic personality disorder".' Peter Beresford, 'Social Work and a Social Model of Madness and Distress: Developing a Viable Role for the Future', *Social Work & Social Sciences Review* 12(2) (2005), 59–73, 63.

41. Kimberly White and Ryan Pike, 'The Making and Marketing of Mental Health Literacy in Canada', in LeFrançois et al. (eds), *Mad*, 239–64, 240.

42. Mark Osteen, 'Autism and Representation: A Comprehensive Introduction', in Mark Osteen (ed.), *Autism and Representation* (London: Routledge, 2010), 1–48, 3.

250 pages'.[43] Anne Louise Chappell sees such marginalization of mental illness within disability studies as akin to 'suggesting that the analyses of society offered by feminism are applicable only to white women',[44] a focus that (black) womanist interpretation has sought to challenge.

Advancing a moderating position, others have recently argued that 'neurodiversity', a category which understands autism, bipolarity and so on not as pathological disorders (in need of cure) but rather 'natural and valuable form[s] of human diversity',[45] holds some promise in bridging disabled and mad-identified groups in producing mad/neurodiverse forms of knowledge and praxis. In Steve Graby's words,

> [The neurodiversity movement] is particularly well placed to bring together broader categories of marginalised people(s) into a (necessarily loose, but nonetheless potentially hugely important) solidarity network of movements fighting for radical acceptance of all types of human diversity, under a broad banner of 'anti-normalisation' and challenges to supposedly 'universal' assumptions about 'human nature' that privilege majority and historically dominant groups.[46]

Brigit McWade, Damian Milton and Peter Beresford offer a similar vision in their initiation of a dialogue between disability studies, mad studies and neurodiversity which might, in their opinion,

> move us beyond the limitations of identity-based politics that create 'insiders' and 'outsiders'. In doing so it should bring us into conversation with other disenfranchised groups, such as refugees and asylum seekers, people without work, lone parents, and organised activist groups … [it will] move us beyond a focus on individual suffering towards building collective identities in order to address inequalities, such as disablement, disenfranchisement, marginalisation and impoverishment. The aim is to stop thinking about how we are the same and begin to work with our differences collectively.[47]

43. Stuart Murray, *Representing Autism: Culture, Narrative, Fascination* (Liverpool: Liverpool University Press, 2008), 8.

44. Anne Louise Chappell, 'Still Out in the Cold: People with Learning Difficulties and the Social Model of Disability', in Tom Shakespeare (ed.), *The Disability Reader: Social Science Perspectives* (London: Continuum, 1998), 211–20, 213.

45. Nick Walker, 'Neurocosmopolitanism'. Available online at: http://neurocosmopolitanism.com/neurodiversity-some-basic-terms-definitions/.

46. Steve Graby, 'Neurodiversity: Bridging the Gap between the Disabled People's Movement and the Mental Health System Survivor's Movement?', in H. Spandler et al. (eds), *Madness, Distress and the Politics of Disablement* (Bristol: Policy Press, 2015), 231–43, 241.

47. Brigit McWade, Damian Milton and Peter Beresford, 'Mad Studies and Neurodiversity: A Dialogue', *Disability & Society* 30(2) (2015), 305–309. Available online at: http://dx.doi.org/10.1080/09687599.2014.1000512.

Akin to disability studies' critical interrogation of the capitalist frameworks that render those bodies unable to work as 'other', so mad studies seeks to reveal neoliberalism and biomedical psychiatry's commonalities, in constructing human distress as 'mental illness' – an individual rather than a social/structural concern – leading to the so-called healthification of social problems.[48]

Recovering historical and cross-cultural perspectives on madness are vital tasks within mad studies, for, as Shainl Diamond proposes to think and act beyond the present means 'recognising that madness is constructed differently in various historical and cultural contexts, and that there is no real basis of inherent or natural characteristics that define an eternal Mad subject'.[49] Crucially, mad studies scholarship is careful to guard against the flattening construction of a singular mad experience. It engages diverse testimonies of 'experts by experience – people whose lived experiences … underpin their standpoints and contributions'.[50] These experiences/testimonies are variously evoked by the 'history, culture, political organising, narratives, writings and most importantly, the people who identify as Mad; psychiatric survivors; consumers; service users; mentally ill; patients; neurodiverse; inmates; disabled – to name a few of the "identity labels" *our* community may choose to use'.[51] The importance of these perspectives has been central to the discipline from its inception. For it is at heart a discipline firmly critical of distant 'abstracted academism' and one which is resolutely committed to activism and change.[52] Judi Chamberlain, often hailed as a foremother of the mad movement in North America, powerfully attests to this, in her celebrated memoir *On Our Own: Patient Controlled Alternatives to the Mental Health System* (1978), when she writes:

> For too long, mental patients have been faceless, voiceless people. We have been thought of, at worst, as subhuman monsters, or, at best, as pathetic cripples …

48. LeFrançois et al., 'Introduction', 16.

49. LeFrançois et al., 'Introduction', 15.

50. Peter Beresford, 'Foreword', in LaFrancois et al. (eds), *Mad*, ix–xii, xi.

51. My italicization. Note how 'our' fronts experience and identity as central to this discipline. Lucy Costa cited in Brigit McWade et al., 'Mad Studies', 306. Christopher Dingwall-Jones' clarification of terminology is useful in this respect. He writes, 'The term "mental health system survivor", or simply "survivor" is used more commonly among activists critical of psychiatry, and especially psychopharmacological treatments. However, not all who experience psychic distress share the hostility towards mental health institutions implied by these terms. Indeed, there is even controversy over the terms "mental health" and "mental illness", both from people who support a more thoroughgoing biomedical approach, and who therefore use the term "brain disease" to suggest a specific physical aetiology for distress, and from those who are more critical of the medical model, and who argue that "mental illness" closes the still open question of causation.' Christopher Dingwall-Jones, 'Antic Dispositions: The Representation of Madness in Modern British Theatre', PhD Thesis, University of Kent (2014). Available online at: https://kar.kent.ac.uk/48042/1/130C%20D J%20Final%20(Amendments,%20Redacted).pdf, 6.

52. Beresford, 'Foreword', ix.

> It is only in this decade with the emergence and growth of the mental patients' liberation movement, that we ex-patients have begun to shake off this distorted image and to see ourselves for what we are – a diverse group of people, with strengths and weakness, abilities and needs, and ideas of our own. Our ideas about our 'care' and 'treatment' at the hands of psychiatry, about the nature of 'mental illness' and about new and better ways to deal with (and truly help) people undergoing emotional crises differ drastically from those of mental health professionals.[53]

In short, the sorts of transgressions initiated within mad studies, from which I will draw direct inspiration within this project, enable readers to critically question damaging and oppressive Western medical and cultural discourses surrounding madness. For, in the words of Robert Menzies, Brenda LeFrancois and Geoffrey Reaume, whether we identify as Mad or distressed or not, such viewpoints will offer 'a chance to liberate our thoughts from old, unhelpful assumptions and conceptual frameworks and test out others against our own experience, knowledge and understanding'.[54]

Space, Embodiment and Performance

Critical attention to the means by which spatial and ideological arenas and structures are physically and discursively invoked will also be an important consideration within this book. Productions of spatio-temporal frameworks inevitably pattern constructions of 'normative' bodies and minds within cultures. They also frequently dictate the marginalization and stigmatizing of those 'other' bodies and minds which are perceived to transgress these. As Elizabeth Teather notes, '[T]he social construction of disabling differences as markers of inferiority or otherness have, at both macro and micro scales, helped to situate certain bodies as "out of place" in society and in the spaces of everyday life.'[55] From ancient cemeteries to high-gated Victorian madhouses, from post-asylum psychiatric care facilities to care within communities, discourses of madness are frequently inscribed topographically. Erving Goffman was particularly attuned to the ways in which the bodies incarcerated within asylums experienced a 'mortification of the self' through loss of civil identity and intense surveillance and regulation.[56]

53. Judi Chamberlain cited in Mel Starkman, 'The Movement', in LeFrançois et al. (eds), *Mad*, 27–37, 30.

54. Beresford, 'Foreword', xi.

55. Elizabeth Kenworthy Teather, *Embodied Geographies* (London: Routledge, 1999), 151.

56. Erving Goffman, *Asylums: Essays on the Social Situation of Mental Patients and Other Inmates* (Chicago: Aldine, 1961), 47. Strategic agency of the 'patients' was also observable within Goffman's work: 'The patient curling up at the window, looking outside through the bars,

Embodied performances are also frequently appealed to in representational, cultural and ideological understandings of madness.[57] All too often, negative stereotypical images of madness call to mind 'raving, dribbling, staring, rocking, flailing, twitching "mad" characters'.[58] The visual spectacles witnessed in 'hysteria', 'fits', contortions and rages[59] form links between bodily actions and negative cultural estimations. Harpin and Foster warn, however, that such sensationalized stereotypical images 'sustain a diagnostic gaze towards individuals and offer up superficial surface behaviours as decipherable clues to inner enigmas'.[60] What is missing, in disability activist Petra Kuppers's opinion, is the embodied 'self-presentation' of those 'mad' experts by experience, and the means by which they often rebelliously refigure and reclaim their own somatic agency.[61] Christopher Dingwall-Jones similarly bemoans that much historical work has focused on the body as 'an intellectual and discursive concept' rather than on the specific 'lived' bodies of individuals.[62] The so-called cognitive turn in performance studies signals a renewed interest in the ways in which space and bodies interact and how embodiment inevitably influences perceptions and conceptions of alternative identities. What Dingwall-Jones terms 'intercorporeal encounter(s) with madness' as opposed to widely perpetuated stereotypical iconographic, cultural and metaphorical encounters between 'sane' and 'mad' also underscores the importance of critical attention to specific, subversive and resistant mad embodiments and performances. Attention to lived performances also belies a purposeful decentring of anachronistic Cartesian distinctions between mind and body, for constructions of madness and sanity in ancient world contexts too, often cannot be conceptualized in distinction from embodied experience.[63]

Overview of Book

The main aim of the following chapters, then, is to identify and refigure various prejudicial assumptions and interpretations perpetuated within Western biblical

pressing the nose of his whole body against the outside, and in this way somewhat removing himself from the ward and somewhat freeing himself from its territorial restriction' (237–8).

57. The front cover of Michel Foucault's celebrated book *Folie* (1961), features in the Wellcome Collection's *Bedlam: The Asylum and Beyond* exhibition. This is entirely appropriate, for this work is among the most important and influential texts within the field. On spatiality and madness, see also Andrew Scull's, *Museums of Madness* (London: Allen Lane, 1979) and *The Insanity of Place/The Place of Insanity* (London: Routledge, 2006).

58. Harpin and Foster, 'Introduction', 4.

59. Petra Kuppers, *Disability and Contemporary Performance: Bodies on the Edge* (London: Routledge, 2003), 124.

60. Harpin and Foster, 'Introduction', 4.

61. Kuppers, *Disability*, 124.

62. Dingwall-Jones, 'Antic', 9.

63. Dingwall-Jones, 'Antic', 9.

studies concerning madness. Contemporary 'm/Mad' perspectives will seek to retrieve some of the strategies, agencies and identities within biblical interpretation, which are so often eclipsed behind psy-pathological labelling and/or stereotypical negative estimations.

Chapter 1, 'Ivory Towers and the Banishment of Bedlam: Reason, Right Minds and Sane Privilege in Biblical Studies', will attempt to launch a meta-critical exposure of sane prejudice and sane privilege – 'the invisible advantages granted to people who have never been psychiatrized, or perceived as mad'[64] – within the identity and discourses of Western biblical scholarship. This includes the ways in which the medical model's language of mental illness is discursively leaked into scholarly rhetoric (and casual cultural slurs) to undermine another's position as invalid, 'irrational' or marginal, and the frequent rehearsal of damaging stereotypes and psychiatric 'diagnoses' of morally ambivalent or negatively perceived characters within biblical literatures.

Chapter 2, 'The Curious Incident of a Jew in the Night-Time: Autistry and an Encounter with Nicodemus', will seek to reappropriate autism as a 'neurodiverse' identity and in so doing, challenge the widespread 'cultural marginalization of autistic subjectivities'.[65] 'Autistic presences', it will be submitted, find resonance within Jn 3:1–15 not within a single character, but rather the wider narrative discourse itself, and its neurodivergent positioning of the audience.

Chapter 3, '"Ex-centric Women": Intersecting Marginalities and the Madness Narratives of Bessie Head, a Canaanite Woman and Pythian Slave Girl', seeks to take heed of recent criticisms regarding the Eurocentric nature of madness constructions, by exhibiting the Africana 'mad' writer Bessie Head's work alongside two female biblical characters. Head's work is used not just to elucidate the sanist and sexist oppression these characters have respectively endured but also to comment on the other interconnecting practices of subjugation (racism, colonialism, servitude and slavery) which they border and, at times, critically resist.

Chapter 4, 'Gatekeeping the Madness of Jesus and Paul: Negotiating Mythologies of Madness in an Age of Neoliberalism', will seek to pay attention to the 'sanist' protection of celebrated biblical figures such as Jesus and Paul and probe the cultural mythologies that link 'positive' stereotypes of madness, including individual genius and creativity, with these figures. Such attributes, it will be proposed, resonate with the meritocratic and voluntaristic ethos of neoliberalism and as such serve to sustain constructions of these characters as 'able' representatives of contemporary neoliberal contexts.

64. PhebeAnn Wolframe 'The Madwoman in the Academy, or, Revealing the Invisible Straightjacket: Theorizing and Teaching Saneism and Sane Privilege' *Disability Studies Quarterly* 33(1) (2013). Available online at: http://dsq-sds.org/article/view/3425/3200.

65. James McGrath, 'Autistic Criticism: An Autistic Reading of BBC1's The Syndicate (2015) and the Cultural State of Asperger Syndrome'. Available online at: http://www.rowmaninternational.com/cultural-studies/autistic-criticism-an-autistic-reading-of-bbc1s-the-syndicate-2015-and-the-cultural-state-of-asperger-syndrome.

Chapter 5, 'Madness, the Affect Alien and the Gospel of Mark: Critically Probing a Happiness Turn in Biblical Studies', will destabilize and question the widespread prizing of happiness, well-being, therapy and 'mental health' in neoliberal, North Atlantic societies. Cultural constructions of happiness/well-being which exclude, marginalize, cure and/or obliterate the complex experiences and relationships of individuals and communities rendered 'other' by normative constructions are directly challenged here.[66] The Gospel of Mark is purposively read with a Hearing Voices Network Group, which resists psy-framings of their auditory and visual experiences as disordered. The Gospel of Mark is also itself rendered an 'affect alien' – an [un]happiness archive – by the ways in which it determinedly occupies, rather than seeks to overcome, distress and grief.

My conclusion, entitled 'Beyond Bedlam? Keeping Open[ing] Minds in Biblical Interpretation', will sum up the ways in which the exhibits presented within this book could refigure understandings of 'madness' within Western biblical studies and indicate how m/Mad-identified perspectives can begin to deconstruct the sane/insane and able/disabled binaries so common therein.

I hope that this book is received (for it certainly was conceived) as 'a *for*, not an *against* book'.[67] It critiques, but also constructs and models (through its selected engagements with m/Mad culture and sources) the emergence of 'survivor research engagement' and collaboration in the academy.[68] Moreover, through its encounter with mad studies, this book purposefully positions its focus not on spectacles of madness, but rather more directly on the 'cultures, institutions and language which makes madness [and sanity] matter so much'.[69] It joins forces with those postmodern projects which seek to question and deconstruct 'totalising knowledge' (such as the medical model and *DSM-5*) and which are often perceived to 'stand in isolation from [their] socio-political context'.[70] Such knowledge, however, always involves discursive and political positioning;[71] moreover, it is by the power afforded to such positions that those constructed as 'other' are routinely censored, silenced and/or contained.

66. James O. Pawelski, 'Today, Tomorrow, and the Day after Tomorrow: A Case Study for the Theology of Joy Project'. Available online at: http://faith.yale.edu/sites/default/files/pawelski_today_tomorrow_and_the_day_after_tomorrow.pdf, 2.

67. Beresford, 'Foreword', xi; emphases in the original.

68. Beresford, 'Foreword', xi.

69. Ian Parker et al., *Deconstructing Psychopathology* (London: Sage Publications, 1995), 14.

70. Dwight Fee, 'The Broken Dialogue: Mental Illness as Discourse and Experience', in Dwight Fee (ed.), *Pathology and the Postmodern: Mental Illness as Discourse and Experience* (London: Sage Publications, 2000), 1–17, 4.

71. Fee, 'The Broken', 4.

Chapter 1

Ivory Towers and the Banishment of Bedlam: Reason, Right Minds and Sane Privilege in Biblical Studies

Behind a thick black curtain in the exhibition space of the Wellcome Collection's 'Bedlam: The Asylum and Beyond' (2016) the viewer encounters Javier Téllez's video installation *Caligari and the Sleepwalker* (2008). This piece was first produced for the 'Rational/Irrational Exhibition' at the House of World Cultures in Berlin[1] and drew inspiration from Robert Wiene's silent horror picture, *The Cabinet of Dr Caligari* (1920). Wiene's original film featured a suited narrator, Francis, telling the story of Dr. Caligari and a somnambulist he hypnotizes to commit murders. At the close of the film, Francis is revealed as a psychiatric patient. He is subsequently straitjacketed by the asylum director who vows to cure him of his disturbing delusions. The narrative, while first presented to the audience as 'reality', is thus ultimately rendered 'hallucinatory'. Téllez's reception and reinterpretation of the original movie subversively destabilizes the (often problematic) boundaries erected between sanity/insanity and rationality/irrationality. His script does not centre on a crime (so redolent of negative stereotyping associating criminality with psychiatric pathology) but rather the identity and insights of the sleepwalker, Cesare, a being from 'Slave Star'. The script was written in collaboration with patients of the Vivantes Klinik, a psychiatric unit in Berlin, who were asked to respond to the original movie. Included within Téllez's film are not only dramatized performances of these conversations, but the patients themselves feature as the cast. Pedro Reyes in his review of Téllez's work thus states: 'Téllez's project build[s] a bridge between these two worlds, opening the possibility of creative collaborations with the so-called mentally ill, he avoids the pieties associated with art therapy by warning us that he seeks "not a therapeutic practice to cure the insane but rather one to *cure the sane of their lucidity*"'.[2] Curing 'the sane of their lucidity' is perhaps most provocatively hinted at through the set of Téllez's film – Erich Mendelsohn's astrophysical observatory, the Einstein Tower, at Potsdam. This tower functions

1. Kunsthaus Baselland, 'Javier Tellez'. Available online at: https://artmap.com/baselland/exhibition/javier-te-llez-2009.

2. My italicization; Pedro Reyes, 'Bomb: Artists in Conversation Javier Téllez' (2010). Available online at: http://bombmagazine.org/article/3379/javier-t-llez.

symbolically as a proverbial 'ivory tower', an image which has frequently denoted Western academic pursuits. In Marvin Finkelstein's words:

> Here was a necessarily elevated social institution that could serve as the trusted source of credible, valuable, and objective knowledge for a modern society. The university remains symbolic of such a location, both lofty and insulated, where the best and brightest might undertake the sacred pursuit of knowledge unscathed by the exigencies of daily life that might somehow taint the noble cause of scholarship.[3]

Only Caligari and the sleepwalker feature inside the tower, the rest of the time it provides an ominous backdrop to the questions posed to the sleepwalker from the patients external to (/excluded?) from it. These questions (and answers) include 'What is Slave Star?' ('A psychiatric hospital'), 'How do you perceive?' ('Through love') and most tellingly, 'Where will the next disaster happen?' ('Here!').

By way of analogy with the exclusionary tendencies of the proverbial ivory tower of Western academia, here I intend to probe biblical studies' analogous banishment of 'madness' through the methodological, epistemological and discursive privileging of reason, rationality and 'right' minds. This stance, and its suspicion of anything perceived to fall short of these ideals, is, it is argued, symptomatic of a certain disciplinary (and exclusionary) 'sanism', which has been defined by the American lawyer Michael Perlin as 'an irrational prejudice' due to a person's perceived mental or emotional disability and 'based primarily upon stereotype, myth, superstition, and deindividualisation'.[4]

Voices in biblical studies have increasingly identified latent sexist, racist, imperial and neocolonial impulses. However, no one has, to my knowledge, ever explicitly broached the ways in which 'sanism' and the stigma it frequently projects onto those perceived to be different from a [sanist] norm (whether literary characters or living interpreters) also operates within the discipline. In probing sanist dimensions and assumptions of Western biblical scholarship, I will be drawing inspiration from 'mad' reading strategies to evaluate the extent to which the discipline reproduces the following sanist impulses: (a) naturalizes psychiatric discourses of madness, applies and assumes psy-identifications (actual and metaphorical) as uncontested givens and perpetuates stereotypes about those perceived as mentally ill or mad as 'other'; (b) leaks madness into other intersectional marginalities including gender, race, class and sexuality and so on. For, as Perlin notes:

> Sanism is as insidious as other 'isms' and is, in some ways, more troubling, since it is largely invisible and largely socially acceptable. Further, sanism is

3. Marvin Finkelstein, 'The Ivory Tower in a Flat World: The University and Applied Sociology in the Global Economy', *Journal of Applied Social Science* 1(1) (2007), 16–22, 16.

4. Michael Perlin, cited in John Parry and Eric Drogin, *Criminal Mental Health and Disability Law, Evidence and Testimony* (Chicago: American Bar Association, 2007), 48.

> frequently practiced, consciously or unconsciously, by individuals who regularly take liberal or progressive positions decrying similar biases and prejudices that involve sex, race, ethnicity or sexual orientation. Sanism is a form of bigotry that 'respectable people can express in public' ... To sustain and perpetuate sanism, we use pre-reflective 'ordinary common sense' (OCS) and other cognitive-simplifying devices such as heuristic reasoning in an unconscious response to events both in everyday life and in the legal process.[5]

(c) Perpetuates negative stereotypes and stigma in relation to mental difference (violence, danger, sin etc.). This is sometimes referred to as 'sane chauvinism' or 'mentalism' and is often integrated into the language used (irrational, insane, schizophrenic, bipolar etc.) to refer to positions to which the speaker objects.[6]

Here (albeit highly selective) cameo illustrations of sanism from within the discipline of biblical studies are offered by way of example.[7] First, the ways in which the guild constructs its normative identity as 'sane' in its rationalistic outlooks, methodologies and values will be demonstrated. Second, the ways in which (negative) madness stereotypes and psychopathological categories are employed discursively within scholarly rhetoric to undermine another's work as 'irrational' will be illustrated through assessments of Morton Smith's (character and) work on the Secret Gospel of Mark.[8] Third, in relation to actual biblical exegesis, the projection of damaging sanist stereotypes to 'classify' morally ambivalent or negatively perceived characters within biblical literatures (Saul, Nebuchadnezzar, Ezekiel, Herod etc.) and consolidate their presumed social/political deviance[9] will be investigated. The leaking of biomedical discourses into interpretations of demonic possession narratives and enforced cure (/normalization) of such

5. Michael Perlin, 'You Have Discussed Lepers and Crooks: Sanism in Clinical Teaching', *Clinical Law Review* 9 (2003), 683–704, 684.

6. PhebeAnn Wolframe, 'Reading through Madness: Counter-psychiatric Epistemologies and the Biopolitics of (In)sanity in Post-World War II Anglo- Atlantic Narratives', PhD Thesis, McMaster University (2014). Available online at: https://macsphere.mcmaster.ca/bitstream/11375/13900/1/fulltext.pdf.

7. These examples have been purposefully selected due to their explicit adoption and use of the language of madness to denote the culturally 'other' and/or employment of psychiatric-related discourses, ideas, terminology and/or categories.

8. Peter Jeffrey, *The Secret Gospel of Mark Unveiled: Imagined Rituals of Sex, Death, and Madness in a Biblical Forgery* (New Haven: Yale University Press, 2007).

9. On 'psycho-sciences to denote modern Western established mainstream clinical psychiatry (20th–21st century) including, but not especially concentrating on, Freudian psychoanalysis as a part of that mainstream'. See Annina Yla-Kapee, 'Telling Madness: Narrative, Diagnosis, Power and Literary Theory', Thesis, Tampere University (2014). Available online at: https://tampub.uta.fi/bitstream/handle/10024/96148/978-951-44-9557-1.pdf?sequence=1, 22.

individuals will also be probed.[10] Finally, inspired by mad studies, some pointers for an awareness-raising of sanism and sane privilege within the biblical studies discipline will be offered.

Reason, Right Minds and Ivory Towers: Biblical Studies as a 'Sane[ist?]' Discipline

European (and, more broadly, Western) critical biblical studies had its genesis in an Enlightenment scientific paradigm which posited the scholar as a 'rational subject positioned outside of time and space'.[11] This perspective has frequently been envisaged spatially and architecturally as the occupation of 'an ivory tower'. Freed from the shackles of church authority, the Enlightenment focus on professional objectivity with regard to sources and methods (and based on rationality and reason) belied a social location which, according to Elisabeth Schüssler Fiorenza, 'was institutionalized in the modern university as the positivist paradigm of knowledge that gives primary importance to evidence, data, and empirical inquiry – that is to the *logic* of facts'.[12] The scientism which privileged the historical critical method in biblical studies has also influenced broader Western thinking, including the implicit assumption that modern medical/disease concepts are more 'advanced' (civilized?) than alternative worldviews. It is no coincidence that historical exegesis frequently drew upon anatomical/medical terminology to describe its methodologies. Indeed Stephen Moore has graphically pictured both the human cadaver and the textual body of the Bible laid out for inspection on the pathologist's and historical critic's slab: both 'dissected' by reason in order to identify and subdue them.[13]

B. McLean contends that despite a proliferation of postmodern approaches in recent years, it is still true to say that biblical studies is subject to an 'ongoing tyranny of historicism in the form of historical positivism' which has the 'effect of normalizing the outmoded epistemological framework of the Enlightenment with the result that those alternative forms of knowing continue to be marginalized and excluded'.[14] The historical critical method, which assumes that a singular meaning of a text can be exhumed, is still taken as the un-named core of the discipline. As Sandra Gravett attests: 'There is an entire structure built around historical

10. On disability-critical responses to the 'curative' model, see Alison Kafer, *Feminist, Queer, Crip* (Bloomington: Indiana University Press, 2013), 27.

11. Elisabeth Schüssler Fiorenza, *Democratizing Biblical Studies: Toward an Emancipatory Educational Space* (Louisville: Westminster John Knox Press, 2009), 92.

12. Schüssler Fiorenza, *Democratizing*, 68; my emphasis.

13. Stephen Moore, *God's Gym: Divine Male Bodies of the Bible* (New York: Routledge, 1996), 57–72.

14. B. H. McLean, *Biblical Interpretation and Philosophical Hermeneutics* (Cambridge: Cambridge University Press, 2012), 7.

critical scholarship ... It is only after you get tenure and are successful in historical criticism that you can even open up this [the unquestioned norm of historical criticism] conversation.'[15] Accordingly, those readings drawn from feminist, postcolonial, 'global', queer or disability standpoints are still routinely rendered 'perspectival' and/or 'marginal'.[16]

In the Enlightenment era, 'prejudice' denoted judgements which could not be legitimated by reason. Thus, reason was 'assigned the role of emancipating humanity from normalizing tendencies of religious prejudice ... replacing falsehood and superstition with true, rational, verifiable knowledge'.[17] Yet, as Hans-Georg Gadamer (ironically) pointed out, ultimately 'the Enlightenment's attack on prejudice is *itself part of the prejudice of the Enlightenment*'.[18] For, if reason and rationality were the era's revered qualities, then unreason and un-rationality were (prejudicially?) identified as their nemeses. Michel Foucault's attention to the ways in which 'madmen were perceived and treated by intellectuals and officials all over Europe'[19] is instructive here. In his opinion, the age of reason heralded 'catastrophe for the living metaphors of unreason'.[20] Foucault's magnum opus *Madness and Civilisation* (1961) saw that for reason to exist as a definable quality it needed to be diametrically set against and apart from unreason. As such, in Michael MacDonald's words, 'the great value of Foucault's work lies in his insight that madness was a speculum in which *normal people* saw their own image reversed and distorted'.[21] In an associated vein, Catherine Lutz has pointed out how the body, emotions and the feminine were also regularly dismissed and rejected as 'irrational' in Western scholarly discourse and, one could add, grafted onto stereotypical assumptions regarding madness – 'excitability as madness', 'sadness-as-madness', 'badness-as-madness' and so on.[22] In Lutz's words:

> As both an analytic and an everyday concept in the West, emotion, like the female, has typically been viewed as something natural rather than cultural, irrational rather than rational, chaotic rather than ordered, subjective rather than universal, physical rather than mental or intellectual, unintended and uncontrollable, and hence often dangerous. This network of associations

15. See A. K. M. Adam, Richard Ascough, Sandra Gravett, Alice Hunt, Dale Martin, Edward Wimberly and Seung Ai Yang, 'Should We Be Teaching the Historical Critical Method?', *Teaching Theology and Religion* 12 (2009), 162–87, 178.

16. Adam et al., 'Should', 178.

17. McLean, *Biblical*, 184.

18. Gadamer, cited in McLean, *Biblical*, 185; original emphasis.

19. Michael MacDonald, *Mystical Bedlam: Madness, Anxiety and Healing in Seventeenth-Century England* (Cambridge: Cambridge University Press, 1983), xvii.

20. MacDonald, *Mystical*, xi.

21. MacDonald, *Mystical*, 38; my emphasis.

22. Erick Fabris, *Tranquil Prisons: Chemical Incarceration under Community Treatment Orders* (Toronto: University of Toronto Press, 2011), 29.

> sets emotion in disadvantaged contrast to more valued personal processes, particularly to cognition or rational thought, and the female in deficient relation to her male other.[23]

Rejection of the emotional as irrational also ultimately served to uphold the dominant status quo and silence those incensed by injustice. Protesters ('resistant women', 'racial others', 'homosexuals') regularly have their political activism dismissed as a type of madness and are consequently interrogated and cured psy-medically.[24] Matthew Schlimm, citing Lutz, accordingly notes: 'Emotion becomes an important metaphor for perceived threats to established authority [and is associated with] those groups which have traditionally "been conceived of as passionate beings incapable of sustained rationality" including "infants, children, adolescents, *mental patients*, primitive people, peasants, immigrants, Negroes, slum dwellers, urban masses, crowds, and most of all, women"'.[25]

Schüssler Fiorenza, and others striving towards more democratic models within biblical studies, are acutely aware of how the privileging of rationality and reason has dangerously concealed ideological biases, power plays and prejudices against other forms of embodiment, contextuality, subjectivity and knowing. For, the 'the unexamined assumption of academic discourse equates white, male and Western reality with human reality'.[26] Therefore, it is often unconsciously assumed that 'natural differences exist between wo/men and other colonized peoples as rationally inferior, marginal, subsidiary, or derivative'.[27] When such figures are perceived to be making their voice heard, they are often 'judged as unnatural, aggressive and disruptive' (/mad?) acting contrary to an 'objective and scholarly' (/sane?) persona.[28] She contends that biblical studies has not sufficiently fostered an acknowledgement of, or problematized, 'to what end biblical studies as a scholarly inquiry is constructed in certain circumstances and how it serves particular interests'.[29]

23. Catherine A. Lutz, 'Engendered Emotion: Gender, Power, and the Rhetoric of Emotional Control in American Discourse', in R. Harre and W. G. Parrot (eds), *The Emotions* (Thousand Oaks, CA: Sage, 1996), 152–70. Available online at: http://www.brown.uk.com/brownlibrary/EMOT.htm.

24. Michael O'Rourke (ed.), *The Ashgate Research Companion to Queer Theory* (Farnham: Ashgate, 2009), 124.

25. Lutz, cited in Matthew Richard Schlimm, 'From Fratricide to Forgiveness: The Ethics of Anger in Genesis', PhD Thesis, Duke University (2008), 57; my italicization. Available online at: http://dukespace.lib.duke.edu/dspace/bitstream/handle/10161/890/D_Schlimm_Matthew_a_200812.pdf?sequence=1.

26. Schüssler Fiorenza, *Democratizing*, 34–5.

27. Schüssler Fiorenza, *Democratizing*, 34–5.

28. Schüssler Fiorenza, *Democratizing*, 34–5.

29. Schüssler Fiorenza, *Democratizing*, 37.

Schüssler Fiorenza, too, in her call for the democratizing of biblical studies, urges biblical scholarship to explore and engage 'both the exclusionary spaces and the democratizing potentials of the Bible that it becomes methodologically aware of its social location in a democratic society, and that it reflects on its democratic sociopolitical contexts'.[30] It is of course true to say that from the 1970s onwards biblical studies has increasingly witnessed a proliferation of methodological approaches stimulated by concerns seemingly 'external' to the high spaces of the university. Previously marginalized voices within the academy have increasingly challenged structural norms of the discipline. Within such perspectives, the proverbial ivory tower is no longer lauded for its lofty, detached outlook, but rather increasingly viewed as an 'incontestably bad place'.[31] Illustrative of such dimensions, Schüssler Fiorenza, for example, writes critically about the strict separation of scholars interpreting the Bible in their ivory towers, from those outside the academy:

> One often finds the assumption that the critical interpretation of the bible is restricted to the 'ivory tower' of elite universities or denominational seminaries. This stumbling block overlooks the fact that all wo/men who read or hear the bible are always already interpreting it. Interpretation is not done by ivory tower academics only and it is not their prerogative. Moreover, such an assumption forgets the old adage 'knowledge is power'.[32]

In a related vein, others wanting to engage biblical interpretation within ecclesial contexts talk about the 'attempt to free the Bible from its recent captivity in the cold ivory towers of academia'.[33] Socially engaged scholars are extolled for their ground-level activism. Laurel Dykstra and Ched Myers's edited volume on social justice references Jack Elliott's work on the experience of the stranger and sojourner in 1 Peter, which is directly informed by his association with the Sanctuary Movement in the 1970s and the Central American refugees escaping from US-sponsored wars in the 1980s. Elliott is hailed not only as 'a pioneer in social-science scholarship in biblical studies' but more importantly as one who 'gives lie to the notion of ivory-tower scholarship'.[34] Two-thirds world scholarship has also challenged the Western ivory tower as an abstract, disengaged, colonial and white-ist symbol.

30. Schüssler Fiorenza, *Democratizing*, 2.

31. Steven Shapin, 'The Ivory Tower: The History of a Figure of Speech and Its Cultural Uses', *British Journal for the History of Science* 45 (2012), 1–27, 23.

32. Elisabeth Schüssler Fiorenza, *Wisdom Ways: Introducing Feminist Biblical Interpretation* (New York: Orbis Books, 2001), online version, no pages.

33. A. K. M. Adam et al., *Reading Scripture with the Church: Toward a Hermeneutic for Theological Interpretation* (Grand Rapids: Baker Academic, 2006), 131.

34. Laurel Dykstra and Ched Myers (eds), *Liberating Biblical Study: Scholarship, Art, and Action in Honor of the Center and Library for the Bible and Social Justice* (Oregon: Wipf and Stock, 2011), 195.

Zimbabwean scholar Canaan Banana thus defiantly states: '[M]y theology is not manufactured from the ivory tower or white elephant pinnacles of bourgeoisie individualistic mentality. My theology originates from the ghetto. It emanates from mundane situations and crises.'[35] While the ivory tower has been 'scaled', 'breached', 'bridged' and 'leaned'[36] within such sociopolitical movements, it is also still largely true to say that rational modes of thinking and intellectual reasoning continue to be the normative hallmarks of Western biblical scholarship.

To take just one example, the Society of Biblical Literature (SBL), the largest international association of scholars working in biblical studies, self-identifies as 'an interdisciplinary, humanistic, academic society that includes scholars of history, literature, archaeology, anthropology, theology, and more'.[37] The assumption of the primacy of the historical notwithstanding here (those 'other' exegetical pursuits falling outside the remit of history or theology are presumably indicated in the 'and more') other features also inherently indicate an implicit sanist normativity for the discipline. First, the self-description of the discipline as 'humanistic' adopts a term which has been problematized by critical race and disability theorists in recent years for its exclusionary/oppressive dynamics. Rosi Braidotti traces the origins of 'humanism' to the European Enlightenment and its construction of the human as an 'an ideal of bodily perfection',[38] 'a rational animal endowed with language',[39] 'implicitly assumed to be masculine, white, urbanized, speaking a standard language, heterosexually inscribed in a reproductive unit and a full citizen of a recognized polity'.[40] Dan Goodley notes that this humanistic vision had both Eurocentric and imperialist impulses; 'those outside of Europe (including many in the colonies) became known as less than human or inhuman'.[41] He traces

35. Canaan Banana, *Come and Share: An Introduction to Christian Theology* (Gweru: Mambo Press, 1991), xi.

36. Shapin, 'The Ivory Tower', 1–27. See also Brett Stockdill and Mary Yu Danico (eds), *Transforming the Ivory Tower: Challenging Racism, Sexism, and Homophobia in the Academy* (Hawaii: University of Hawaii Press, 2012); and Raymond V. Padilla and Rudolfo Chdivez Chaivez, *The Leaning Ivory Tower: Latino Professors in American Universities* (Albany: State University of New York Press, 1995).

37. Society of Biblical Literature (SBL) website at: https://www.sbl-site.org/aboutus/welcome.aspx. SBL also defines its core values as follows: 'Accountability; Openness to Change; Collaboration; Professionalism; Collegiality; Respect for Diversity; Critical Inquiry; Scholarly Integrity; Inclusivity; Tolerance.' These values are commendable, yet while practical moves have been made to enact these values in relation to gender, race and so on (with specific groups founded to facilitate equality and diversity in these areas) the society has largely ignored neurodiversity, neuro-atypicality or mental distress in its visions of inclusion.

38. Rosi Braidotti, *The Posthuman* (London: Polity Press, 2013), 13.

39. Braidtotti, *Posthuman*, 141.

40. Braidotti, *Posthuman*, 65.

41. Dan Goodley, Rebecca Lawthom and Katherine Runswick Cole, 'Posthuman Disability Studies', *Subjectivity* 7 (2014) 342–61.

a correlative move in humanism's familiar relationship with the medical and psy-discourses which seek to 'colonize' (and exclude) the 'mentally disordered' and 'disabled'.[42]

Second, and in specific relation to the SBL's core values of 'critical enquiry', Margaret Price reveals how, after the political movements of the 1960s, academic discourse began to replace the language of 'reason' and 'rationality' with 'criticality' and 'critical thinking'; in both instances, the ideal of the humanist subject as normative remained constant.[43] She also notes how such language is easily aligned with contemporary Western medical models: 'rational', 'critical' – all assume the humanist and associate psy-discourses as both authoritative and benign.[44] Collegiality and productivity, too, are often values which are defined over and against madness – 'academic discourse also presumed the necessity of a "sound" and "agile" mind in order to maintain collegiality and productivity'[45] – Hilary Clark talks about the challenges of 'passing as an academic' given the shame attached to mental illness within the academy. She reveals how those not holding tenured roles adopt tactics of silence around their experiences in order to safeguard their identity and career prospects.[46] Elizabeth Ellsworth also identifies the implicit sanist oppression played out through seemingly benign academic values such as 'sharing' and critical 'dialogue'. In her words, '[V]oices … [in the academic spaces of conferences, lecture theatres, seminars etc.] do not and cannot carry equal legitimacy, safety and power in dialogue.'[47] Moreover, the neuro-atypical/-diverse 'are still required to pantomime our way through work, embodying – or enminding – as best we can the "good man speaking well" '.[48]

The general descriptor of 'academic' and 'academic society' has also been seen to mark a substantive and ideological gulf between academic discourse and madness. Price, in her incisive study of the rhetorics of mental disability in higher education, shows how both the academy and psy-discourses seek to control, censor, heal or expel 'mad' subjects. In her words, '[A]cademic discourse operates not just to omit, but to abhor mental disability – to reject it, to stifle and expel it.'[49] She poignantly asks, '[W]hat does this mean for those of us with atypical (some would say "impaired") minds that work, learn, and teach in this location?'[50] In her work, Price interviewed a number of so-called independent scholars in trying to expose the structural prejudice they too are often subject to[51]

42. Goodley et al., 'Posthuman', 344.

43. Margaret Price, *Mad at School: Rhetorics of Mental Disability in Academic Life* (Michigan: University of Michigan Press, 2011), 39.

44. Price, *Mad*, 37.

45. Price, *Mad*, 140.

46. Hilary Clark discussed in Price, *Mad*, 131.

47. Elizabeth Ellsworth, cited in Price, *Mad*, 40.

48. Ellsworth, cited in Price, *Mad*, 41.

49. Price, *Mad*, 8.

50. Price, *Mad*, 8.

51. Price, *Mad*, 226.

through their place 'outside' the ivory tower. Within biblical studies, James McGrath, in a 2014 biblioblog[52] post, exemplifies such predispositions when he cautions the guild about independent scholars 'who dabble in academic enquiry … but who are not employed in institutions of higher education'.[53] He cites two reasons for this, the first is practical: professional academics find it hard to 'keep up' with literature so this is exacerbated for the independent scholar with limited resources and access to institutional libraries and so on. The second is more (suspiciously) ideological: 'just as one should not simply accept a view offered by a professional scholar, how much more so should one not simply accept something that is asserted by someone who may have even less expertise?' He revealingly goes on to note that independent scholars may have contributions to make by working on [marginal] texts 'that deserve attention but which might not lead to a book contract'. The Ascension of Isaiah is given as an example of this. He also writes that 'when it comes to the Secret Gospel of Mark, there have likewise been people outside of the usual areas of scholarly focus who have contributed to the discussion'.[54] Whether this is an attempt to promote the marginalization of this particular text in the academy and/or the people who work on it remains an open question.

In a discipline that implicitly upholds sanist constructions and values (and biblical studies is not alone in this, for it is a key feature of much of the Western academy), it is perhaps no surprise that in a recent study by Andrew Village, which attempted to profile the typical SBL member, the following insights emerged. Village writes: 'There was an overall preference for introversion over extraversion, thinking over feeling and judging over perceiving'; 'scholars showed a much higher preference for thinking than the clergy. This was true for both sexes, which is unusual because women in most populations show a preference for feeling over thinking.'[55] Notwithstanding the problematic gender assumptions uncritically made here, when attempting to profile users in terms of the exegetical methods they employed, Village noted the following in relation to 'postmodern' as opposed to historical approaches:

> [I]ntuitives [as opposed to thinkers] were particularly likely to work with cultural studies, autobiographical, postcolonial, and postmodern criticisms. It seems

52. James Crossley reveals that biblioblogging is a popular phenomenon in the world of biblical scholarship and an important medium through which to detect certain disciplinary trends. Crossley notes that most biblioblogers are male, white and evangelical. Moreover, they often echo 'dominant trends in the American Mass media concerning US foreign policy' and therefore manufacture consent to dominant (and dominating) paradigms. Crossley, *Jesus*, 39.

53. James McGrath, 'Independent Scholars', Patheos.com. Available online at: http://www.patheos.com/blogs/religionprof/2014/12/independent-scholars.html.

54. McGrath, 'Independent'.

55. Andrew Village, 'Psychological Type Functions and Biblical Scholarship: An Empirical Enquiry among Members of the Society of Biblical Literature', *Mental Health, Religion & Culture* 18(7) (2015), 605–21.

> that the intuitive function is suited to methods that draw on multidisciplinary discourses that cross methodological boundaries. There was also a link between preference for feeling-type judging and the broad areas of reader-centred and ideological criticism. This may be because these areas are developing more values-based ethics of interpretation which require application of the feeling rather than the thinking.[56]

Once more the core historical work of the discipline is featured as 'thinking' and the more 'marginal' approaches are identified as 'intuitive' (/emotional). Whether these results are representative or entirely accurate, they do nonetheless show tendencies in the ethos of a discipline, fostered through its practices and contexts which are, as Schüssler Fiorenza contends, also indelibly reflective of webs of power. She notes how 'it becomes important to explore the concept not just in terms of the ethos of the individual biblical scholar but also in terms of the professional ethos of the discipline that determines the social self-identity, positioning and socialization of the emerging biblical scholar'.[57] Discussion here has revealed a privileging of rationality, criticality and latent Eurocentrism and colonialism of humanistic ideals, all of which still reverberate through the field of biblical studies. Such features inevitably plot not only an ideal of 'biblical scholarship' but also systematically exclude, silence and erase the lived experiences of those 'others' who are deemed unfit (too mad?) for occupation of the ivory tower.

Pathologizing Discourses and Scholarship

Just as psy-discourses and pathologizing labels have been projected onto 'patients' in the mental health system, so in Western scholarly debate psy-discourses are selectively employed to discredit those with whom one disagrees.[58] Here, as an (albeit conveniently exaggerated) example, I am going to survey some of the sanist rhetoric which has been employed with regard to Morton Smith, in Peter Jeffrey's volume *The Secret Gospel of Mark Unveiled: Imagined Rituals of Sex, Death and Madness in a Biblical Forgery* (2007).[59] It is not my purpose to establish or assess

56. Village, 'Psychological', 620.

57. Schüssler Fiorenza, 'Introduction', in Schüssler Fiorenza and Kent Harold Richards (eds), *Transforming Graduate Biblical Education: Ethos and Discipline* (Atlanta: SBL, 2010), 1–18, 6.

58. Certain practices are hailed as being good for the 'health' of the discipline, while others are perceived as damaging and unhealthy.

59. Peter Jeffery, *The Secret Gospel of Mark Unveiled: Imagined Rituals of Sex, Death and Madness in a Biblical Forgery* (New Haven: Yale University Press, 2007). Jeffrey is primarily a medievalist, liturgist and musicologist. He worked at Princeton when he wrote the book and now works at Notre Dame University. He has been recognized as an important voice

the persuasion or otherwise of Jeffrey's case (nor indeed of his subject matter). Rather here my focus is exclusively on exposing how sanism is prevalent within Jeffrey's rhetorical and discursive rejection not only of Smith's claims, but also of Smith's very credibility as a 'rational' interpreter based on his projected psychiatric state (at least as much as this is discernible from the authorial persona that Jeffrey perceives Smith to be constructing within his written works).[60] I suggest that three main 'normative' (/humanistic) assumptions held by Jeffrey are perceived by him to be transgressed in Smith's discovery and writings. These are, first, methods of 'critical' scholarship (which Smith is alleged to have contravened through pretence and forgery of the document); second, Christian faith ('Smith was a seminary trained priest, who, very early in his career, chose a life in academia'[61] and gradually came to 'adopt a position' more akin 'to atheism'[62]); and, third, heterosexuality (Smith's manuscript, Jeffrey alleges, purposefully forefronts homoerotic elements).[63] The salacious use of the terms 'imagined', 'forgery' and 'madness' in the title of his book ultimately indicates Jeffrey's position vis-à-vis Smith's perceived 'abnormalities'.[64]

Smith's famous discovery of a hitherto unknown Greek text in Mar Saba monastery in 1958 – a Letter of Clement of Alexandria to Theodore with extracts from a so-called Secret Gospel of Mark, reproduced in the eighteenth century in the back pages of a separate volume – pictures Jesus raising an affluent youth from the dead and subsequently spending the night with him. The manuscript has evoked heated dispute and widespread conjecture among scholars. This was not only regarding its contents and meaning, but also its very authenticity and, more

in Secret Gospel of Mark scholarship; indeed his book was reviewed in a panel session on Psychology and the Bible at the 2009 SBL, and he has contributed to subsequent biblical studies volumes on the theme. See also Jeffrey's essay in Tony Burke's edited collection, *Ancient Gospel or Modern Forgery?: The Secret Gospel of Mark in Debate* (Oregon: Wipf and Stock, 2011).

60. In Peter Jeffrey's own words: 'In order to keep the focus securely on the authorial persona, I scrupulously restricted my remarks to publicly available texts, mostly by Smith himself.' Jeffrey, 'The Secret Gospel of Mark Unveiled: Reply to Scott G. Brown' (2008). Available online at: http://music2.princeton.edu/jeffery/Review%20of%20Biblical%20LiteratureJeffery%20reply%20to%20Brown.pdf, 19.

61. Anthony Le Donne, *The Wife of Jesus: Ancient Texts and Modern Scandals* (London: Oneworld Publications, 2013), 82.

62. Le Donne, *Wife*, 82.

63. Shawn Eyer, 'The Strange Case of the Secret Gospel According to Mark', *Alexandria: The Journal of the Western Cosmological Traditions* 2 (1995), 103–29, 109.

64. 'In an article entitled "Stalemate in the academy" Charles Hedrick has recently argued that "Secret Mark has yet to be given a full and impartial hearing". It "appears to have been discredited and shunted aside to a great degree for other than scholarly reasons". These reasons had to do with discomfort about Smith's theory that Jesus practised magical rites, particularly the hint that these rites may have included homosexual acts.' Hedrick cited in Jeffery, *Secret*, 30.

specifically, whether it was a hoax perpetuated by Smith himself. The latter is the opinion forwarded by Jeffrey in his assessment of the case, who applies the lenses of liturgy and a kind of 'forensic analysis of Smith's writings and life history'[65] in his profiling and interrogation of the document and its founder.

Jeffrey joins the voices of those who have made odd personal jibes at Smith's embodiment and/or persona in their rejection of him as deviant. Shawn Eyer in his review of some of the more peculiar, almost comical, scholarly responses to Smith's work cites as an example Joseph Fitzmyer, who 'saw it worthwhile to point out that Morton Smith was bald'. Eyer, thus ironically declares: '[W]hatever importance we may attach to the thickness of a scholar's hair, it seems that detached scholarly criticism fails when certain tenets of faith – even "enlightened" liberal faith – are called into question.'[66] The ways in which 'sane chauvinism' is built into the language of such personal jibes and employed as a discursive tool to 'other' Smith's position are not hard to find; Eyer notes how frequently 'words like "strange" or "dangerous" [are used] to describe things that are really only *different*'.[67]

The adoption of psychiatric insights not only as biological givens, but also tools by which to delegitimize the case of those with whom one disagrees, is apparent. Smith's work and writing itself is identified (and questioned) by Jeffrey's imposition of psychiatric labels:

> Smith's later account is *more bi-polar*. Though the Smith of 1960 recognised several items that 'may be of importance'... . the Smith of 1973 would say 'I was gradually reconciling myself to my worst expectations and repeating every day that I should discover nothing of importance.' Yet, somehow finding the unknown letter from Clement of Alexandria shot him suddenly to the other extreme.[68]

An assumed 'irrationality' and logical incoherence of the subject matter is also projected by Jeffrey onto both Clement's letter and Smith's accompanying work. He writes:

> I had great difficulty organizing this book; in some ways it was the most difficult thing I have ever tried to write. Almost every section of the book as it now stands was somewhere else in an earlier draft. Eventually I came to the conclusion that, since the subject was an act of deception, it was bound to keep collapsing in on itself. A 'real' subject, I think, would have an inherent structure, so that one could write a coherent narrative simply by describing that structure.[69]

65. Nicole Kelley, 'Review of Jeffrey's The Secret Gospel of Mark Unveiled', *Magic, Ritual, and Witchcraft* 4 (2009), 114–17.

66. Eyer, 'Strange', 110.

67. Eyer, 'Strange', 110; my emphasis.

68. Jeffrey, *Secret*, 9; my emphasis.

69. Jeffrey, *Secret*, 241.

A naturalized view of psychiatry is also detectable in Jeffrey's arguments. In a response to a largely critical review of his work, Jeffrey posits himself as a person with therapeutic 'counselling training' who is therefore uniquely tooled to comment not only on Smith's state of mind (albeit solely through Smith's written persona) but also destabilize Smith's case on that basis. Note particularly how emotions are linked with irrationality in his following statement:

> What can it mean when the discovery of a text about falsehood, conflict and sexuality is recounted in a personal memoir full of statements about false memories, conflict, sexuality *and insanity*? But my book was the first to make real headway with such questions. As the first person with counselling training and experience to address the problem, I was in a position to 'hear' the *contradictions, deceptions, emotions and silences*, in Smith's authorial 'voice' with somewhat more clarity than others have ... I actually approached this sensitive matter with considerable restraint: In order to keep the focus securely on the authorial persona, I scrupulously restricted my remarks to publicly available texts, mostly by Smith himself.[70]

Littered throughout the work are other psychiatric conjectures concerning Smith's assumed state of mind, and its lack in relation to rationality and reason; Jeffrey notes how 'extreme mood swings and bouts of amnesia raise doubts about his [Smith's] truthfulness'.[71] Moreover, 'dissociative episodes ... are a persistent and troubling feature of Smith's literary persona, whether or not they had anything to do with the man himself'.[72]

In a post-publication author interview, Jeffrey, when questioned explicitly about 'innuendos and suggestions that Morton Smith was mentally ill' tellingly replied:

> Everyone exhibits psychiatric symptoms to some degree. Everyone is a little narcissistic, a little paranoid, a little psychotic, a little bipolar, etc. These characteristics are classified as mental illnesses only when they become so pronounced that they interfere with normal functioning, though it is also true that some very ill people are capable of extraordinary productivity. It is therefore appropriate to note such tendencies in any discussion of any historical figure, and doing so need not be tantamount to an allegation of mental illness ... I don't

70. Jeffrey, 'Reply to Scott G Brown', 14; my emphasis.

71. Jeffrey, 'Reply to Scott G Brown', 18.

72. Jeffrey, *Secret*, 29. Note, however, that Smith's actual words need not be read in this psychiatric light at all. He states: 'The experience I shall never forget – it was probably the high point of my life. But the other things that must have been happening at the same time were simply gone, hidden by the blaze of the facts like stars in the day ... I think I remember the strange feeling of walking around the unchanged world, doing the usual things, unnoticed and unnoticeable, with all this going on inside my head.' Morton Smith, cited in Jeffrey, *Secret*, 29.

> believe [however] anyone with experience listening to mentally ill people could possibly read Smith's *The Secret Gospel* (Harper) memoir without wondering about Smith's personal issues. The book is, in fact, the weirdest publication I ever read, full of many of the kinds of things we are trained to look for: sudden and extreme changes of mood that seem like excessive reactions to the events that provoked them, an exaggerated sense of self-importance, memory lapses at key points, hostility disguised as humor, bizarre theories about what constitutes truth, sanity, or reality. The fact that some of these also appear in the Mar Saba letter of Clement, as well as in Smith's own voice, is surely relevant.[73]

Perhaps the most potent admission regarding Jeffrey's embrace of a psychiatric model is implicit within his remarks that characteristics of Smith 'hardly inspire confidence in what his books aim to tell us', particularly since, in Jeffrey's words, 'Smith made many bizarre and irresponsible statements identifying Christianity with mental illness, even while he repeatedly denigrated the value of psychiatry'.[74] In this statement, Jeffrey is no doubt referring to Smith's 1949 article, 'Psychiatric Practice and Christian Dogma', in which Smith (at this point still a minister within the church) discusses the irreconcilability of Christian faith with personal crises which are all sexual in nature (male sexual preferences, a relationship with a divorcee whose ex-husband was still alive and female masturbation).[75] However, crucially, the article does not, as Jeffrey alleges, 'identify Christianity with mental illness' but rather confirms how Christianity perpetuates certain normative constructions of sexuality, which dangerously marginalize those who do not subscribe to them. This is despite Smith claiming within the article that he 'doesn't see that if two adult males enjoy one another sexually, any harm is done to anybody'[76] and that the individual 'doesn't seem to be unstable, keeps his job, gets on well in society, has lots of normal friends, and seems generally happy'.[77] Smith also acknowledges the fact that a Christian counsellor would nonetheless be duty bound to point out the following to the individual:

> He must be told that homosexuality is a sin far more serious than fornication, and that unwillingness or inability to repent of it automatically debars the sinner from the sacraments. Whether or not psychological or social arguments against homosexuality are used, it must be made clear that the sin is not a matter for dispute nor for private judgment, but is established by the Christian

73. Jeffrey, 'Frequently Asked Questions about Morton Smith, the Secret Gospel of Mark, and my book, *The Secret Gospel of Mark Unveiled*', Interview. Available online at: http://music2.princeton.edu/jeffery/smithfaq.html.

74. Jeffrey, *Secret*, 29.

75. Albert I. Baumgarten, *Elias Bickerman as a Historian of the Jews: A Twentieth Century Tale* (Tübingen: Mohr Siebeck, 2010), 206.

76. Smith, cited in Le Donne, *Wife*, 86.

77. Smith, cited in Le Donne, *Wife*, 86.

> tradition which individuals can only accept or reject. Finally, for the good of the congregation no less than for his own good, he must sooner or later be made to choose between his new attachment to the Church and his previous sexual adjustment, *even though there be great probability that he will find no other adjustment so satisfactory*.[78]

Smith's ultimate rejection of Christianity and abandonment of the priesthood – which is cast by Jeffrey as itself a 'kind of psychological crisis'[79] rather than a social liberation or indeed anything else – and Smith's suspicion of psychiatry was no doubt influenced in part by both Christianity and psychiatry playing a part in leaking 'madness' into other intersectional marginalities, including sexual preference. For homosexuality (like madness) was in the past pathologized and categorized as a psychiatric disorder.[80]

Jeffrey's own strategic seepage of madness into sexual categories amounts, in the words of Scott Brown in his review of Jeffrey's volume, to 'exegetical violence'.[81] Jeffrey reads the Secret Gospel of Mark within histories of sexology, and ultimately concludes that it amounts to a 'tale of sexual preference … structured to create the impression that Jesus practiced homosexuality'.[82] Its provenance is not ancient but rather redolent of a twentieth-century author who is assumed to reflect 'a homoerotic subculture in English universities' and 'encoded contemporary homosexuality in the vocabulary of Platonic boy-love'.[83] Brown points out how the caricature of Smith's Jesus as a 'gay magician' does not take seriously Smith's own position, which in his opinion was far more nuanced and

> did no more than raise the question of whether the baptism he perceived to be occurring in LGM 1:11–12 involved physical symbolism of spiritual union with Jesus, in view of the fact that the other rite that Jesus instituted involved physical

78. Morton Smith, 'Psychiatric Practice and Christian Dogma', *Journal of Pastoral Care* 3 (1949), 17; my italicization.

79. Jeffrey, *Secret*, 184.

80. Similarities in the construction of madness and homosexuality are not incidental. 'Although homosexuality was removed from DSM and ICD in the 1970s and 1980s, the ripples radiating from homosexual psychopathologic discourse have not been easily dislodged … The INS enforced homosexual immigration exclusion until 1990 with the passage of the 1990 immigration act.' Barbara Rockenbach and Tom Mendina (eds), *Ethics and Electronic Information: A Festschrift for Stephen Almagno* (North Carolina: McFarland, 2002), 31, 34–5.

81. Scott G. Brown, 'Review, the Secret Gospel of Mark Unveiled: Imagined Rituals of Sex, Death, and Madness in a Biblical Forgery', *RBL* (9/15/07). Available online at: http://www.bookreviews.org/pdf/5627_5944.pdf.

82. Jeffrey, 91, cited in Brown, 'Review'.

83. Jeffrey, 213, cited in Brown, 'Review'.

> symbolism of spiritual union with Jesus in the form of ingesting bread and wine that represented his body and blood.[84]

Furthermore, Scott writes, 'To the best of my knowledge, Smith's last word on the subject, conveyed in a letter to Ian Wilson, was that no existing evidence, including the longer Gospel, could answer whether Jesus' baptism had a sexual element.'[85] Scott concludes his review of Jeffrey's project with uncertainty about 'what could lead a person to imagine so much depravity and falsity in a noncanonical Gospel and the person who discovered it?'[86] An appeal to Foucault is insightful in beginning to answer Scott's question. Unreason, in Foucault's opinion, was not madness, but rather the manifestation of difference or abnormality within a 'discourse that functions and circulates within and against those of a normative nature'.[87] Similarly, for Foucault, 'mental illness' was not an unchanging 'fact' across cultures, but rather specifically constructed within particular discursive formations. In Erik Fabris's words:

> The splitting of social life and the interactions into 'mad' and 'sound' (sane and insane, healthy and ill, rational and irrational) is necessary for the containment of certain acts and experiences. This hegemonic, ideological or dividing move has been called sanism and mentalism, though the latter can be regarded as a more general form of discounting any mental 'difference'. It might also be called European androcentric rationalism, but while this identifies oppression it does so without clearly identifying its expressed target, madness.[88]

Jeffrey's whole project was a discursively strategic scheme to distinguish both the Secret Gospel of Mark and Morton Smith as 'mad' – implying 'someone or something fell from [a] socially graced or normal state'[89] – highlighting Morton Smith's apparent transgression of normative patterns of scholarship, faith and sexuality. The paternalistic, sanist statements from Jeffrey's acknowledgements, pages and so on and the projection of Smith as emotional, tortured and other, indicate as much:

> When Morton Smith's life story is accurately and fairly told, it may well be evident that his feelings of rage were understandable, even amply justified. But the way he chose to express them in his publications was not … I have sat with some

84. Brown, 'Review'.
85. Brown, 'Review'.
86. Brown, 'Review'.
87. Fabris, *Tranquil*, 27.
88. Fabris, *Tranquil*, 29.
89. Luke Heighton, 'Reason Dazzled: Klimt, Krakauer and the Eyes of Medusa', in Gemma Blackshaw and Sabine Wieber (eds), *Journeys into Madness: Mapping Mental Illness in the Austro-Hungarian Empire* (Oxford: Berghahn Books, 2012), 145.

> extremely psychotic people who wanted me to validate things that were both false and intentionally hurtful; I know how hard it is to acknowledge someone's pain while refusing to condone his desire to pass it on to others. But that is what we must do. It is tragic that Smith's long-ago impostures, like antique landmines from a half-forgotten war, are still injuring innocent and well-intentioned scholars. The time has come to break the circle of hurt, by shelving the Secret Gospel under twentieth-century fantasy fiction where it belongs.[90]

This case provides a cameo example of how psy-discourses can at times be (prejudicially) employed to discredit and marginalize those with whom one disagrees. Such sanist modes of discourse, and their particular characterizations of 'madness', ultimately are designed to reinforce and perpetuate the speaker's/author's own specific cultural ideals of normalcy.[91] Such discourses amount to what mad studies has hailed as 'epistemic violence' by which an individual is stigmatized and ideologically disqualified as a 'legitimate knower'.[92] Refracted through psy-discourses Jeffrey renders Smith as the stereotypical 'mental patient': 'a dangerous person is someone who is unpredictable, who cannot be trusted, who threatens the public order and who consequently needs to be controlled'.[93]

Pathologizing Discourses and Biblical Characters

A cursory look at the ways in which a selection of recent biblical studies reference guides define 'madness' (particularly as they see it embodied in biblical characterizations) is a palpable means to try to gauge some of the broad ways in which the discipline has negotiated the topic. While nearly all entries begin with the caveat that cross-cultural cleavages between the ancient and contemporary Western worlds (and their linguistic and conceptual assumptions) should be duly acknowledged – 'The ancients depicted the supernatural origin, moral nature and behaviours that characterized madness rather than its psychological makeup'[94]; 'The modern psychological understanding of madness simply did not exist in biblical times'[95] – nonetheless many still go on to echo certain psy-discourses and/or concepts in their interpretations of selected biblical characters, belying

90. Jeffrey, *Secret*, 19.

91. Heighton, 'Reason', 145.

92. Maria Liegghio, 'A Denial of Being: Psychiatrization as Epistemic Violence', in LeFrançois et al. (eds), *Mad*, 122–9.

93. Liegghio, 'Denial', 126.

94. Richard Spencer, 'Madness', in David Noel Freedman and Allen C. Myers (eds), *Eerdmans Dictionary of the Bible* (Grand Rapids: William Eerdmans, 2000), 843.

95. Leland Ryken, James C. Wilhoit and Tremper Longman III, 'Madness', in Leland Ryken, James C. Wilhoit and Tremper Longman III, *Dictionary of Biblical Imagery* (eds) (Westmont, IL: IVP, 1998), 524.

an implicit cultural absorption of Western medical models. Interesting, too, is the fact that if one runs database searches on 'madness and the Bible', time and again the same 'morally ambivalent' biblical characters are thrown into view – Saul, Nebuchadnezzar, Ezekiel, Herod, and so on – along with various psy-related commentaries they have been subject to in recent biblical interpretations.[96] Thus, it is variously claimed: Saul, in his rebellion against God is punished by an evil spirit and in this 'exhibited evidence of psychoses, including hysteria'[97] and, moreover, his '"evil spirit from the Lord" may have been a form of manic-depression'[98]; Nebuchadnezzar, boasting of his own accomplishments, is reduced to bestial madness by God and is thought to 'exhibit symptoms of depressive or psychotic delusion'[99]; Jesus is shown to frequently deliver from demons 'those who exhibit apparently psychotic behaviour'.[100] The irrationality of these characters' respective madness seems to be based, at least in part, on assumptions concerning their moral excesses and/or emotions: 'Saul is plagued by paranoid jealousy of David ... [and] become[s] violent'; 'Nebuchadnezzar's pride becomes overwhelming',[101] 'bizarre, disturbing and grandiose'.[102] In a similar vein, the demon-possessed of the gospels are viewed as those with 'disorders' who 'strip themselves, live in tombs and behave violently'. Moreover, it is claimed: 'Other kinds of "madness" are the foolish ignorance of wicked teachers and religious leaders [who are] unreasonably evil and selfish, [marked by] foolhardiness and delirious frenzy and eccentricity.'[103] Psychobiographical commentaries that adopt modern medical models of mental illness as hermeneutical keys to interrogate biblical figures have also functioned

96. William Todd Schutz notes that the aim of 'psychobiography is simply stated, though immensely difficult to achieve: the understanding of persons'. William Todd Schutz, 'Introducing Psychobiography', in William Todd Schultz, *Handbook of Psychobiography* (Oxford: Oxford University Press, 2005), 3; Christopher Cook, 'The Prophet Samuel, Hypnagogic Hallucinations and the Voice of God – Psychiatry and Sacred Texts', *British Journal of Psychiatry* 203 (2013), 380–80; Christopher Cook, 'Psychiatry in Scripture: Sacred Texts and Psychopathology', *The Psychiatrist* 36 (2012), 225–9; Steven Shawn Tuell, 'Should Ezekiel Go to Rehab?: The Method to Ezekiel's "Madness"', *Perspectives in Religious Studies* 36 (2009), 289–302; David Halperin, *Seeking Ezekiel: Text and Psychology* (Pennsylvania: Pennsylvania State University Press, 1993); Aryeh Kasher and Eliezer Witztum, *King Herod: A Persecuted Persecutor: A Case Study in Psychohistory and Psychobiography* (Berlin: De Gruyter, 2008).

97. Ryken et al., 'Madness', 524.

98. 'Madness', in W. R. Browning, *A Dictionary of the Bible* (Oxford: Oxford University Press, 2009). Available online at: http://www.oxfordbiblicalstudies.com/article/opr/t94/e1180.

99. Ryken et al., 'Madness', 524.

100. Ryken et al., 'Madness', 524.

101. Ryken et al., 'Madness', 524.

102. Spencer, 'Madness', 843.

103. Spencer, 'Madness', 843.

as a convenient vehicle for sanist stereotyping. Saul Olyan, commenting on the embodied performance of David's feigned madness, speculates that this evoked 'potential indicators of mental disability' including autism-spectrum disorders:

> Frequently attention-seeking behaviors often associated with severe mental retardation and autism, strikes me as more plausible, particular in a narrative context in which David is attempting to feign mental disability publicly. If David is indeed drumming while drooling, he is portrayed as acting in ways indicative of severe mental retardation in a most public place – at the city gate or palace gate.[104]

David Halperin pictures Ezekiel as a talented yet intensely anguished figure, torn apart by internal turmoil concerning sexual desire and phobia. Moreover, this psychopathology is viewed as profoundly disturbing to the normative Western reader and ultimately discredits confidence in his prophetic testimony:

> Ezekiel 'as he really was' – as I imagine him – is very far from a lovable person. He emerges in these pages as an extreme exemplar of morbidity … It is hard to contemplate this *pathology without revulsion*, harder still to imagine so *hideous a system of delusion* dominating one of the great figures of the bible. *It is hardest of all to accept this portrait of Ezekiel and still think of him as a moral or religious authority.*[105]

Aryeh Kasher and Eliezer Witztum, similarly, in their co-written psychobiography of Herod the Great, diagnose this historical figure through the lens of 'Paranoid Personality Disorder'. Herod, troubled by persecutory delusions and irrational emotions, enviously executes those (including members of his own family) who are perceived as threats to his rule. They claim that later '[h]is [Herod's] condition subsequently deteriorated into what is known in modern psychiatric terminology as "Delusional Disorder" … [manifest in] psychotic levels, causing grave damage and ultimately even a loss of judgement, insight and the ability to comprehend reality. At times, these were compounded by depressive states that exacerbated his condition'.[106] Donald Capps, in his 2008 book *Jesus the Village Psychiatrist*,[107] evocatively (and anachronistically) identifies Jesus as 'a village psychiatrist' and attempts to 'diagnose' the interrelationship between physical, psychiatric and emotional dimensions of identity in the figures that he healed. Capps pictures the lot of the first-century Galilean peasant as fraught with anxiety-prompting

104. Olyan, *Disability*, 68.

105. All these phrases are redolent of sanist rhetoric. Halperin, *Seeking*, 12; my emphases.

106. Kasher and Witztum, *King*, xv.

107. Donald Capp, *Jesus the Village Psychiatrist* (Louisville: Westminster John Knox Press, 2008).

pressures: colonization, taxation, food scarcity, sexual exploitation, violence, banditry and inter- and intra-familial strife and aggression. Accordingly, the paralytic's symptoms (Mk 2:1-12) are demonstrative of 'psychosocial conflicts of the Jewish people, especially Jewish males'[108] who were systematically degraded by enforced menial occupations. The blindness of the man of Bethsaida (Mk 8:22-26) and Bartimaeus (Mk 10:46-52) are linked with uncontrolled emotion, particularly sexual envy, evidenced in wider cultural beliefs surrounding the evil eye.[109] The demon-possessed boy (Mk 9:14-29) kicking and foaming at the mouth reflects self-directed aggression against an overbearing Galilean father who stood in 'a long tradition of training sons to fight in defence of the homeland'.[110] Others, too, have slipped into psychopathological discourses in relation to the 'demon possessed': Craig Evans, for example, declares 'many mental illnesses were (mis)interpreted as being brought on by demon possession or some form of demon influence'.[111]

Diagnosing the long gone dead, leave alone those who are known to us only as characters in ancient literary texts, is, of course, a precarious (historical) enterprise, magnified further by the projection of alien (and disputed) frameworks onto such traditions. Justin Meggitt asserts that those who do not share 'a prior commitment to [classic] psychoanalytic assumptions' will find work such as Capps's 'unacceptably speculative'.[112] Meggitt himself submits that 'from what limited information we can deduce about the disorders that Jesus encountered it seems unlikely that their aetiologies were predominantly psychosomatic'.[113] In a different vein, Darla Schumm, working at the biblical studies and disability studies frontier, pertinently questions the stigmatizing imposition of Freudian categories surrounding sexuality onto these characters and their family relationships and 'a somewhat dangerous and implicit suggestion that physical disease and disability is often a result of a mental imbalance'.[114] Moreover, the enforced healing (/normalization) of such individuals, exhibits a 'curative' medical model (and compulsory normativity).[115]

108. Capp, *Jesus*, 51.

109. Capp, *Jesus*, 73–6.

110. Capp, *Jesus*, 2.

111. Craig Evans, *Luke* (Understanding the Bible Commentary Series) (Grand Rapids: Baker Books, 2011), online edition, no pages.

112. Justin Meggitt, 'The Historical Jesus and Healing: Jesus' Miracles in Psychosocial Context', in Fraser Watts (ed.), *Spiritual Healing: Scientific and Religious Perspectives* (Cambridge: Cambridge University Press, 2011), 17–43, 29, 21.

113. Meggitt, 'Historical', 30.

114. Darla Schumm, 'A Review of Jesus the Village Psychiatrist', *Journal of Religion, Disability and Health* 14 (2010), 419–21, 419.

115. Alison Kafer, *Feminist, Queer, Crip* (Bloomington: Indiana University Press, 2013), 27.

Otto Wahl likewise notes how psy-labelling is frequently used to 'characterize people rather than to name their disorders'.[116] Persons/characters 'diagnosed' with psychosis ideologically transform into 'psychotics' with all the damaging implications and assumptions that that label evokes (in a way that cancer does not signify the person as 'the cancerous').[117] In Wahl's words, '[U]se of such terms … subtly dehumanize the person implying that the [social or mental] disorders define the individual rather than describe a fluctuating or temporary psychiatric condition.'[118] That is not to say, of course, that these biblical interpreters have complete confidence in their biomedical 'diagnoses' of biblical characters, but rather that they seem to echo psychiatric insights from their own Western cultural contexts (which often ideologically associate particular experiences and conditions with deficit, negativity and excess) to further consolidate the perceived 'otherness' and/or moral offence of these biblical characters.

S. Tamar Kamionkowski, too, offers salutary warnings of the uncritical imposition of a 'Western psychiatric gaze' in projects such as these. She writes, 'Human nature is variable, norms are not absolute, and what seems strange in one culture appears perfectly normal in another.'[119] A Western psychiatric gaze has also been critically implicated in 'colonialist contest[s] between so-called civilised and primitive bodies'[120] where a pathologizing of persons or behaviours deemed morally questionable is symptomatic of a privileging of 'a Western norm of rationality'.[121] In Victoria Pitts's words, the 'willingness to apply the language of pathology – a powerful social [and sanist] discourse that has historically been used as a tool of socialization and control – [is] uncritical

116. Otto Wahl, *Media Madness: Public Images of Mental Illness* (New Brunswick: Rutgers University Press, 1995), 21.

117. Wahl, *Media*, 21.

118. Wahl, *Media*, 21.

119. S. Tamar Kamionkowski, *Gender Reversal and Cosmic Chaos: A Study in the Book of Ezekiel* (London: Bloomsbury, 2003), 77.

120. Victoria Pitts, *In the Flesh: The Cultural Politics of Body Modification* (New York: Palgrave Macmillan Press 2003), 77.

121. Matthew Bell, *Melancholia: The Western Malady* (Cambridge: Cambridge University Press, 2014), 103. Rationality is of course also privileged in the discourses of psychiatry: 'Cognitive science distinguishes between two kinds of rationality: instrumental and epistemic. Instrumental rationality concerns the extent to which decisions and actions approximate the best ways to achieve appropriate goals. Epistemic rationality concerns the extent to which beliefs and thought processes are formed in coherence with logical rules – and correspond to the structure of the world as it is intersubjectively assumed. Thus, rationality is a normative concept, which means that it corresponds to a certain ideal of adequacy and efficiency. It is not clear how the flagrant irrationality of psychosis relates to possible irrationality as described by cognitive science.' Rasmus Revsbech, Erik Lykke Mortensen, Gareth Owen, Julie Nordgaard, Lennart Jansson, Ditte Sæbye, Trine Flensborg-Madsen and Josef Parnas, 'Exploring Rationality in Schizophrenia', *British Journal of Psychiatry* (2015), 98–103, 98.

and dangerous'.[122] In this respect, the works reviewed here do variously forward types of sanist framings and are reflective of 'imperialistic pathologizing'.[123]

Sane Privilege in Biblical Studies

The examples introduced here are symptomatic of broader trajectories of sane prejudice and sane privilege evident within the Western biblical studies discipline, in which the sane subject – rational, reasonable, logical and dispassionate – is 'rendered invisible resulting in unearned entitlements and conferment of dominance'[124] while those perceived to fall outside that norm are frequently dismissed through psy- and pathologizing discourses. PhebeAnn Wolframe, in her evocative article 'The Madwoman in the Academy', critically interrogates the 'use [of] such discourses to describe not only people who have been psychiatrized, but also those who have been marginalized in other ways'[125] and, inspired by work on white privilege, notes how the 'sane' and normative academic (white, male, heterosexual, able-bodied) frequently assumes his identity to be 'morally neutral, average, and also ideal'.[126] Wolframe's suggestive listing of the contents of the 'knapsack of sane privilege' (purposefully adopted and adapted here for my own discipline of biblical studies) makes for salutary reading[127]:

(a) *I consider 'sane' people (both as characters in biblical texts and peers in scholarship) and particularly those who embody other forms of privilege (on account of sex, race, ability and class) largely positively.* The mad, in contrast, are stereotypically associated with negative tropes of otherness and are frequently identified as irrational, emotional, deficient, morally questionable and violent and so on.
(b) *I am never asked to represent or give the voice of 'sane' people:* 'Token' sane people are not needed as they constitute the majority. However, the 'token mad person' (like the token female, black or disabled character or scholar) is often assumed to represent the 'otherness' of an entire group.
(c) *It is unlikely that, as a 'sane' academic, my personal background (medical history, political affiliation, race, sexual orientation, gender performance, clothing, hairstyle and aspects of my physical and verbal presentation) will be seen as crucial for understanding my work.* Yet mad people's histories are often exhibited before others and their views and practices are often read

122. Pitts, 'Flesh', 77.

123. Donnelly, *Vogue*, 12.

124. Claire Maxwell and Peter Aggleton, 'Introduction', in Claire Maxwell and Peter Aggleton (eds), *Privilege, Agency and Affect: Understanding the Production and Effects of Action* (Basingstoke: Palgrave Macmillan, 2013), 1–11, 4.

125. Wolframe, 'Madwoman'.

126. Wolframe, 'Madwoman'.

127. Wolframe, 'Madwoman'.

symptomatically against the backdrop of these histories, which are accordingly understood as reflections of their madness and/or deviance.

(d) *Being understood as sane (either as a character in biblical texts and/or as a scholar), and particularly if one is privileged in other ways, means that one need not be subject to cures or other 'normalization' practices.* Yet 'mad' persons and characters are frequently forced into 'curative treatments' (healings etc.) and to embody and perform 'normative' practices of the culture/discipline (including standard bodily performances, speech and practices etc.) in which they operate. Price notes how frequently 'persons [like herself] with mental disabilities are presumed not to be competent, or understandable, or valuable, or whole'[128] and are consequently exiled from the ivory tower. She writes: 'The instruments of exclusion are not visible or dramatic – men in white coats dragging people away – but quiet, insidious: We flunk out and drop out. We fail to get tenure.'[129] The infrastructure of higher education in her view thus discriminates against those who do not adequately fit the implicit norms of reason, rationality and sense and so on. These representations 'reify the belief that madness and sanity are two extremely separate spaces – one dangerous, one safe. To extend the metaphor of academe as an ivory tower, these representations attempt to form a moat which both *defines* and tries to *protect* academe as a sanctuary of reason. The moat separates the "normal", non-crazy people, from the crazies.'[130]

Those neurodiverse or 'mad' academics within the academy are therefore habituated and conditioned to 'pass' as normal; never revealing their non-rational 'deviancies' from the norm. As Price notes: '[T]he necessity of passing for survival perpetuates the conventional view of academe as an "ivory tower" ... threatened (from the outside) by the destructive force of insanity.'[131]

(e) *As a sane academic, I fit in. I do not feel cut off, out-of-place, outnumbered, unheard, distanced or feared.* Sara Ahmed's work on 'killjoy' feminist bodies marked by otherness or deviation from patriarchal social norms,[132] notes Wolframe, is relevant here. Mad bodies, likewise, frequently make normative 'sane' bodies uncomfortable through their otherness. In Wolframe's words, '[O]ur protests against sanist assumptions are also often seen as killing the joy of those who are "only trying to help" (generally by reinforcing psychiatric discourse) or who feel they have legitimate reasons to fear or ostracize mad people.'[133]

128. Price, *Mad*, 26.

129. Price, *Mad*, 6.

130. Margaret Price, 'Assaults on the Ivory Tower', Lecture at Leeds University (2008); emphases in the original. Available online at: http://pf7d7vi404s1dxh27mla5569.wpengine.netdna-cdn.com/files/library/price-Leeds-talk.pdf.

131. Price, *Mad*, 7.

132. Sara Ahmed, *The Promise of Happiness* (Durham: Duke University Press, 2010), 50.

133. Wolframe, 'Madwoman'.

The privileging of rationality and reason in both academic and psychiatric discourses[134] inevitably involves the prejudicial marginalization of other ways of being and knowing.[135] As Wolframe appositely warns, sane privilege can be a distinct disadvantage when it prevents acknowledgement of the value of alternative perspectives, including those of the 'mad'.[136] 'Mad', though 'once a reviled term that signalled the worst kinds of bigotry and abuse', now transgressively reappropriated functions as 'a critical alternative to "mental illness" or "disorder" as a way of naming and responding to emotional, spiritual and neuro-diversity',[137] signalling 'an identity, a stance, an act of resistance [and] a theoretical approach'.[138] Working within the 'mad studies' field, Shayda Kafai attempts to deconstruct the discursive binary opposition between sane and mad by purposefully conceptualizing what she terms a 'Mad Border Body' which is 'a dual inhabitant' moving between and within both sanity and madness. In her words:

> The mad border body reminds us, just as the mestiza and queer border body do, that identity categories are not given but constructed; identities are created in the act of edging, in the in-between living that dominant culture often scrutinizes and assumes invisible … The mad border body challenges the belief that madness is an 'individual pathology … [a] permanency of defect' (Wilson and Beresford 144). This body challenges the notion of permanent rigidity, the belief that madness diminishes one's ability to access full personhood. Thus, the role of the mad border body is to re-examine the ableist belief that one is either sane or mad, that one body cannot possess the attributes of both categories.[139]

134. Psychiatry and biblical studies both value objectivity. 'Psychiatry seeks objective criteria as a basis for its diagnoses and treatments. Whilst some of what must be accepted as objective evidence is necessarily somewhat subjective (another person's account of the thoughts that they observe within their own minds, for example) the aspiration is to be as objective as possible. Transcultural psychiatry acknowledges further that objectivity is especially vulnerable where a psychiatrist from one culture confidently asserts the abnormality of experiences, beliefs or behaviour of a person from another culture. Thus, determination of the abnormality of religious experiences, beliefs and behaviours requires reference to the cultural norms of the particular faith tradition and its local community, as well as to the self understanding of the individual.' Cook, 'Psychiatry', 225–9.

135. Karin Olson, Richard A. Young and Izabela Z. Schultz (eds), *Handbook of Qualitative Health Research for Evidence-Based Practice* (New York: Springer, 2016), 217.

136. Wolframe, 'Madwoman'.

137. LeFrançois et al., 'Introducing', 10.

138. Jennifer Poole and Jennifer Ward, 'Breaking Open the Bone: Storying, Sanism and Mad Grief', in LeFrançois (eds), *Mad*, 94–104, 96.

139. Shayda Kafai, 'The Mad Border Body: A Political In-betweeness', *Disability Studies Quarterly* 33 (2013). Available online at: http://dsq-sds.org/article/view/3438.

This poses the question, how can one begin to deconstruct the normate rational mindset in Western academia in general, and biblical studies in particular, and to craft an alternative 'mad border' subject, which deconstructs the gulf between sanity and madness? Here, three proposals to this effect are offered which will foreground my arguments in later chapters.

First, the rhetorical fiction of 'rationality' and 'reason' needs to be deconstructed. Philosopher Raphael Sassower, in his provocative work *A Sanctuary of Their Own: Intellectual Refugees in the Academy* (2000) has similarly warned that '[t]he voice of reason could bar potential actions and could confine us all to the cradle of rationality from which we exit only feet first. When there are exceptions, when individual academics do defy the rules of their games, they are in too small a minority, marginalized and patronized'.[140] He radically proposes that the ivory tower should be recast as a sanctuary (/asylum?) in which academics may 'madly' pursue certain questions and address moral issues from 'diverse' and 'different' (rather than 'deviant' or 'other') spaces of knowing.[141] Undoubtedly there are, and have been, mad and/or neurodiverse interpreters within biblical studies, but the fact that none have 'come out' in their writings as such[142] and continue to 'pass' as 'normal' belies a certain normalizing/rationalizing script, which scholars feel duty bound to enact. Rather, 'mad talk' should be a legitimate channel by which people 'can narrate their knowledge'.[143]

Second, the abstraction and separation between reason and emotion needs to be questioned. As studies of privilege, agency and affect within academic contexts have similarly noted:

> Logos and pathos are intertwined not positioned as opposites … although commitments to intellectual pursuits might appear to be about the purely ideational or rational, it is difficult to sustain this separation since the strengths of these commitments comes from the second-order emotional commentary … intellectual commitments academics make are not the binary opposite of our emotions but intertwined with them.[144]

140. Raphael Sassower, *A Sanctuary of Their Own: Intellectual Refugees in the Academy* (Lanham: Rowman and Littlefield, 2000), 13.

141. Sassower, *Sanctuary*, 13.

142. In marked contrast to, for instance, queer perspectives, which have increasingly been revealed within the academy. See, for example, Halvor Moxnes' autobiographical foreword in his *Putting Jesus in His Place: A Radical Vision of Household and Kingdom* (Louisville: Westminster John Knox, 2003).

143. Liegghio, 'Denial', 128.

144. Sue Clegg, 'The Space of Academia: Privilege, Agency and the Erasure of Affect', in C. Maxwell and P. Aggleton, *Privilege, Agency and Affect: Understanding the Production and Effects of Action* (New York: Palgrave Macmillan, 2013), chapter 4, digital version, no pages.

Emotions are neither more fundamental than reason in developing theories and interpretations, nor less important; rather, each of these human aspects reflects elements of human experience and knowing inseparable from other elements.

Third, as Sara Heinämaa argues in her study of European rationality's break with modernity, the Western scientific tradition enshrined in reason needs in postmodern times to embrace the particularity of discourse and experience. She urges for the 'develop[ment of] new conceptual means for articulating rationality in a situation in which truth itself is increasingly regarded as relative to specific cultures, traditions, and historical situations'.[145] The construction of 'mad' counter-discourses (like cultural models of disability)[146] in which the voices of experience, rather than the dominant voices of sanist culture or medicine/psychiatry, are heard is one such example of such particularity. Caroline Knowles likewise agrees that

> [t]he concept of voice invokes a politics of recognition and places the theorization and experience of the unheard at the centre of the research activity ... the use of voice in the task of social analysis positions lives as a key source of social knowing. The voice narrating the story of its life in a particular broad set of circumstances opens a window onto that life, other lives and broader social circumstances in which they are cast.[147]

Mad voices also caution against psy-pathological discourses leaking into other terrains: the so-called psychiatrist within. We need to be aware of how our own voice and words prop up (even unconsciously) models of oppression. We must proceed cautiously asking: 'Whose discourse are we adopting? In whose interest is it? What does it make visible and what does it remove from sight? Who does it touch and how?'[148] What Mark Osteen terms 'an empathetic scholarship', which involves the determined juxtaposition of contemporary mad culture with biblical texts and interpretations, provides a useful stimulant for thinking differently in regard to both texts and madness.[149] As I argued elsewhere: 'We can imaginatively speak with, rather than for those who cannot speak for themselves by immersing

145. Sara Heinämaa, *European Rationality in the Break from Modernity: Studies in Phenomenology and Hermeneutics*. Available online at: http://www.helsinki.fi/erbm/description/index.html.

146. On the relative absence of mad perspectives in contrast to disability perspectives/voices in academic discourse, see Robyn Lewis Brown, 'The Absence of Psychiatric C/S/X Perspectives in Academic Discourse: Consequences and Implications', *Disability Studies Quarterly* 33 (2013). Available online at: http://dsq-sds.org/article/view/3433/3198.

147. Caroline Knowles, *Bedlam on the Streets* (London: Routledge, 2000), 11.

148. Bonnie Burstow, 'A Rose by Any Other Name: Naming and the Battle against Psychiatry', in LeFrançois et al. (eds), *Mad*, 79–90, 90.

149. Reflective and critical questions prompted from encounters with mad perspectives may include: what material and ideological effects do mad perspectives offer within biblical studies? How does madness intersect with other marginalities? Does madness illuminate relationships between 'psychiatry and colonialism, patriarchy, eugenics and neoliberalism?'

ourselves in the experiences and stories of those in other cross-cultural settings who have experiences similarly marginalisation on account of their perceived [differences].'[150] If Western biblical scholarship is ever to overcome sanism and sane privilege it must cease 'banishing Bedlam' from its ivory tower and rather, akin to Téllez's collaborative work with the patients of the Vivantes Klinik who questioned many of the sanist stereotypes endemic to the original version of *The Cabinet of Dr Calagari*, radically connect with the mad experiences, identities, practices and performances that could potentially transform it. Of course, in responding to that vision, one needs, first, citing Téllez's provocative words on the subject, to 'cure *the sane* of their lucidity'.[151] The meta-critical exposure of implicit sanist assumptions within the biblical studies discipline outlined here, I hope, is one small first step towards responding to such a call.

How does madness destabilize assumptions surrounding 'truth and subjectivity'? Wolframe, *Reading*, 5.

150. Louise Lawrence, *Sense and Stigma in the Gospels: Depictions of Sensory-Disabled Characters* (Oxford: Oxford University Press, 2013), 5.

151. Reyes, 'Bomb'; my italicization.

Chapter 2

The Curious Incident of a Jew in the Night-Time: Autistry and an Encounter with Nicodemus

The Western public's fascination with autism has rightly been hailed as 'a phenomenon'[1] Since its formal identification as a 'disorder' in the mid-twentieth century,[2] both diagnoses and awareness of autism have burgeoned, so too have the condition's cultural and metaphorical currencies. The success of Mark Haddon's award-winning mystery novel *The Curious Incident of the Dog in the Night-Time* (2003),[3] told from the viewpoint of a 15-year-old protagonist Christopher Boone, who dazzles at maths but finds interaction with people puzzling,[4] bears witness to this widespread appeal. Stuart Murray goes as far as to suggest that Haddon's novel has 'become ubiquitous as *the* contemporary marker of the details of autistic presence, a *fiction* that is increasingly read as *factual*.'[5] This is in spite of the fact that it is not penned by an autistic author[6] and in some reviewers' opinions, uncritically rehearses hardbound stereotypes including 'incapacity to read the thoughts, emotions and actions of others'[7] and the narrow interests of the

1. Irene Rose, 'Review of Stuart Murray, Autism and the Contemporary Sentimental: Fiction and the Narrative Fascination of the Present', *Disability Studies Quarterly* 30(1) (2010). Available online at: http://dsqsds.org/article/view/1072/1251.

2. See Adam Feinstein, *A History of Autism: Conversations with the Pioneers* (Chichester: Wiley Blackwell, 2010).

3. Mark Haddon, *The Curious Incident of the Dog in the Night-Time* (New York: Doubleday, 2003).

4. Although Christopher Boone is never explicitly diagnosed within the novel, his 'condition' did feature on the book's blurb.

5. Stuart Murray, 'Autism and the Contemporary Sentimental: Fiction and the Narrative Fascination of the Present', *Literature and Medicine* 25(1) (2006), 24–45, 37; my emphases.

6. Petra Kupper discusses Eric Chen's rewriting of passages from the novel in light of his own autistic experience. See Petra Kupper, 'Dancing Autism: The Curious Incident of the Dog in the Nighttime and Bedlam', *Text and Performance Quarterly* 28(1–2) (2008), 192–205.

7. Murray, *Autism*, 27. As the *Oxford English Dictionary* rather starkly puts it: 'a mental condition, present from early childhood, characterized by great difficulty in communicating and forming relationships with other people and in using language and abstract concepts'.

so-called high-functioning autistic savant.[8] Haddon himself never specified within the novel the condition that Christopher Boone was presumed to have, and has recently voiced alarm that his book has been received in some quarters as a virtual textbook on autism. In his words:

> I'm a little worried if people are saying, 'If you want to work out how to treat people on the spectrum, read this novel' … I also get a bit worried when people say, 'I've got Asperger's, my family have never understood me but I gave them your book and it opened a window' … I want to say, 'I wish the people in your life had been able to make the leap of imagination to understand your world without having to go into a bookshop and buy a book'.[9]

The reception of Haddon's novel serves as a fitting example of how autism is not self-evident within public consciousness but rather, as Anne McGuire submits, is 'made intelligible to us via multiple discursive contexts (e.g., the ways in which autism gets written about in the newspaper; what images we are presented with …). These contexts work to give autism a particular and contingent shape and structure; they allow autism to appear as it does' and, in turn, serve to *re*-produce its 'taken-for-granted representations'.[10]

Medical models of the condition are also part of its discursive construction. The most recent edition of *The Diagnostic and Statistical Manual of Mental Disorders* (*DSM-5*) released in 2013, subsumes a number of conditions under the heading 'Autism Spectrum Disorders' and promotes a deficit model in regard to the following areas: (a) 'social-emotional reciprocity': ranging from isolation to peculiar social approach, failures in back and forth conversation patterns and concentration on narrowly defined interests; (b) 'nonverbal communicative behaviors used for social interaction' including 'abnormalities in eye contact and body language or deficits in understanding and use of gestures'; (c) 'developing, maintaining, and understanding relationships' from 'difficulties adjusting behavior to suit various social contexts … to absence of interest in peers'.[11]

Oxford English Dictionary. Available online at: http://www.oxforddictionaries.com/definition/english/autism.

8. On the language of functioning, see Stuart Murray, 'Autism Functions/The Function of Autism', *Disability Studies Quarterly* 30(1) (2010), no pages. Available online at: http://dsq-sds.org/article/view/1048.

9. Anita Singh, 'Mark Haddon – Don't Use Curious Incident as an Autism Textbook', *The Telegraph*, 1 June 2015. Available online at: http://www.telegraph.co.uk/culture/culturenews/9311242/Mark-Haddon-dont-use-Curious-Incident...as-an-autism-textbook.html.

10. Anne McGuire, 'Representing Autism: A Sociological Examination of Autism Advocacy', *Atlantis* 35(2) (2011), 62–71, 62. Available online at: http://journals.msvu.ca/index.php/atlantis/article/viewFile/918/9143.

11. *DSM-5* cited online at: https://www.autismspeaks.org/what-autism/diagnosis/dsm-5-diagnostic-criteria.

Building on these medical 'deficit' constructions, the 'autistic spectrum' has also furnished contemporary discourses with a metaphorical arsenal to censor and exile those identities and practices it deems 'other'.[12] In Murray's words, '[T]he figure of the autistic individual … is the *personification* of difference … the alien within the human, the mystical within the rational, the ultimate enigma.'[13] Ann Jurecic powerfully reveals some of the ways in which these negative cultural resonances are given expression when she states:

> I have heard casual insults – 'Don't be autistic!' – as well as offhand references to 'autistic personality', 'ethical autism' and 'autistic economics'. In addition, fed by our limited, distorted understanding of what it means to have autism … [it] appears to have become a disturbing new metaphor for the postmodern self, disengaged from the world and from others. This metaphor may imply that we identify with the alienation of autism, but our appropriation of the diagnosis to represent the emptiness of contemporary lives and our transformation of the word 'autistic' into an insult suggest a prejudice fuelled by a profound discomfort with and fear of neurological difference.[14]

Theological discourses, too, have not been immune to discursive employments such as these. Andrew Pinsent, for example, has recently adopted the term 'spiritually autistic' to denote 'a person [who] … might be in full possession of the virtue of wisdom (she might even be aware that God exists and be capable of following instructions from God), but she would lack attention of union of the soul with God and [would be] unable to share in God's stance toward wisdom'.[15]

12. This could also be related to some of the negative social constructions which have often surrounded the condition – including 'refrigerator mothers' assumed to be emotionally 'cold' in their approach to their children. Douglas Biklen writes, 'As I have written in my own work on the sociology of autism, metaphor is ubiquitous, beginning with the very term autism, which implies that the person is an island to him or herself.' Douglas Biklen, 'Review of Representing Autism: Culture, Narrative, Fascination', *Journal of Literary & Cultural Disability Studies* 3(1) (2009), 107–109. Available online at: http://muse.jhu.edu/journals/jlc/summary/v003/3.1.biklen.html.

13. Stuart Murray, 'Autism and the Contemporary Sentimental: Fiction and the Narrative Fascination of the Present', *Literature and Medicine* 25(1) (2006), 24–45, 25; emphasis in the original.

14. Ann Jurecic, 'Neurodiversity', *College English* 69(5) (2007), 421–42, 422.

15. Andrew Pinsent, 'Wisdom and Evil', in Paul K. Moser and Michael T. Mcfall (eds), *The Wisdom of the Christian Faith* (Cambridge: Cambridge University Press, 2013), 99–120, 113. Jonathan Marlowe adopts a similar trope in a sermon when he states: 'John's gospel suggests that *spiritual autism* may be the condition that afflicts us. Like Nicodemus and the woman at the well, we are too concrete, too literalistic, too focused on the minutia of our pet projects and daily tasks to lift up our eyes and see the world outside us, to see the heavenly world from which Jesus has come bearing gifts, and to which he desires to take

In critically responding to both the medical 'deficit model' and pejorative discursive and cultural employments such as those noted above, certain advocacy perspectives have recently sought to reappropriate autism as a 'neurodiverse' identity – advancing 'a willingness to make room for difference as difference'[16] – within life and discourse.[17] Such standpoints 'see autism as a different way of thinking, worthy of celebration in its own right, not a malady to be cured'.[18] Taking cues from such perspectives and related sources (autobiographies etc.) – what Mark Osteen and others have rendered 'autistry'[19] – here I want to probe another 'curious incident in the night-time'. This time it involves a Jew named Nicodemus who has recently been subject to both hypothesized autistic diagnoses and/or negative discursive inflections (frequently employing stereotypical traits) associated with the condition. In critically responding to these flat appropriations of Nicodemus's character, I adopt what James McGrath has termed an 'autistic criticism', whereby one seeks to 'promote the agency and recognition of autistic perspectives on cultural texts' and, in so doing, challenge the widespread 'cultural marginalization of autistic subjectivities'.[20] McGrath points out how literary characters understood by interpreters to be somewhere 'on the spectrum are usually positioned as *other* to the audience, as well as to the characters surrounding them'[21] with neurotypical addressees thus perpetuated as 'the norm'. Can, however, alternative readings be constructed through interactions with contemporary autistry's voices and

us' (my emphasis). Jonathan Marlowe, 'Spiritual Autism' (2005). Available online at: http://theivybush.blogspot.co.uk/2005/02/spiritual-autism.html.

16. Ralph James Savarese, 'Parent & Sibling Roundtable: Neurodiversity and Caregiving', *Disability Studies Quarterly* 30(1) (2010), no pages. Available online at: http://dsq-sds.org/article/view/1061/1236.

17. 'Neurodiversity' is often credited as being coined by sociologist and autism advocate Judy Singer. She argued that '[t]he "neurologically different" represent a new addition to the familiar political categories of class/gender/race' in her essay 'Why Can't You Be Normal for Once in Your Life?', in Marian Corker (ed.), *Disability Discourse* (Buckingham: Open University Press, 1999), 59–67. Although Singer herself later wrote, 'I am not sure if I coined this word, or whether it's just "in the air", part of the zeitgeist.' Singer, cited in J. Meyerding, 'Thoughts on Finding Myself Differently Brained' (1998), no pages. Available online at: http://mjane.zolaweb.com/diff.html.

18. Anna P. Kroncke, Marcy Willard and Helena Huckabee, *Assessment of Autism Spectrum Disorder: Critical Issues in Clinical, Forensic and School Settings* (New York: Springer, 2016), 32.

19. See Mark Osteen, *Autism and Representation* (New York: Routledge, 2008), esp. 97–179.

20. James McGrath, 'Autistic Criticism: An Autistic Reading of BBC1's The Syndicate (2015) and the Cultural State of Asperger Syndrome', no pages. Available online at: http://www.rowmaninternational.com/cultural-studies/autistic-criticism-an-autistic-reading-of-bbc1s-the-syndicate-2015-and-the-cultural-state-of-asperger-syndrome.

21. McGrath, 'Autistic', no pages; my emphasis.

literatures? Moreover, can these 'autistic presences' find resonance within Jn 3: 1-15, not with a single character, but rather the wider narrative discourse (and its positioning of the audience) itself?

In short, my aims are threefold: first, to challenge 'diagnostic' readings of Nicodemus's autism (or metaphorical spiritual autism), which inscribe his character (and the autistic condition) with stereotypical negative tropes and deficits. Second, through interaction with autistry's sources, to identify traits of the condition from those neuro-diverse lived voices who do not inscribe their 'autistic' identity with deficits but rather with abilities. Third, to show how these 'autistic presences' actually have much in common with Jesus and the audience within John's Gospel, rather than a single 'disabled' and/or 'othered' character.

Nicodemus . . . On the Spectrum?

Given recent moves in a variety of disciplines, in both sciences and the arts, which have sought to retrospectively 'diagnose' various historical and literary characters as autistic, or marked by autistic-like traits,[22] it is perhaps unsurprising that similar attempts have also begun to have been made in relation to biblical figures.[23] Nicodemus, a famously enigmatic character who

22. For diagnosis of historical and/or literary characters, see Uta Frith, *Autism: Explaining the Enigma* (Oxford: Blackwell, 2003). For example, Frith diagnoses a monk named Brother Juniper in a twelfth-century text by St. Francis. She notes that he is portrayed as having a very literal understanding of Franciscan virtues which leads to misunderstanding and seems incapable of empathetic interconnection with other characters (19–21). Kristina Chew's recent essay notes that 'applying concepts of neurodiversity and cognitive difference … to pre-twentieth century texts poses not only interpretative but ethical challenges'. She nevertheless attempts such an analysis of 'Homer's epic poetry using concepts from neurodiversity to highlight how intellectual and physical disability are therein represented'. She looks at how neurodiversity might be studied in the ancient world by focusing on specific ranges of words in poems including speechless and much travelled/versatile to identify certain neurodiverse elements. See Chew, 'Odysseus and "the Fools": Applying Concepts of Neurodiversity to the Ancient World', in Alexandra Perry and Chris Herrara (eds), *Ethics and Neurodiversity* (Newcastle: Cambridge Scholars Publishing, 2013), 276–85.

23. Neurologists Stephen Matthew and Jeyaraj Pandian, for example, have attempted to identify Samson as exhibiting autistic traits including 'abnormal eating' evidenced in the incident of consuming bees and honey in the carcass of the lion and a propensity for extraordinary physical feats and for violence. They write, 'In Chapter 14, he tears a lion with his bare hands "as he would have a rent a kid" (verse 6); in Chapter 15, he kills a 1000 Philistines with the jawbone of an ass; and in Chapter 16 in his final act, he causes the house in which he was held captive to fall by pushing against two pillars that he was tied to, killing more men than he ever did in his life, and in doing so sacrificing his own life. It is possible that Samson was able to perform these feats as he may have been insensitive to pain, which is occasionally seen among autistics. A study of hospitalized individuals carried

confounds simple categorization, has been variously numbered among these. Nicodemus is first introduced in the fourth gospel as 'a Pharisee' and 'leader of the Jews' who comes to Jesus by night (3:1). He addresses Jesus as 'Rabbi' and goes on to hail him as a 'teacher who has come from God' (3:2). However, Nicodemus questions Jesus's reference to 'being born from above' (3:3) by asking 'how can anyone be born after having grown old? Can one enter a second time into the mother's womb and be born?' (3:4). Jesus continues by explaining the importance of 'being born in the Spirit' and eventually declares, 'Are you a teacher of Israel and you do not understand these things?' (3:10). Nicodemus's second (albeit brief) appearance is in chapter 7, where the Jewish authorities are featured wishing to arrest Jesus but Nicodemus interjects with the following statement: 'Our law does not judge people without first giving them a hearing to find out what they are doing, does it?' (7:51). Finally in chapter 19, Nicodemus features in the entombment scene, bringing 'a mixture of myrrh and aloes weighing about a hundred pounds' (19:40) to prepare Jesus's body. The narrator reminds the reader that Nicodemus first came to Jesus 'at night' (19:39) and he is accompanied at the tomb by Joseph of Arimathea, who it is claimed 'was a disciple of Jesus, though a secret one, because of his fear of the Jews' (v.38). In all three instances, in Jouette Bassler's terms, 'Nicodemus makes appearances that seem to be fraught with significance but the nature of that significance remains elusive. He appears often enough to evoke curiosity but not, it seems, often enough to satisfy it'.[24]

While estimations of Nicodemus's character have been mixed in biblical scholarship,[25] with debates variously probing the extent to which he negatively embodies opponents/outgroups or conversely a more positive identity as 'a

out in Sweden had reached the conclusion that individuals with autism or autism spectrum disorders are prone to acts of violence.' See Stephen Mathew and Jeyaraj Pandian, 'Newer Insights to the Neurological Diseases among Biblical Characters of Old Testament', *Annals of Indian Academy of Neurology* 13(3) (2010), 164–6.

24. Jouette M. Bassler, 'Mixed Signals: Nicodemus in the Fourth Gospel', *Journal of Biblical Literature* 108(4) (1989), 635–46, 635.

25. Gabi Renz sees him as an 'ambiguous disciple'. See Gabi Renz, 'Nicodemus: An Ambiguous Disciple? A Narrative Sensitive Investigation', in John Lierman, *Challenging Perspectives on the Gospel of John* (Tübingen: Mohr Siebeck, 2006), 255–82. Craig Koester similarly writes: 'Some see Nicodemus moving in a positive direction from his initial confusion at Jesus' words to his tentative defence of Jesus, to his final act of claiming Jesus' body for burial, which is understood to convey his own faith. Others read the evidence negatively, noting that he is initially depicted as an unbeliever, speaks only of what the law requires, and makes no claims about Jesus, and finally demonstrates his lack of understanding by piling the spices used for the dead on a Jesus who is the resurrection and the life (19:38–42).' Craig Koester, 'Theological Complexity and Characterization of Nicodemus in John's Gospel', in Christopher W. Skinner (ed.), *Characters and Characterization in the Gospel of John* (New York: Bloomsbury, 2013), 165–81, 166.

"true" disciple, that is "another" of the loved and loving in-group',[26] it is also true to say that even within more affirmative readings, a certain discursive 'othering' surrounding his encounters and communications is often detectable. Andreas Köstenberger sees Nicodemus's coming by night to bely a certain 'covertness of operation and fear of publicity'.[27] Craig Blomberg underscores his 'ignorance' in relation to Jesus's metaphorical language.[28] Wayne Meeks identifies the 'ludicrous "one hundred pounds" of embalming spices [which] indicate clearly enough that he has not understood the "lifting up" of the Son of Man'.[29] And Jouette Bassler states that while Nicodemus may be in transition to faith, ultimately he is rendered 'other' as he 'moves through the narrative with one foot in each world, and in this Gospel, that is just not good enough'.[30]

The negative traits surrounding this character's interactions, frequently identified in biblical scholarship, could at least in part have fed (albeit largely unintentionally) into wider cultural 'diagnoses' of this character as autistic in various popular cultural forums and church resources. These frequently plot Nicodemus according to the famed 'triad of impairments'[31] associated with the condition in the following areas: (a) *social interaction* – isolation ('he approached Jesus alone ... at night ... in the quiet') and repetitive and routinized behaviours ('he reached for the rule book when Jesus was on trial'); (b) *social/verbal communication* – misunderstanding and literalism ('he did not understand metaphors'); (c) *social imagination and understanding* – a certain social awkwardness ('[he brought] too many herbs and spices to the tomb').[32] Several of these retrospective 'diagnostic' readings are no

26. Mary Marshall, 'Becoming "Another": Nicodemus and his Relationships in the Fourth Gospel', in Ulrich Schmiedel and James Matarazzo, *Dynamics of Difference: Christianity and Alterity: A Festschrift for Werner Jeanrond* (London: Bloomsbury, 2015), 33–40, 35.

27. Andreas J. Köstenberger, *John* (Grand Rapids: Baker Academic, 2004), 120.

28. Craig Blomberg notes, 'Whatever possible historical reasons–fear, secrecy, convenience–which may have prompted this timing, John surely sees it as symbolic of Nicodemus' spiritual darkness.' Craig Blomberg, 'The Globalization of Biblical Interpretation: A Test Case John 3–4', *Bulletin for Biblical Research* 5 (1995), 1–15, 6.

29. Wayne Meeks, 'The Man from Heaven in Johannine Sectarianism', *Journal of Biblical Literature* 41 (1972), 44–72, 55. In Michael Goulder's words Nicodemus's action is 'an extravagant error'. Michael Goulder, 'Nicodemus', *Scottish Journal Theology* 44 (1991), 153–68.

30. Bassler, 'Nicodemus', 646.

31. Susan Douglas, *Understanding Actions, States, and Events: Verb Learning in Children with Autism* (Berlin: Walter de Gruyter, 2012), 21.

32. These quotations are all drawn from Ann Memmot, a church disability officer. She does note more positively that Nicodemus is 'there when others weren't, and was one of Jesus' friends'. Ann Memmot, 'Enabling Church 2014 – Presentation Slides', Torch Trust. Available online at: http://churchesforall.org.uk/wp-content/uploads/2014/04/Enabling-Church-presentations-handout-17pt.pdf. A recent blog post (rather worryingly replying to a thread entitled 'Has Aspergers Anything to do with Devils?') on a Christian forum is also illustrative of such identifications: 'Nicodemus was arguably a man with Aspergers

doubt well-intentioned (many are by ecclesial authorities tasked with disability enablement and inclusion). Presumably, they seek to recover biblical exemplars to make affirmative connections with those within contemporary communities living with an autism diagnosis. However, frequently (and akin to criticisms of Haddon's project) these externally imposed identifications uncritically rehearse culturally received stereotypes of the condition, which are noticeably defined by their deviance from a 'neurotypical' norm. Such identifications are thus reflective of 'a history of being interpreted, often pejoratively, based on what [this character] look[s] like and how well [he] perform[s] in particular situations, according to particular normate standards'.[33]

Uncritical 'diagnostic' readings are, of course, problematic on more fundamental levels. Mark Osteen notes that such projects never broach the question of whether 'diagnosing the dead is permissible or even possible', leave alone literary characters.[34] Shirley Dent voices a similar concern in her review of a recent project which seeks to diagnose Jane Austen's character Mr. Darcy with Asperger's syndrome. In her opinion,

> There is little point in reading literature backwards through our contemporary concerns in an attempt to consolidate and console our current lives. Darcy is Darcy not because he is autistic but because his reserve and restraint are what an early 19th-century female author admired. And the best comfort and consolation we can give to those who live with autism is not to look backwards but to look forwards with all that society, medicine and literature has to offer.[35]

Syndrome … He approached Jesus away from the crowds, had a job where rules and regulations would have been very important, couldn't understand metaphors, reached for the rule book when Jesus was being tried rather than use emotional reasoning, and at the burial he turned up with 100 times more burial herbs than he needed.' See http://www.christianforums.com/threads/has-aspergers-anything-to-do-with-devils.7245937/page-3.

33. Douglas Biklen, *Autism and the Myth of the Person Alone* (New York: New York University Press, 2005), 66.

Ronnie Thibault similarly notes how '[c]ommon frameworks throughout the clinical and professional fields of autism contextualize autistic experience through diagnostic categories of difference constructed by physicians, psychologists, neurologists, educators, and service providers. These characterizations are determined through standard observational criteria such as delayed communication and language, repetitive physical behaviors, and marked deficits in social skills (Centers for Disease Control). While this deficit mindset influences how television programs, movies, websites, awareness campaigns, journalists, print media and other cultural industries represent autism and sway public assumptions about autistics'. R. Thibault, 'Can Autistics Redefine Autism', *Trans-Scripts* 4 (2014), 57–88, 58.

34. Mark Osteen, 'Autism and Representation: A Comprehensive Introduction', in Osteen (ed.), *Autism*, 1–48, 12.

35. Shirley Dent, 'Don't Diagnose Fictional Characters', Guardian Book Blog (2007). Available online at: http://www.theguardian.com/books/booksblog/2007/apr/04/dontdiagnosefictionalcharacters.

Osteen, similarly, warns about the inherent dangers of such diagnostic processes, not least in respect to the 'dilution of autism and all that it implies'.[36] However, unlike Dent's hasty rejection of the worth of any project looking at the past and its literatures in this way, Osteen is more open to experimental 'autistic' readings, which should not involve diagnoses of characters but rather identification of 'autistic presences', in analysis of historical and literary records.[37] He is however also convinced that such projects must consciously move outside deficit medical models, to engage in more appropriate disability-critical hermeneutics. Murray too notes:

> Given that there have always been people with autism there is an arguable logic to re-reading narratives in [this light] … The difficulty lies in establishing how extending an idea of autism that respects the nature of the condition might find expression at a time when it also has to read in terms of its increased use of metaphor, and how it interacts with the knowledge prevalent at a time before the category of autism itself came into being.[38]

Autism is heavily freighted with power-laden ideological assumptions which are socially constructed and culturally produced and 'always reflect power relationships between the defined and those who do the defining'.[39] In constructing an alternative to the 'deficit model', autistry urges interpreters to engage with 'perspective[s] of people classified as autistic and to interpret the multiple meanings of autism with an eye to placing the perspectives of labelled people in the foreground'.[40]

Engagement and employment of 'autistry' and 'autistic criticism' necessarily entail the following features. First, it should chart 'how people labelled autistic perceive others' representations of their bodies and performances and probe how they themselves experience and interpret their bodies'.[41] Second, it should expose and critique the pathologization and negative metaphorical use of autism. Third, it should name and recognize the instability and shifting nature of the concept in

36. Thibault voices a similar position when he writes: 'Diagnostic interpretations, socially accepted idioms and media assumptions saturate representations that at times disregard the heterogeneous nature of Autistic individuals and exclude their lives from the cultural landscape.' Thibault, 'Can Autistics', 58.

37. Osteen, 'Autism', 12.

38. Murray, *Autism*, 10.

39. Thibault draws heavily on Biklen's work in the following formulations. See Thibault, 'Can Autistics', 46–7.

40. Biklen purposefully names such a methodology as a 'critical phenomenology model': 'for it presumes that ideas about autism derive from many sources, always reflect power relationships between the defined by those who do the defining and shift over time and in relation to social and cultural contexts'. Biklen cited and discussed in Thibault, 'Can Autistics', 46–7.

41. Thibault, 'Can Autistics', 66.

different contexts. And, fourth, through privileging autistic voices, it should offer tools to creatively reimagine autistic perspectives on literary texts and historical records which move beyond 'dominant systems of representation [which] … reproduce stigmatizing assumptions that characterize autistics as isolated lone "objects" of pity and despair'.[42]

Ralph Savarese has recently underscored the importance of engaging autistry sources and the neurological postcolonialities, sensory-perceptions and social worlds these variously evoke. He names such approaches as 'neurocosmopolitan'. By this he means 'not just a [hermeneutical] openness to neurological difference but, rather, a denaturalisation even a dethronement of privileged neurotypicality'.[43] By cultivating an estrangement from one's own taken for granted assumptions, one is enabled not only to engage empathetically with, but also to 'forestall unfavourable judgments' about an 'other'.[44]

Autist life writing and autobiographies are particularly important sites for constructing such perspectives. Ian Hacking suggests that these compendiums, which witness to embodied cultural experiences, have the potential to move 'autistic people from being *thin* people, who are assumed to have very little emotional life, to *thick* people, who have lives that are … rich in their depth and breadth'.[45] Autobiography as a genre would also seem to belie a certain self-awareness, visualization and a desire to interact with the broader context which subverts the flat triad of impairments centred on deficiencies of communication, social interaction and functional behaviour so often associated with autism. Indeed, Oliver Sacks, commenting on Temple Grandin's celebrated autobiographical book *Emergence: Labelled Autistic* (1986),[46] witnesses to this when he hails this text as 'unprecedented because there had never before been an insider narrative of autism; unthinkable because it had been medical dogma for forty years or more, that there was no "inside", no inner life in the autistic'.[47] Hacking cautions, however, that autobiography can only give insight into one individual's perceptions and that any attempt to essentialize an autistic 'mind' or 'identity' on the basis of such texts is

42. Thibault, 'Can Autistics', 61.

43. 'Ralph Savarese, 'What Some Autistics Can Teach Us about Poetry: A Neuro-cosmopolitan Approach', in Lisa Zunshine (ed.), *The Oxford Handbook of Cognitive Literary Studies* (Oxford: Oxford University Press, 2015), 393–417, 394.

44. Savarese, 'What Some', 394.

45. Ian Hacking, cited by John Swinton, 'What Does Autistic Love Look Like? Reflections on Autistic Love', in Hans S. Reinders (ed.), *Authenticity and Community: Essays in Honor of Herman P. Meininger* (Antwerp: Garant, 2011), 141–56, 151; my emphasis.

46. Backcover of Temple Grandin (co-written with Margaret Scarino), *Emergence: Labelled Autistic* (New York: Grand Central Publishing, [1986] 2005). Sacks elsewhere asks, 'How could an autistic person write an autobiography? It seemed a contradiction in terms.' Oliver Sacks, *Anthropologist on Mars* (New York: Vintage Books, 1995), 253.

47. Sacks cited in Francesca Happé and Uta Frith, *Autism and Talent* (Oxford: Oxford University Press, 2010), 219.

erroneous. Reviewing four autobiographies, Hacking notes that '[the] ... metaphor of autistic spectrum "fruit salads" [is apropos]. To quote a common adage: "If you know one autistic person, you know *one* autistic person"'.[48]

Others have noted difficulties in adopting the life-writing autobiographical genre, not least because it is often positioned to 'address a non-autistic audience' and thus seeks to 'explain' the condition to outsiders. Stuart Murray avers that 'this might offer a context for its difference, in that it is less challenging and more palatable to a mainstream audience'.[49] Thomas Couser also cautions that to make such narratives commercial, they often display elements of a 'triumph narrative': '"supercrip" and the "heroic overcomer" – the savant and the recovered autistic'.[50] These limitations acknowledged, nevertheless these sorts of accounts can aid to some degree in not only decentring aspects of neurotypicality, but also finding resonances and connections of autistic experience with broader cultural patterns. In appealing to autist autobiography here, therefore, I am acutely aware that I am not interacting with flesh and blood authors but rather their texts and what 'these words are doing to public understanding[s] of autism',[51] just as I am dealing with receptions and interpretations of the Bible and elements of bodily performances observable in these textual traditions. For, as Francisco Ortega submits, '[t]he cerebral subject [in literature and culture] is an "anthropological figure" that has no reality prior to its performative embodiments'.[52]

By listening to voices of experience, here I will seek to join those voices who challenge models which stereotypically define the autistic (a) as isolated, alone and metaphorically in darkness and (b) as overly literalistic and unable to understand metaphorical or figurative language. By this method, I can hope, in part, to seek to overcome wholly negative constructions of the condition imposed from 'outside'[53] which have not only inflected understandings of 'autism' but also inevitably steered the positioning of characters on a 'spectrum' of deficits.

'Alone' and 'by Night': Autistry, Isolation and Metaphors of Identity

The etymology of autism infers isolation as central to its character: 'the autist is only himself (cf. the Greek word *autos*)'.[54] A 'basic desire for aloneness' was crucial to Leo Kanner's original 1943 description of the condition and cultural receptions

48. Ian Hacking, 'Autistic Autobiography', in Happé and Frith (eds), *Autism*, 200; my emphasis.

49. Murray, *Autism*, 36.

50. Couser, cited in Osteen, 'Autism', 16.

51. Happé and Frith, *Autism*, 197.

52. Francisco Ortega, 'The Cerebral Subject and the Challenge of Neurodiversity', *BioSocieties* 4 (2009), 425–45, 426.

53. Victoria McGeer, 'The Thought and Talk of Individuals with Autism: Reflections on Ian Hacking', *Metaphilosophy* 40(3–4) (2009), 26–1068.

54. Biklen, *Autism*, 51.

have accordingly viewed autism as 'connot[ing] the aloneness and separation of those frequently described as living as if "in a world of their own"'.[55]

Nicodemus's approach to Jesus, alone and by night, has accordingly been cited by those proposing an autism diagnosis (either medical or metaphorical) for his character as reflective of the condition. It is relatively simple to challenge such a flat portrayal. While the approach itself could be perceived as isolationist, it does nevertheless show Nicodemus initiating the encounter and purposefully marks his broader social connections in its characterization of him as 'a Pharisee' and 'leader of the Jews' (3:1). His use of the plural pronoun 'we' (3:2), also echoed in Jesus's speech (3:11), may also denote a certain collective consciousness (although it could conversely be read as a reversal or mixing of pronouns common in autism).[56]

Temple Grandin, an animal scientist at Colorado State University, is perhaps one of the best known autistic advocates in the world. She witnesses that rather than producing innate isolationism, powerful sensory reception often causes individuals to withdraw from contexts and groups of people 'to block out an onslaught of incoming stimulation',[57] but this does not preclude a desire for intense encounters with other beings in more tranquil settings. Challenging the 'isolationist' deficit model from within, Biklen likewise observes how autistic autobiographical accounts frequently 'reveal people in search of connections with the world'.[58] Joyce Davidson and Mick Smith, in their plotting of emotional geographies of autism, likewise state: 'Connections are, for a significant number of ASD authors, often experienced most readily and most intensely with(in) a natural world that apparently offers some respite from the disruptive, intrusive, and communicatively overburdened social world. These personal geographies are characterized by rich, rewarding, and meaningful relationships … imbued with many varied phenomenal and emotional resonances.'[59]

Perhaps the 'night' references in the Nicodemus narrative could therefore be reconceptualized as a space of quietness, freedom from distraction and minimal sensory stimulation. Others, echoing this position, have noted a more positive association of the night with rabbinic study (*Str.* B 2, 419–20) and intense concentration.[60] It is perhaps not insignificant that Nicodemus's approach follows the most sensorially overloaded and chaotic scene of the gospel: Jesus in the temple, turning over tables and driving out people, sheep and cattle (2:13–22).

55. Joyce Davidson and Mick Smith, 'Autistic Autobiographies and More-Than-Human Emotional Geographies', *Society and Space* 27 (2009), 898–916, 898.

56. Theo Peters and Chris Gillberg, *Autism: Medical and Educational Aspects* (New Jersey: Wiley, 1999), 11.

57. Temple Grandin with Margaret Scariano, *Emergence: Labeled Autistic* (Florida: Costello, 1986), 9.

58. Biklen, *Autism*, 49.

59. Davidson and Smith, 'Autistic Autobiographies', 899.

60. Colin G. Kruse, *The Gospel According to John: An Introduction and Commentary* (Grand Rapids: Wm. B. Eerdmans Publishing, 2004), 104.

Far more emphasis in professional commentaries has of course been put on the metaphorical correlates of both Nicodemus's solitude and nocturnal approach – what could be termed 'spiritual autism'. Colin Kruse notes that '"by night" suggests he was in a state of spiritual darkness when he approached Jesus'.[61] Likewise, D. A. Carson proposes that '[t]he best clue lies in John's use of night elsewhere: in each instance (3:2; 9:4; 11:10; 13:30) the word is either used metaphorically for moral and spiritual darkness, or, if it refers to night-time hours, it bears the same moral and spiritual symbolism. Doubtless Nicodemus approached Jesus at night, but his own "night" was blacker than he knew'.[62]

Metaphorical projections have also been endemic to both popular cultural constructions of autism and, in somewhat different ways, to autistic autobiographical texts themselves. Mitzi Waltz in her article 'Metaphors of Autism, and Autism as Metaphor: An Exploration of Representation' sets out to identify such uses. She writes that negative metaphors (including darkness to represent misunderstanding) are frequently and simplistically imposed by those outside, which has 'the obvious effect of rendering their subjects as less than human'.[63] In contrast, Waltz notes that the metaphors used by people with autism in their writings often 'position themselves as normal but different' – strangers, or even as aliens – but that those identifying as autistic, frequently see the 'rigid social structures and expectations of mainstream culture' as the problem rather than themselves. Temple Grandin, for example, famously describes herself as 'an anthropologist on Mars'[64]: she is not the alien from another planet, rather the 'normal' world is the foreign terrain (Mars). It is this arena 'that she must work to understand, in the manner of an anthropologist studying a foreign culture'.[65]

It is striking that this 'autistic' self-description finds more resonance within Johannine discourse with the Word, who comes from above to a world that does not know him (1:10), rather than Nicodemus or any other character. Wayne Meeks's classic article 'The Man from Heaven in Johannine Sectarianism' (1972) extrapolated this metaphorical Christology and linked the alien identity of Jesus with the Johannine community exiled from the synagogue: 'the alienation in turn is explained by further Christological development of the alien status of Jesus, this

61. Kruse, *The Gospel*, 105.

62. D. A. Carson, *The Gospel According to John* (Downers Grove: IVP, 1991), 186.

63. Mitzi Waltz, 'Metaphors of Autism, and Autism as Metaphor: An Exploration of Representation', Paper presented at the *Making Sense of Health and Disease*, 2nd Global Conference. Available online at: http://www.persons.org.uk/mso/hid/hid2/hid03s11a.htm.

64. Temple Grandin, cited in Oliver Sacks, *An Anthropologist on Mars* (New York: Alfred Knopf, 1995).

65. Joseph Straus, 'Autism and Postwar Serialism as Neurodiverse Forms of Cultural Modernism' in Blake Howe, Stephanie Jensen-Moulton, Neil Lerner, Joseph Straus (eds), *The Oxford Handbook of Music and Disability Studies* (Oxford: Oxford University Press, 2016), 684–706, 697.

in turn pushed the group into further isolation'.[66] Within the Nicodemus discourse, therefore, the metaphorical emphasis that shows most commonality with autistic life-writing comes from Jesus himself. Jesus's and his community's (rather than Nicodemus's) alien status is embodied in his question, 'Are you a teacher of Israel and yet you do not understand these things? ... Truly I tell you, we speak of what we know and testify to what we have seen yet you do not receive our testimony' (3:9–11). Aligned to this, and challenging an isolationalist model, recent work on autistry also notes how 'works written *by* autistic people [frequently] feature metaphors of doors, windows and other images of separation but it's a separation with the possibility of some kind of contact'.[67] Grandin notes that visual symbols of doors and windows frequently helped her to conceptualize relationships in this foreign terrain. Like glass 'they shatter easily and have to be approached carefully'[68] but do offer openings to interaction with others. This openness towards the outside world again is most keenly demonstrated in Jesus's own self-descriptions within not only this particular discourse – 'so must the Son of Man be lifted up, that whoever believes in him might have eternal life' – (3:14–15) but also Jesus's own self-identifications in the broader gospel – 'I Am the Gate. Whoever enters by me will be saved, and will come in and go out and find pasture' (10:9).

To sum up thus far, while 'alone', 'by night' and 'darkness' have frequently been cited as evidence of Nicodemus's presumed [spiritual] autism, what discussion here has shown is that autistry sources challenge the deficit 'isolationist' model in a number of ways. These include seeking solace as avoidance of sensory stimulation; intense emotional geographies with other beings but often on an immediate level; and a conception not primarily of an autistic person as 'alien' but rather the otherness of the (normative/majority) contexts they inhabit. Furthermore, these reconfigurations find more resonance with the Christology of John's gospel than with the character of Nicodemus.

Jonathan McNabb, an autist activist, has recently stated that he 'find[s] the basic stumbling block ... [to be] the assumption most neurotypical people have that [the] neurotypical worldview is neutral and normative ... Autism is then seen in contrast to this given, natural, neutral and normal society'.[69] This presumption of neurotypicality certainly seems to have been evidenced by commentators and other popular presentations which persist in negatively 'othering' Nicodemus (but not Jesus) along these lines. Autistry sources however can 'reculturise autism, exposing the epistemological impacts of dominant representations. These

66. Jerome H. Neyrey, *An Ideology of Revolt: John's Christology in Social-Science Perspective* (Oregon: Wipf & Stock Publishing, 2007), 117.

67. Steven J. Venturino, *The Complete Idiot's Guide to Literary Theory and Criticism* (USA: Alpha, 2013), electronic version, no pages; my emphasis.

68. Grandin, cited in Tatyana B. Glezerman, *Autism and the Brain: Neurophenomenological Interpretation* (New York: Springer, 2013), 112.

69. Jonathan McNabb, 'I Dont Want to Be a Pioneer I Just Want to Be Me'. Available online at: http://archive.autistics.org/library/nopioneer.html.

counter-representations also encourage examination of larger assumptions about normality, impairment and difference'.[70] By figuring these 'autistic presences' within Johannine discourse, we start to see how the gospel can be used to recalibrate and question the so-called neurotypical position of its audience and interpreters and could in turn play a part in glimpsing 'a shared culture free from the "tyranny of the normal" '.[71]

'Entering the Womb a Second Time': Autistry and Literalism

One of the most dominant tropes in biblical scholarship, which also likely feeds into popular constructions of Nicodemus's character according to a deficit autistic model, is his presumed literalism and misunderstanding of metaphor. Nicodemus's questions about being born again and entering for a second time a mother's womb (3:3–4) are almost unanimously read as evidence of his 'obtuseness [and] dimwittedness'.[72] In the words of Larry Jones, 'Nicodemus attempted a literal and wooden interpretation of [Jesus's] words and missed the point.'[73]

Deficiencies in so-called theory of mind (the ability to grasp another's intentions) are often cited as the reason behind an autistic incapacity to grasp figurative language, metaphor, irony and symbolism. Lisa Zunshine, however, rightly cautions against 'casually pronouncing some texts, individuals or groups somehow deficient in their mind-reading ability'.[74] Ralph Savarese goes further when he states that 'the potency of mindblindness' is in effect 'a trope of dehumanization … [because] ascribing an impoverished mental state to a person is a step necessary for imagining him or her as Other'.[75]

Autistry's autobiographical sources can challenge these stereotypical projections in a number of ways. The writings of Tito Rajarshi Mukhopadhyay, a 21-year-old Indian author and poet, whom medical models would categorize as 'non-verbal', 'low functioning' and 'severely autistic'[76] is such an example. His work reveals a rich and evocative use of literary forms including symbolic language, which is crucially

70. McNabb, 'I Dont'.

71. Straus, 'Autism and Postwar', 696.

72. Kenneth H. Maahs, *The John You Never Knew: Decoding the Fourth Gospel* (Bern: Peter Lang Publishing, 2006), 67.

73. Larry Paul Jones, *The Symbol of Water in the Gospel of John* (Sheffield: Sheffield Academic Press, 1997), 70.

74. Lisa Zunshine, *Why We Read Fiction: Theory of Mind and the Novel* (Columbus: Ohio State University Press, 2006), 11.

75. Ralph Savarese and Lisa Zunshine, 'The Critic as Neurocosmopolite; Or, What Cognitive Approaches to Literature Can Learn from Disability Studies: Lisa Zunshine in Conversation with Ralph James Savarese', *Narrative* 22 (2014), 17–44, 24.

76. Ralph Savarese, 'More Than a Thing to Ignore: An Interview with Tito Rajarshi Mukhopadhyay', *Disability Studies Quarterly* 30 (2010), no pages. Available online at: http://dsqsds.org/article/view/1056/1235.

connected to his embodiment. In his *How Can I Talk if My Lips Don't Move?* (2008) Mukhopadhyay writes about his synaesthesia (simultaneous perception by a number of senses) and shows how this feeds into his vivid descriptions and understandings. Describing one individual Mukhopadhyay writes: 'In the beginning, Deepa's presence was just the sound of her voice, which tasted like a tamarind pickle. As days passed, her presence became a peacock blue, dipped in the taste of tamarind pickle.'[77] Mukhopadhyay also writes about remembering faces through symbols. His teacher is remembered 'as a yellow plastic bowl with a wide circumference'.[78] Savarese accordingly notes that here we witness the production of figurative and symbolic literary forms based on perceptual experience: 'So significant is his sensory integration … that his writing [is] an aesthetic defamiliarization.'[79] Oliver Sacks, writing on the back cover of Mukhopadhyay's *The Mind Tree* (2003), likewise writes (albeit somewhat paternalistically) that 'it has usually been assumed that deeply autistic people are scarcely capable of introspection or deep thought, let alone of poetic or metaphor[ical] leaps of the imagination … Tito gives the lie to all of these assumptions and forces us to reconsider the condition of the deeply autistic'.[80]

Also challenging stereotypical assumptions with regard to autistic perceptions of figurative language is Grandin, whose autobiographical works have been celebrated for displaying her propensity for visual thinking or, as the title of one of her best-known books indicates, *Thinking in Pictures* (1996).[81] In her experience,

> [w]ords are like a second language to me. I translate both spoken and written words into full-color movies, complete with sound, which run like a VCR tape in my head. When somebody speaks to me, his words are instantly translated

77. Tito, cited in Savarese and Zunshine, 'The Critic', 24.

78. Savarese and Zunshine, 'The Critic', 24.

79. Savarese and Zunshine, 'The Critic', 20.

80. Oliver Sacks on the backcover of Tito Rajarshi Mukhopadhyay, *The Mind Tree* (New York: Arcade Publishing, 2003).

81. Grandin notes that this capability has been invaluable to her career as a designer of livestock containment equipment: 'I credit my visualization abilities with helping me understand the animals I work with. Early in my career I used a camera to help give me the animals' perspective as they walked through a chute for their veterinary treatment. I would kneel down and take pictures through the chute from the cow's eye level. Using the photos, I was able to figure out which things scared the cattle, such as shadows and bright spots of sunlight. Back then I used black-and-white film, because twenty years ago scientists believed that cattle lacked color vision. Today, research has shown that cattle can see colors, but the photos provided the unique advantage of seeing the world through a cow's viewpoint. They helped me figure out why the animals refused to go in one chute but willingly walked through another.' Temple Grandin, 'Thinking in Pictures with 2006 Updates from the Expanded Edition Chapter 1: Autism and Visual Thought', no pages. Available online at: http://www.grandin.com/inc/visual.thinking.html.

> into pictures. Language-based thinkers often find this phenomenon difficult to understand, but in my job as an equipment designer for the livestock industry, visual thinking is a tremendous advantage ... I value my ability to think visually, and I would never want to lose it.[82]

In her evocative account of reciting the Lord's Prayer as a child she articulates this vivid visual processing and reveals a penchant for figurative perception:

> The power and the glory were represented by a semicircular rainbow and an electrical tower. These childhood visual images are still triggered every time I hear the Lord's Prayer. The words 'thy will be done' had no meaning when I was a child, and today the meaning is still vague. Will is a hard concept to visualize. When I think about it, I imagine God throwing a lightning bolt. Another adult with autism wrote that he visualized 'Thou art in heaven' as God with an easel above the clouds. 'Trespassing' was pictured as black and orange NO TRESPASSING signs.[83]

Grandin also reveals how visualized images help her relate abstract concepts such as peace or honesty: 'I thought of peace as a dove, an Indian peace pipe, or TV or newsreel footage of the signing of a peace agreement. Honesty was represented by an image of placing one's hand on the Bible in court. A news report describing a person returning a wallet with all the money in it provided a picture of honest behavior.'[84] On the strength of autobiographical evidence such as this, Anna Thiemann, Annette Kern-Stähler and others have recently proposed[85] that, contrary to popular belief, autistic discourses are not overly literalistic and do indeed employ metaphoric and figurative language albeit in specific ways, often connected to space and embodiment. Savarese accordingly adopts George Lakoff and Mark Johnson's appeal to a 'philosophy in the flesh' – cognition that is embodied and presented according to sensory/material perception – to articulate an autistic poetics that, crucially, is not seen as a deficit, but rather difference and (even) advantage.[86]

Visual-spatial reasoning – 'the ability to present a problem visually and the use of visual imagery to solve it'[87] – was also the means by which ancient rhetoric was

82. Grandin, 'Thinking', no pages.

83. Grandin, 'Thinking', no pages.

84. Grandin, 'Thinking', no pages.

85. Anna Thiemann and Annette Kern-Stähler, 'Metaphor and (Dis)Embodiment: Inside the Autistic Mind', *REAL: Yearbook of Research in English and American Literature* 24 (2008), 215–31.

86. Ralph Savarese, 'Toward a Postcolonial Neurology: Autism, Tito Mukhopadhyay, and a New Geo-poetics of the Body', *Journal of Literary & Cultural Disability Studies* 4 (2010), 273–89.

87. Digby Tantam, *Autism Spectrum Disorders through the Life Span* (London: Jessica Kingsley Publishers, 2011), 153.

employed to evoke particular visual images and sensations within (often largely illiterate) hearers. Ekphrasis, as taught in Greco-Roman rhetorical schools, was a discourse that brought a subject described in words 'vibrantly before the eyes of the audience'.[88] This 'visual verbalising'[89] frequently included 'brief sketches so that persons and actions and times and places and seasons may be brought before the eyes with clarity … and in turn [transform] the audience of the written word into spectators'.[90] Kuan Wang notes that this definition 'is very different from that given by modern literary criticism, which [more narrowly] defines ἔκφρασις in relation to visual art, such as "the verbal representation of visual representation" or "words about an image"'.[91] Recent work on so-called rhetography, which V. K. Robbins defines as 'the progressive, sensory-aesthetic, and/or argumentative texture of a text … that invites a hearer/reader to create a graphic image or picture in the mind that implies a certain kind of truth and/or reality',[92] is also instructive here.

L. Gregory Bloomquist has adopted such a 'rhetographical' approach in his recent reading of Nicodemus's imaging of being born again and entering, though old, a second time a mother's womb. A typical inference among exegetes is that Nicodemus harbours a fundamental confusion about being born 'again' as opposed to 'above', which is rooted in these distinct renderings of ἄνωθεν (3:3)[93] although the term ἄνωθεν can also more broadly denote 'from the beginning', 'from an earlier time' or 'from the very first'.[94] Through this binary opposition of meanings and associated ideological spheres frequently cited in relation to them (physical/spiritual, above/below, worldly/heavenly) as Christopher Skinner's comment exemplifies, commentators presume a rhetorical and discursive 'othering'

88. Hui Kuan Wang, 'Sense Perception and Testimony in the Gospel According to John', PhD thesis, Durham University (2014). Available online at: http://etheses.dur.ac.uk/10844/1/Finall_Thesis_20141115.pdf?DDD32+. Accessed 1 March 2016. See also Bradley Arnold, *Christ as the Telos of Life: Moral Philosophy, Athletic Imagery, and the Aim of Philippians* (Tübingen: Mohr Siebeck, 2013), esp. pp.127ff.

89. Tamar Yacobi, 'Fictive Beholders: How Ekphrasis Dramatizes Visual Perception', in Ellen Spolsky (ed.), *Iconotropism: Turning toward Pictures* (Pennsylvania: Bucknell University Press, 2004), 70.

90. Jo-Ann Brant, *John* (Grand Rapids: Baker Academic, 2011), 69.

91. Wang, 'Sense'. See also Michael Squire's work. He submits that Reformation theology and its legacy subordinated the image to the word in ways that are 'misleading and anachronistic for the Greco-Roman world. Second, he builds on this critique by exploring complex interplays of text and image in Roman culture'. See Michael Squire, *Image and Text in Graeco-Roman Antiquity* (Cambridge: Cambridge University Press, 2009), xxvi, 516.

92. Vernon K. Robbins, *The Invention of Christian Discourse: From Wisdom to Apocalyptic* (Blandford Forum: Deo Publishing, 2008), xxvii.

93. Christopher William Skinner, *John and Thomas: Gospels in Conflict? A Study in Johannine Characterization* (Oregon: Pickwick Publications, 2009), 219.

94. UBS, *BibleWorks 9 Software for Biblical Exegesis & Research* (Norfolk, VA: BibleWorks, 2011).

of Nicodemus's character through '[his] focus on the literal [which] creates misunderstanding and [consequently] places the reader in a position of privilege'.[95] However, could Nicodemus's words be seen as providing a rhetographical 'picture' of childbirth as a visual field for the hearer to penetrate Jesus's words? Moreover, given the sensory experiences cited in Grandin's and Mukhopadhyay's respective biographies, could it be the dark tightness of the womb, which is fundamental in this image? Bloomquist notes that foetuses, while assumed to have eyes in ancient medicine, 'were considered to be unable to see anything while in the womb'. He links this with the experience of one who is not born. Bloomquist therefore posits the rhetography of the image establishing:

> The twice-born or second-born, as the offspring of God are born into a new family, the royal family of God. Once born, they will, as Jesus says, be able to see what in the womb they can neither see nor even imagine. For John, only those who are twice-born – again, from above, by water and the spirit – into a womb-less existence are born as children into God's royal family, having, like Jesus himself, God as their father.[96]

Nicodemus's question and visual-spatializing of the womb thus illustrate that '[h]umans – or at least the humans with whom Jesus is concerned – live in a kind of enwombed existence. These humans have eyes, but they cannot see. Some of them are, however, poised to see when they are born'.[97] In this respect, rather than Nicodemus being distanced as totally 'other' from the gospel's hearers, or indeed belying rejection of Jesus's words – which Kenneth Maahs sees being 'register[ed], half mockingly, [by] the absurdity of his response which is an obstetric *reductio ad absurdum*'[98] – his visualization actually allows the audience (akin to Grandin's concrete visualizing of abstract concepts) to figure the intangible notion of which 'being born again/from above' speaks. This interpretation is bolstered as Jesus does not correct a presumed misperception on Nicodemus's part, 'but merely reiterates that those who are not born of water and Spirit cannot enter the kingdom of God'.[99]

The multiple meanings frequently associated with ἄνωθεὺ ('above' denoting spatial orientation and 'again'/'from the beginning' denoting temporal orientation) also (literally) take on different dimensions when put alongside autistry sources. Lakoff and Johnson's work on 'orientational metaphors' (charting how concepts

95. Christopher Skinner, *Reading John* (Oregon: Cascade Books, 2015).

96. L. Gregory Bloomquist, 'Eyes Wide Open, Seeing Nothing: The Challenge of the Gospel of John's Non-visualizable Texture for Readings Using Visual Texture', Saint Paul University Faculty of Theology. Available online at: http://www.religion.emory.edu/faculty/robbins/Pdfs/Bloomquist%20Sawyer%20presentation.pdf.

97. Bloomquist, 'Eyes'.

98. Maahs, *The John*, 67.

99. Robert Jensen, *Baptismal Imagery in Early Christianity: Ritual, Visual, and Theological Dimensions* (Michigan: Grand Rapids, 2012), 143.

are spatially related to one another) reveals how simple directional words such as '"up-down, in-out, front-back, on-off, deep-shallow, central-peripheral" often arise from physical experiences of the world and then end up being imposed on abstract concepts such as happiness and sadness'.[100] However, Grandin reveals how 'spatial words such as "over" and "under" had no meaning for [her] until [she] had a visual image to fix them in [her] memory'.[101] Ralph Savarese goes further and explains how 'different operational metaphors that spatially situate (or fail to situate) the person' are important in autistic autobiography.[102] Mukhopadhyay's use of the preposition 'around', for example, in his tellingly titled book *The Mind Tree*, provides an insight into what Savarese has termed a 'postcolonial neurology' for the word implies 'a very different experience of relational embodiment' (which in contrast to vertical axes plots a more horizontal field of experience) and points to 'a new geography of the possible'.[103]

> Speaking as that giant banyan tree, Tito writes, 'The silence *around* tells me that it is night' and, further, 'When the dust blows with the wind and when the crows settle down on my branches, I can make out that it is midday.' Almost startled by its own consciousness, the tree remarks, 'My concerns and worries are trapped within me somewhere in my depths, maybe in my roots, maybe in my bark or maybe all *around* my radius.' Tito's mind facilitate[s] a kind of diffusion of thought and feeling. All *around* my radius, he speculates.[104]

While vertical orientation is of course central to John's discourse (3:3; 3:7; 3:13) no less significant are orientating visualizations of a horizontal nature: 'the wind blows where it chooses, and you hear the sound of it, but you do not know where it comes from or where it goes. So it is with everyone who is born of the Spirit' (3:8). While many again have taken this image as impenetrable for a presumed 'literalist' such as Nicodemus, with him being presumed to miss the double voiced nature of πνεῦμα, denoting both wind and spirit,[105] in visual-thinking terms, the image of wind gives a different orientational perspective – that does not plot a vertical axis, nor trace origins or destinations ('you don't know where it comes from or where it goes'), but rather can be physically sensed ('you hear the sound of it'). John's Jesus will also go on to concretely visualize his identity in a number of similar

100. Savarese, 'Toward', 273.

101. Grandin, 'Thinking', no pages.

102. This is of course relevant in regard to critiques of the use of the metaphor in relation to 'high' and 'low' functioning autism. See Ralph Savarese and Emily Savarese, '"The Superior Half of Speaking": An Introduction', *Disability Studies Quarterly* 30 (2010). Available online at: http://dsq-sds.org/article/view/1062/1230.

103. Savarese, 'Toward', 279.

104. Savarese, 'Toward', 281; my emphases.

105. David Sten Herrstrom, *The Book of Unknowing: A Poet's Response to the Gospel of John* (Oregon: Wipf and Stock, 2012), 32.

sensorially figurative ways which, like Mukhopadhyay's writings, envisage a far less vertical orientation and instead acknowledge a more concrete, experiential and participatory orientation, to use Mukhopadhyay's own terms, 'an aroundness'. Jesus as bread of life (6:35) will be ingested by others; as light of the world (8:12) he will, as the theory of extramission in the ancient world proposes, touch others with his rays; as 'gate of the sheep' (10:7) he will take others into him and as the true vine (15:1) akin to Mukhopadhyay's *Mind Tree*, will consider others to be part of his form, branches and roots.[106]

The sensory perceptions, material visualizations and more fluid conceptions of body boundaries so integral to many autistic autobiographical accounts therefore once more find resonance here with John's Christology and the broader gospel's discursive communicative strategies. Autistry here challenges readers to move beyond a literalist/metaphorical binary towards not only a 'visual' but also multisensory reading of texts. In the words of Alex Purves in his recent study of *Synaesthesia and the Ancient Senses* (2014) 'what we seek to recapture here is the reader who reads not just to *make sense*, but in order *to sense*'[107] and evoke language as an 'intersensory experience'.[108]

'The Curious Incident of a Jew in the Night-Time': Autistry and Interpretation

Discussion here has been less about the characterization of a specific literary character as autistic and rather more about the myriad ways in which neurotypical culture (in both popular domains and professional biblical studies) continues to create and perpetuate narratives about an autistic 'other' (whether that is conceived literally or metaphorically). Diagnostic searching for 'autistic' literary and historical identities is a pursuit riddled with hazards and as such should be 'pursued in an appropriately tentative way'.[109] Retrospective diagnostic interpretations, which casually play with labelling characters as autistic, should be critically evaluated and negative (and normative) assumptions about conditions which are often uncritically reproduced in such projects should be exposed and challenged. In the words of Fiona Campbell, scholars should be aware of 'what the study of disability tells us about the production, operation and maintenance of ableism'.[110]

106. The use of 'we' in the chapter may also denote a body which is not bounded as a singularity.

107. Shane Butler and Alex Purves, *Synaesthesia and the Ancient Senses* (London: Routledge, 2014), 3; my emphases.

108. Butler and Purves, *Synaesthesia*, 4.

109. Joseph Straus, 'Autism as Culture', in Lennard J. Davis (ed.), *The Disability Studies Reader* (New York: Routledge, 2013), 460–84, 474.

110. Fiona Campbell, *Contours of Ableism: The Production of Disability and Ableness* (London: Palgrave Macmillan, 2009), 4.

Interaction with autistry's own voices, here accessed in the autobiographical writings of Gardin and Mukhopadhyay respectively, can aid in refiguring encounters and guard against projecting 'the alienated lens' through which the condition is often presented.[111] For, in the words of autistic activist Dawn Prince-Hughes: 'I believe autism can be a beautiful way of seeing the world ... I and others who are autistic do not want to be cured ... much like the deaf community, we autistics are building an emergent culture. We individuals, with our culture of one, are building a culture of many.'[112] In establishing an encounter between autistry sources and Jn 3:1–15 here, rather than gaze voyeuristically on the assumed 'tokenized presence of the disabled character in isolation, as [a] metaphor of insidiousness'[113] I aimed to 'creatively privilege autistic presence ... [and] autistic embodiment'[114] within the narrative discourse itself and chart 'the ways in which the echoes of autism in literature affect meaning and interpretation, especially for the modern reader'.[115] In challenging the deficit model of autism, first, the assumption of isolation, which has variously been projected onto Nicodemus's approach 'alone' and 'by night', was critically assessed. Autistry sources reveal cultural 'contestations over meanings, over borders and boundaries, [and] over the ways [one] make[s] sense of the world'.[116] As such, the rigid picture of a solitary individual was questioned in autistry writings, not only by revealing intense connections with other beings and the natural world, but also the ways in which sensory processing often means that more tranquil settings are sought for encounters with others. Second, the varied metaphors encapsulating autistic identities were explored. Those connecting Nicodemus's (spiritual) autism with darkness were contrasted with metaphors used within autistry sources themselves; these interestingly seemed to coalesce more with Johannine Christology within the gospel (rather than narrowly on the character of Nicodemus) which pictures the majority world (rather than the 'autistic' individual) as the alien territory.

111. Petra Kuppers, 'Dancing Autism: The Curious Incident of the Dog in the Nighttime and Bedlam', *Text and Performance Quarterly* 28 (2008), 192–205, 192–3.

112. Dawn Prince-Hughes, *Songs of the Gorilla Nation: My Journey through Autism* (New York: Three Rivers, 2004), 2–3, 7.

113. Ann Fox and Joan Lipkin, 'Res(Crip)ting Feminist Theater through Disability Theater: Selections from the DisAbility Project', *NWSA Journal* 14(3) (2002), 77–98, 81.

114. Ronnie Thibault, 'A Performative Space for Autistic Embodiment Autistic Aesthetic in Disability Theater' (2012). Available online at: https://sites.google.com/a/uw.edu/thibault-academic-portfolio/bculst501-cultural-studies-as-collaboration-winter-2013/collapsing-boundaries-of-autistic-embodiment-rsvp-cycles-and-the-social-sphere/a-space-for-autistic-embodiment-in-disability-theater.

115. Evelyn Fisher, 'Autism in Literature: The Negotiation between Syndrome and Silent Wisdom' (2010), 12. Available online at: http://aladinrc.wrlc.org/bitstream/handle/1961/9279/Fisher,%20Evelyn%20 %20Spring%20'10%20(P).pdf?sequence=1.

116. Don Mitchell, *Cultural Geography: A Critical Introduction* (Oxford: Blackwell Publishing, 2000), 159.

Finally, the assumed literalism and misunderstanding of metaphor projected onto Nicodemus's question regarding entering the womb a second time, was questioned in light of the figurative receptions of abstracted language as evidenced in autistic autobiographies. This too had resonance with the visualizing of words common in ancient rhetoric and used in part to evoke sensory responses within non-literate hearers. These insights bolstered the claim that not all communication is best served through speech alone. For John the literal 'visualising of a verbal word' is of course fundamental. This is most keenly shown in the prologue which powerfully reveals a 'logos made flesh' (1:14).[117]

What is more, the vertical axes so often emphasized in Jn 3:1-15 (and the associated binaries above/below, light/darkness, understanding/misunderstanding, spirit/flesh) were also balanced with a focus on horizontal axes which prioritize sensory experience, particularly as evidenced in the image of the wind/spirit. The wind's sense of 'aroundness' and participation chimes with Ralph Savarese's work on autistry, which has been particularly helpful in charting the means by which neurodivergent culture and language can chart 'a kind of political or ethical proprioception that not only contests typical arrangements of power and identity but reconfigures them as well'.[118] Dani Ryskamp similarly notes how

> [i]n the play of perception, synaesthesia, metaphor, and metonymy in Tito Mukhopadhyay's *The Mind Tree*, Savarese sees a staunch refusal to allow language to 'cut up the world' or 'cut groups of people from one another'" ... This language maps a new relationship to the world and among individuals even as it resists 'a process of condescending classification'. 'With Tito', Savarese writes, again quoting *The Mind Tree*, 'language steps lightly, provisionally; it neither masters nor replaces the object it names'. By using the language as a guide to destabilizing and ultimately dissolving boundaries between 'self' and 'other'.[119]

In Jn 3:1–15, autistic presences thus have the potential to transform space, time, personhood communication and embodiment.[120] Rather than a single character being 'othered' from a supposedly neurotypical audience, here through detecting autistic presences, perceptual boundaries between subject and object, characters and hearers demand a more 'participatory spectatorship'.[121] In this light, this

117. On Ekphrasis in John's Gospel, see Brant, *John*, 68.

118. Savarese, 'Toward', 283.

119. Dani Alexis Ryskamp, '"Neurodiversity's Lingua Franca?": *The Wild Iris*, *Autobiography of Red*, and the Breakdown of Cognitive Barriers through Poetic Language', *The Hilltop Review* 7 (2014). Available online at: http://scholarworks.wmich.edu/hilltopreview/vol7/iss1/5 2014.

120. Telory Davies Arendell, *The Autistic Stage: How Cognitive Disability Changed 20th-Century Performance* (Netherlands: Sense Publishers, 2015), xxiv.

121. Nicola Shaughnessy, 'Imagining Otherwise: Autism, Neuroaesthetics and Contemporary Performance', *Interdisciplinary Science Reviews* 38(4) (2013), 321–34.

curious incident in the night-time, does not denote a 'reductive representation of autism' but rather can be seen to plot, in the fitting words of Jack Kahn, a neurodivergent 'world-making proposal – an embodiment of a relation to the world which resists the pathologizing conditions that reduce autistic experience'[122] as 'other' to a presumed neurotypical norm.

122. Jack Kahn, 'Racing toward Uncertainty: An Ethico-Aesthetics of Imagination', Pomona College: Claremont, California. Available online at: http://consideringdisability.com/wp-content/uploads/2015/04/Considering-Disability-Journal.97 101.pdf.

Chapter 3

'EX-CENTRIC' WOMEN: INTERSECTING MARGINALITIES AND THE MADNESS NARRATIVES OF BESSIE HEAD, A CANAANITE WOMAN AND PYTHIAN SLAVE GIRL

In the surreal and caustically comical prelude to the British playwright Sarah Daniels's 1990 work *Beside Herself*, the audience encounters 'supermarket hell' with aisles occupied by a host of biblical women – Eve, Delilah, Mrs. Lot, Jezebel, Magdalene and so on – all figures who have variously been marked and marginalized in texts and interpretative histories as 'other'. Eve, in the role of 'prototypal mother', organizes feminist seminars for the women to attend, including 'The burden of guilt and two thousand years of misrepresentation'. Many however, are too distracted having their hair styled by Delilah or picking up tips from Mrs. Noah on hosting a barbecue in inclement weather to pay due attention.[1] Eve perseveres though, in urging them all to break their silence and vocalize how they have been rejected and suffered abuse and trauma for perceived transgressions against fathers, brothers and patriarchal systems.[2] The biblical women are then joined in the aisles by a young mother shouting loudly at her unruly children warning that if they do not behave she will soon need to be 'asking for a padded cell'.[3] To which Mrs. Lot questions, 'What the bleedin' heaven is she on about?' and Jezebel dismissively retorts, 'Take no notice, she's lost her trolley.'[4]

C. Wald sees Daniels's prelude functioning as a humorous and abbreviated version of Foucauldian discourse analysis demonstrating how 'gender-based definitions of [in]sanity are frequently set by hetero-patriarchal norms'.[5] Daniels's prologue serves

1. Pamela Bakker, 'A Critical Analysis of the Plays of Sarah Daniels', PhD Thesis, University of Sheffield (1996), 145. Available online at: https://core.ac.uk/download/files/139/9554313.pdf.

2. See Carina Bartleet, 'Eve's Side of It: Sarah Daniels' Biblical Revision', in Colette Rayment and Mark Levon Byrne (eds), *Seeking the Centre: 2001 International Religion, Literature and the Arts Conference Proceedings* (Sydney: RLA Press, 2002), 191–203.

3. Bakker, 'Critical', 148.

4. Daniels, cited in Bakker, 'Critical', 148.

5. C. Wald, *Hysteria, Trauma and Melancholia: Performative Maladies in Contemporary Anglophone Drama* (London: Palgrave Macmillan, 2007), 116.

to illustrate the common association of women with madness and hysteria and thematically orientates the direction for the drama that ensues.[6] In Wald's words:

> Daniels chooses female figures who to this day serve as cultural icons that embody a sinful, irrational and insane concept of femininity that is indispensible for male sanity, its constitutive other. Rewriting the stories of these biblical women from their own perspective, Daniels … treats the fate of these women with irony, exaggerates or trivialises them, and invents unknown motivations for their ostensibly mad acts. It thus deconstructs the stereotype of sinful and insane femininity and questions the classifications of 'sane' and 'insane' and their association with gender even before the play's main action starts.[7]

Gender has, of course, long occupied a significant place in the annals of madness,[8] the feminine frequently being distanced from normative masculine structures and negatively implicated in dualisms surrounding representation, performance, language and communication. Such structures have been used to perpetuate derisive 'madness' labelling[9] 'of [those female and/or feminized individuals] whose behaviour run[s] contrary to patriarchal definitions of normality'.[10] Daniels's play,

6. Bakker, 'Critical', 148.

7. Wald, *Hysteria*, 116–17.

8. See Jane Ussher, *The Madness of Women: Myth and Experience* (London: Routledge, 2011). Venla Oikkonen similarly attests, 'For more than two thousand years, madness has carried strong associations with female corporeality. While the assumed cause of insanity has varied from the ancient "wandering womb" to the more modern PMS, the gendered associations of madness have not changed significantly. Not surprisingly, one of the main targets of feminist criticism since the early 1970s has been the representations of mad women in cultural and medical texts. While some feminists have criticized these representations for equating women with their bodies by connecting mental instability with menarche, menstruation, pregnancy and menopause (see, for example, Ussher 11, 74), others have pointed out that "madness, even when experienced by men, is metaphorically and symbolically represented as feminine: a female malady."' See Venla Oikkonen, 'Mad Embodiments: Female Corporeality and Insanity in Janet Frame's *Faces in the Water* and Sylvia Plath's *The Bell Jar*', The Electronic Journal of the Department of English at the University of Helsinki 3 (2004). Available online at: http://blogs.helsinki.fi/hes-eng/volumes/volume-3-special-issue-on-literary-studies/mad-embodiments-female-corporeality-and-insanity-in-janet-frames-faces-in-the-water-and-sylvia-plaths-the-bell-jar-venla-oikkonen/.

9. Daniels states, 'I don't think there's anyone in the play who is mentally ill.' Daniels, cited in Bakker, 'Critical', 137.

10. Bakker, 'Critical', 137. Allied to this, the twentieth-century psychiatrist Thomas Szaz provocatively (and controversially) claimed that individual 'mental illness' had no basis in actual psychiatric states, rather, psychopathological classifications were used as mechanisms of social control to contain and suppress marginal members of society. In Thomas Szasz's opinion, 'What is called "mental illness" (or "psychopathology") emerges as the name of the

however, does not simply employ madness as a metaphorical trope or 'narrative prosthesis'[11] to represent the social ills of sexist oppression, but also to illustrate how repressive social systems themselves have the power to wound those subject to them. The manifestation of this wounding often looks quite different (from dominant medical or social models of madness) in the testimonies of a person experiencing it first-hand. The traumatization of Daniels's protagonist, abused by her father, is presented through a character 'doubling device', hence the title of the play *Beside Herself*[12]: 'Eve [played by the same actress who plays Eve in the prologue] represents part of Evelyn's existence that she attempts to block out … The play suggests that Eve is a leftover of the past which "rots" Evelyn's sense of self as long as it is not addressed.'[13] Madness in this perspective entails a forced isolation which itself can be a trigger of distress.[14]

Daniels's work, while very alive to the ways in which gender intersects with constructions of madness, nevertheless uncritically assumes a Eurocentric model of madness. Daniels's female characters accordingly perform acts of resistance to culturally specific Western experiences of oppression – sexism and sanist forms of psychopathological labelling in industrialized/capitalist contexts.[15] Others have recently challenged the broader 'whiteness' of mad studies and urged mad interpreters to consider 'racialized' bodies that often 'already evoke fear, anxiety and disgust and add sanism to the mix'.[16]

Demonstrating this, Sonia Meerai, Idil Abdillahi and Jennifer Poole have coined the term 'anti-Black sanism'. They illustrate how sanist-micro aggressions – 'name-calling, dismissal, and the practices that facilitate the erasure of identity' – are

product of a particular kind of relationship between oppressors[s] and oppressed.' Thomas Szasz, *The Manufacture of Madness: A Comparative Study of the Inquisition and the Mental Health Movement* (Syracuse: Syracuse University Press, 1970), 81.

11. Mitchell and Snyder, *Narrative*, 56.

12. 'From the play's beginning the presence of Eve thus creates a form of traumatised realism that poses a riddle for the audiences. Eve serves as a symptom which invites audiences to speculate about its cause.' Wald, *Hysteria*, 117–18.

13. Wald, *Hysteria*, 117–18. This doubling technique is also seen in other women's madness literatures – including the celebrated Perkins Gilman's story *The Yellow Wallpaper* from 1892.

14. Jennifer Williams, 'Re-membering Madness in Africana Women's Literature', Dissertation, Department of African and African American Studies, Clark Atlanta University (1998). Available online at: http://digitalcommons.auctr.edu/cgi/viewcontent.cgi?article=2195&context=dissertations, 13.

15. See Laura Halperin, *Intersections of Harm: Narratives of Latina Deviance and Defiance* (New Jersey: Rutgers University Press, 2013). See also Alastair Morgan, Anne Felton, Bill Fulford, Jayasree Kalathil and Gemma Stacey, *Values and Ethics in Mental Health: An Exploration for Practice* (London: Palgrave, 2015).

16. Mfoafo-M'Carthy, cited in Sonia Meerai, Idil Abdillahi and Jennifer Poole, 'An Introduction to Anti-Black Sanism', *Intersectionalities* 5 (2016), 18–35, 21.

'compounded when visited on racialized bodies'.[17] They situate anti-Black sanism's roots within the enlightenment prizing of rationality, and the constructions of racialized bodies variously perpetuated within colonization, slavery and psychiatry. These systems, they claim, served to bolster the normality of whiteness and mark anything perceived to be different to European performances, emotions and modes of identity (including indigenous spirituality etc.) as deviant. The African brain was variously compared to that of a 'leucotomized European's' or as 'a European child's cerebrum'.[18] Such viewpoints, they submit, have haunted ongoing pathologization and maltreatment of racialized bodies in mental health, educational and criminal justice systems in the West ever since:

> In the face of a white rationality, the doing of Blackness and the being Indigenous or African/not white is always 'strange', always marginal and subjugated. This occurs in all systems as well as at the intuitive and spiritual level ... It demands that the mad movement and Mad Studies do some considering, too. If ... colonialism operates though exclusion, appropriation, and marginalization of Indigenous knowledge, practice, and peoples, both the mental health system and those who seek to change it must decolonize through inclusion, crediting, and centering Black/African experiences, pain, knowledge, scholarship, and experiences of sanism.[19]

Stephanie LeBlanc and Elizabeth Kinsella similarly warn of the 'epistemic injustice' implicit within 'under-inclusion (or exclusion) from mainstream discourse of the firsthand experiences and perspectives of those that identify as mad'[20] and non-white across the world. Rachel Gorman, likewise, attests to emergent critiques around the lack of critical race and transnational perspectives within disability studies which 'collectively represent an intellectual crisis for disability studies'.[21] For Gorman, exclusion of two-thirds world authors from mad canons starkly 'highlight[s] the pitfalls of an identity-based Mad movement that reproduced a white, Western Mad subject' and absorbed 'white-middle class narratives of disability'.[22] This (could) perpetuate and construct what Jasbir Puar would term (a mad) 'homonationalism'.[23] Shaindl Diamond similarly attests that:

17. Meerai, Abdillahi and Poole, 'Introduction', 21.

18. Meerai, Abdillahi and Poole, 'Introduction', 23.

19. Meerai, Abdillahi and Poole, 'Introduction', 25.

20. Stephanie LeBlanc and Elizabeth Anne Kinsella, 'Toward Epistemic Justice: A Critically Reflexive Examination of "Sanism" and Implications for Knowledge Generation', *Studies in Social Justice* 10(1) (2016), 59–78.

21. Rachel Gorman, 'Mad Nation? Thinking through Race, Class and Mad Identity Politics', in LeFrançois et al. (eds), *Mad*, 269–80, 271.

22. Gorman, 'Mad Nation?', 270.

23. Jasbir Puar, 'Queer Times, Queer Assemblages', *Social Text* 23 (2005), 121–39. Available online at: http://www.uib.no/sites/w3.uib.no/files/attachments/queer_times_queer_assemblages.pdf. Robert Mcruer uses Puar's work in his interrogation of Western

> Encounters with racialized psychiatrized women taught me that psychiatric survivor identity politics do not fit with all people's experiences of the world. This was clear in a conversation I had with Rora, a racialized woman who understood that she was oppressed by psychiatry, but viewed this oppression as deeply intertwined with the racist and sexist violence she had endured throughout her life.[24]

Such work rightly subverts any fixed or essentialized notions of 'mad identity' which do not take into account racialized, colonized, diasporic or classed dimensions of experience.[25]

Responding to such a call, Jennifer Williams, in her evocative study of madness tropes within Africana women's writings, underscores variable cross-cultural attitudes to madness and its causes – including an emphasis on collective ramifications of madness and indigenous spiritual experiences within Africana traditions. The particular ways in which two-thirds world women's literatures can modify Western understandings of madness is vitally important in this respect. Williams shows how 'interlocking oppressive systems' not just based on sexism but also colonialism, racism, classism, servitude and other identity struggles – mark Africana women's literature on madness in very distinct ways.[26] Frantz Fanon's now classic work on how the colonized often manifest particular mental states – 'reactionary psychosis' – as a response to discrimination and colonial control, Williams asserts, continues to be at least in part relevant in this light.[27]

Taking heed of such perspectives, here I will probe the interpretation of two biblical women who have variously been subject, in Western interpretations, to psychopathological and social deviance labelling to denote their otherness. First, 'the hysterical woman of Canaan'[28] who pleads for a daughter 'tormented' by a

disability studies as a kind of homonationalism. See Robert Mcruer, *Crip Theory: Cultural Signs of Queerness and Disability* (New York: New York University Press, 2006).

24. Shaindl Diamond, 'What Makes Us a Community? Reflections on Building Solidarity in Anti-sanist Praxis', in LeFrançois et al. (eds), *Mad*, 64–78, 69.

25. Gorman, 'Mad Nation?', 269.

26. Williams, 'Re-membering', 14.

27. Fanon cited in Alison Howell, *Madness in International Relations: Psychology, Security, and the Global Governance of Mental Health* (London: Routledge, 2011), 52. In a critical vein James Mills writing on madness in colonial India notes that Foucault and Fanon's models are too absolutist: 'The colonizers did not dominate but desired to dominate and the instances where their projects were disrupted and contested emphasize that their domination remained fantasy rather than fact ... neither colonial power or medical power was absolute or dominant.' James Mills, *Madness, Cannabis and Colonialism: The Native Only Lunatic Asylums of British India 1857–1900* (London: Palgrave Macmillan, 2000), 181.

28. Terence Cuneo, 'Liturgy and the Moral Life', in B. Miller, R. Michael Furr, Angela Knobel and William Fleeson (eds), *Character: New Directions from Philosophy, Psychology, and Theology* (Oxford: Oxford University Press, 2015), 583.

demon and is subsequently the recipient of barbed comments by Jesus (Mt. 15:24–28). Second, a Pythian slave girl (Acts 16) possessed by a spirit of divination who has been variously associated with 'melancholy, insanity',[29] 'mental imbalance and schizophrenia'[30] and the demonic by biblical interpreters. While her clairvoyance is presented as financially lucrative for her masters, she is eventually silenced through exorcism by a seemingly irritated Paul (Acts 16:16–18). These characters' multiple marginalities and their respective intersections with perceptions and/or experiences of madness will be critically probed. Taking heed of Williams's warning regarding the Eurocentric nature of madness constructions, the Africana 'mad' writer Bessie Head's work will be used to elucidate not just the sanist and sexist oppression these respective biblical characters endure, but also the other interconnecting practices of subjugation (racism, colonialism, servitude and slavery) which they border and at times critically resist.

In Africana women's literatures, mad borders, as will be seen, can be regarded as liminal spaces offering 'a thin line of respite for the marginal, at which the authority of the centre peters out'.[31] Those rendered as out of place or at the margins – 'ex-centric' (exilic, displaced) – can, at times, destabilize, violate and/or reconceptualize borders to produce, in Edward Soja's terms, 'an assertively different and intentionally disruptive way of (re)interpreting the relation between the centre and the periphery'.[32] Moreover, these 'ex-centric' border transgressions are often played out in what others perceive as 'mad' acts, performances and identities. For, as Susanna Zinato and Annalisa Pes have submitted in their study of madness in postcolonial fiction: 'The freak or mad character's ex-centric vision is a continuous warning against the temptation to believe those discourses that pass themselves off as reflecting or bearing the given, "natural" order of things.'[33]

As Daniels's biblical women in 'supermarket hell' are encouraged to refigure and challenge their patriarchal marginalization in interpretative histories, so here these two biblical women and the (mad) borderlands they correspondingly evoke will likewise be refigured and recast as 'ex-centrics' who, though wounded, still transgress rather than are complicit with the intersecting systems of power that seek to silence them.[34]

29. Abiel Abbot Livermore, *The Acts of the Apostles: With a Commentary* (Boston: James Munroe and Company, 1844), 229.

30. Paul W. Walaskay, *Acts* (Kentucky: Westminster John Knox Press, 1998), 157.

31. Avtar Brah, cited in Jane Campion, 'Writing in the Margins: Exploring the Borderland in the Work of Janet Frame and Anna Ball' *eSharp* 5, Borders and Boundaries, 1–18, 3. Available online at: http://www.gla.ac.uk/media/media_41163_en.pdf.

32. Edward Soja, *Thirdspace: Journeys to Los Angeles and Other Real-and-Imagined Places* (Oxford: Oxford University Press, 1996), 126.

33. Susanna Zinato and Annalisa Pes, 'Introduction', in Susanna Zinato and Annalisa Pes (eds), *Ex-centric Writing: Essays on Madness in Postcolonial Fiction* (Cambridge: Cambridge Scholars Publishing, 2013), 1–24, 3.

34. '"Mad" women writing about madness, all suffer from a double (or triple) alienation: as women writers in a field largely dominated by male writings, and as writers of

Bessie Head's A Question of Power: An Africana Madness Narrative

Madness narratives denote 'firsthand accounts of the experience' of madness (variously understood) in novels, journals, autobiographies and narratives presented by an interlocutor.[35] Anca-Luisa Viusenco characterizes 'madness narratives' as comprising creative writing, pathography and political activism; intentionally telling stories from the position of the subjective experience of madness rather than from a dominant (normalizing) script which renders those perceived as 'mad' as other.[36]

Bessie Head's *A Question of Power* (1974) is a semi-autobiographical madness narrative about biracialism and its associated traumas (social, psychological, communal) in apartheid South Africa. Unbeknown to her, as she was brought up by foster parents, Head was born to a white South African mother and a black native South African father. In her teenage years, her parentage was rather unceremoniously revealed to her by a teacher at a missionary school. Furthermore, it was claimed that her biological mother was insane and institutionalized – 'as she was having a child by the stable boy, who was a native'[37] – and that she is thought to have committed suicide as a result. As an adult, Head experiences displacement and isolation as a single parent in exile in Botswana (due to journal articles she published, which made her politically suspect in South Africa), a journey that Elizabeth, the protagonist of Head's novel, also undertakes.[38] Elizabeth encounters alternate states of consciousness and 'in so doing . . . seek[s] to counter the disturbing effects of the predominant powers (patriarchal, racist, and social class authorities)

"subaltern" (his)stories. Thus, in these cases, writing becomes an act of re-appropriation of one's story and of history, by gendering their own story through the use of specific tropes. This is why writing becomes an act of subversion and transgression – subverting traditional literary genres and tropes, and transgressing generic boundaries.' Nathalie Segeral, 'Reclaimed Experience: Gendering Trauma in Slavery, Holocaust, and Madness Narratives', UCLA Electronic Theses and Dissertations, PhD, French & Francophone Studies (2012), 12. Available online at: http://escholarship.org/uc/item/3xw6t98t.

35. Susan Hubert, *Questions of Power: The Politics of Women's Madness Narratives*, (Newark: University of Delaware, 2002), 19.

36. Anca-Luisa Viusenco, 'The Madness Narrative: Between the Literary, Therapeutic and the Political', *Romanian Journal of English Studies* 10(1) (2013). Available online at: http://www.degruyter.com/dg/viewarticle.fullcontentlink:pdfeventlink/$002fj$002frjes.2013.10.issue-1$002frjes-2013-0030$002frjes-2013-0030.pdf?t:ac=j$002frjes.2013.10.issue-1$002frjes-2013-0030$002frjes-2013-0030.xml.

37. Bessie Head, *A Question of Power* (South Africa: Heinemann, 1974), 16. Adetokunbo Pearse submits that what 'constitutes insanity in this case is the breaking of South Africa's Immorality Amendment Act in 1957'. See Adetokunbo Pearse, 'Apartheid and Madness: Bessie Head's, A Question of Power', *Kunapipi* 5(2) (1983), 81–98, 83. Available online at: http://ro.uow.edu.au/kunapipi/vol5/iss2/9.

38. Williams, 'Re-membering', 72.

on the self'.[39] Head's readers are privy to Elizabeth's experiences of 'madness', itself a crucial deconstruction of racist colonial pictures of African women which claimed that 'they [African women] had not reached the level of self-awareness and introspection required for mental breakdown'.[40] Moreover, Head unpicks the Western construction of Elizabeth's experience as mere 'hallucination' by showing her experiences as common to African indigenous cultures.

> In most indigenous African spiritual systems, communing with those in the spiritual realm is a desired occurrence, for members of the community feel as though their ancestors have lessons to impart and can assist them in the earthly realm. Moreover, most ritualized journeys contain an element of fear that the initiate has to overcome in order to re-emerge as a more self-actualized individual. In *Of Water and the Spirit*, Malidoma Some describes his initiation as a shaman. Recounting the beliefs of his ethnic group, Some proclaims, 'The Dagara believe that contact with the otherworld is always deeply transformational' (Some 1994, 19). Elizabeth's journey through "madness" and the spiritual intervention it entails is essential to catapult her into a more highly evolved state of being.[41]

As Elizabeth is displaced from South Africa to Botswana so too, not just her mind and body but also her space and land needs to be re-construed as 'a discursive space that [she must] retrieve'.[42] Ultimately, Head's novel delves into the philosophical groundings of control, and 'sets forth a humanistic vision'.[43] For Head, as for other Africana women writers, madness thus provides a means by which she comments not only on various alienations and interlocking systems of oppressive powers, but also 'bespeaks a need for re-invention and re-membering'.[44] As such, madness is not only employed as a signifier for experiential wounds but also a powerful stimulant for resistance and reintegration.

Allied resistant and violating strategies will here be explored in relation to the Canaanite woman and the Pythian slave girl. These two characters (separated by books in the biblical corpus) are quite intentionally presented alongside not only Bessie Head's work but also one another – 'beside themselves' – to encapsulate something of what Heather Debling sees Daniels's and other women's madness literatures constructively proposing: namely, a forging of 'homosocial' bonds with other women as central to overcoming the effect of being deemed mad and/or the wounds and suffering this categorization often entails.[45] Their histories are

39. Williams, 'Re-membering', 72.
40. Williams, 'Re-membering', 72.
41. Williams, 'Re-membering', 76.
42. Williams, 'Re-membering', 74.
43. Williams, 'Re-membering', 72.
44. Williams, 'Re-membering', 75.
45. Heather Debling, '"How Will They Ever Heal…?" Bearing Witness to Abuse and the Importance of Female Community in Sarah Daniels's *Beside Herself, Head-Rot Holiday*, and *The Madness of Esme and Shaz*', *Modern Drama* 51(2) (2008), 259–73.

tacitly taken to relate to one another in particular ways and the dialogues initiated here encourage them 'to reclaim experiences ... forge "shared memor[ies] and ... respond to phallocentric [and other oppressive] discourses on the "mad woman," to empower the alienated female "subject" '.[46]

Wounding, Voice and Vocality

Prominent themes which emerge in Head's semi-autobiographical account, which I will adopt here as hermeneutical lenses, are wounding, voice and vocality. Wounding traces the ways in which forms of social oppression (patriarchy, racism, colonialism, servitude etc.) not only mark and marginalize those perceived as 'other' in social constructions but also indelibly inflict wounds and suffering upon individual and collective identities. 'Wounding' demarcates places where 'something buried or hidden splits open, breaches and reveals a memory, a site of pain, of suffering and death' yet crucially 'can also include a joyful sense of new freedom as well'.[47] Madness narratives, such as Head's, frequently attest to distinct associations between subjugation, oppression and social and psychological wounding.[48] Frantz Fanon's seminal work *Black Skin, White Masks* (1952) was one of the first to articulate connections between madness and social oppression, particularly in reference to the (oft-times violent, abusive, humiliating and degrading) practices of colonialism and racism. He noted how Euro-Americans regarded and treated Africans as animal-like: more primitive than whites.[49] Moreover the psychological alienation of these encounters – 'the cultural shock and bereavement ... the physical and psychic trauma of colonial invasion'[50] – was, for the 'colonised subject' (both individually and collectively), damaging and destructive. Fanon writes, 'I began to suffer from not being a white man to the degree that white man imposes discrimination on me, makes me a colonized native, robs me of all worth, all individuality, tells me that I am a parasite on the world, that I must bring myself as quickly as possible into step with the white world.'[51] Elaine Showalter, Hershini Bhana Young and Caroline Brown have also variously attested to how 'class, sexuality, ethnicity and transgression permit the construction of the "mad" other'[52] which denotes a 'metaphor, a symbolic space of negation that

46. Segeral, 'Reclaimed', 19.

47. Dennis Patrick Slattery, *The Wounded Body: Remembering the Markings of Flesh* (New York: SUNY Press, 1999), 16.

48. Jacqueline McDaniel, ' "Madness" in Exile Literature: Insanity as a Byproduct of Subjugation and Manipulation in Bessie Head's A Question of Power', Seton Hall University Dissertations and Theses (ETDs) (2011).

49. Frantz Fanon, *Black Skin, White Masks*, trans. Charles Lam Markmann (New York: Grove, 1967 [original French 1952]).

50. Zinato and Pes, 'Introduction', 1–23, 3.

51. Fanon, *Black*, 98.

52. McDaniel, 'Madness in Exile', 10.

permits the establishing of the parameters of normalcy through the articulation of its opposition'.[53] Susanna Zinato locates such reflexes in Head's narrative. Elizabeth plunges into madness as a result of 'a devastating epic confrontation with abjection ... her hybrid body is the incarnate icon of contamination'.[54] Elizabeth is displaced, but also subject to a certain 'internalization of deep-seated, visceral racist feelings, so that she can be said to be a subject of, as well as, to abjection, in need of purging herself through a process of self-abjection as it were'.[55] Head herself revealed how her wounding was a central structuring device of her work: '[T]he whole process of breakdown and destruction is outlined there ... I'd lost, in *A Question of Power*, the certainty of my own goodness. The novel was written under pressure. I was alarmed.'[56]

Voice is also a particular site where gender and other forms of difference are routinely rehearsed.[57] As Dinah Manisty in her work on madness as a textual strategy submits, in communication 'women are typically situated on the side of irrationality, silence, nature, and body, while men are situated on the side of reason, discourse, culture, and mind'.[58] As a result, as Leslie Dunn notes, '[w]hether [the female voice] is celebrated, eroticised, demonized, ridiculed or denigrated, it is always stigmatized, ideologically "marked" and construed as a "problem" for the (male) social/critic auditor'.[59] While 'voice' has recently been widely adopted in feminist discourse to denote retrieval of muted feminine perspectives and agencies, recent work on embodiment and the female voice has also appealed to Julia Kristeva and Roland Barthes' theorizations, in contending that voice is not just codified by semantic content, but also its sonorous, non-verbal, features (pitch, tone, inflection, pace and cadence). Leslie Dunn purposefully adopts the term 'vocality' in her study of embodied voice for, in her opinion, too often voice is conflated with speech and words as the dominant vehicle of meaning. However,

53. McDaniel, 'Madness in Exile', 10.

54. Zinato and Pes, 'Introduction', 11.

55. Zinato and Pes, 'Introduction', 11.

56. Head, cited in Nettie Cloete, 'Psychological Afflictions as Expressed in Bessie Head's *A Question of Power* and Tsitsi Dangarembga's *Nervous Conditions*', *Uterator* 21(1) (2000), 37–52, 42.

57. Annette Schlichter, 'Do Voices Matter? Vocality, Materiality, Gender Performativity', *Body & Society* 17(1) (2011), 31–52.

58. Dinah Manisty and دانية مانيستي, 'Madness as Textual Strategy in the Narratives of Three Egyptian Women Writers'/الجنون كإستراتيجية نصية في السرد عند ثلاث كاتبات مصريات, *Alif: Journal of Comparative Poetics* 14 (1994), 152–74, 152. See also on sound and gender, Sylvia Mieszkowski, Joy Smith and Marijke de Valck, 'Sonic Interventions', *Journal of International Women's Studies* 2 (2000), 11–12. Also see Mikko Keskinen, 'Her Mistress's Voice: Gynophonocentrism in Feminist Discourses', *Journal of International Women's Studies* 2(1) (2000), 1–15.

59. Leslie Dunn, *Embodied Voices: Representing Female Vocality in Western Culture* (Cambridge: Cambridge University Press, 1996), 9.

human vocality includes all the voice's materializations (e.g. speaking, singing, crying and laughing), each of which, in Dunn's words, 'is invested with social meanings not wholly determined by linguistic content'.[60] Thus, by attending to the sonorous 'grain of the voice',[61] one can start to attend to non-verbal meanings associated with the dynamism, vocalization and audition of a performance.[62] Attesting to this, classicists and ancient historians have similarly noted how the ancient discipline of physiognomy determined whether people would be judged 'sane or insane, male or female, good, evil, trustworthy, depressive, marriageable, moribund, likely or unlikely to make war on us, little better than animals, inspired by God'[63] on account of the sounds they made. Low-pitched manly voices indicated valour and bravery, whereas shrill, high-pitched feminine voices were dismissed as disorderly, volatile and dangerous.[64] In Anne Carson's words:

> High vocal pitch goes together with talkativeness to characterize the person who is deviant from the masculine ideal of self-control. Women, catamites, eunuchs, and androgynies fall into this category. Their sounds are bad and make men uncomfortable. Just how uncomfortable may be measured by the lengths to which Aristotle's willing to go in accounting for the gender of sound physiognomically; he ends up ascribing the low pitch of the male voice to the tension placed on a man's vocal chords by his testicles functioning as loom weights.[65]

As a result, socioculturally, the intonation of female vocality was often inflected within tropes of madness as disorder, to denote threats to social and political order and constancy.[66] In reference to the Bible similarly, feminized speech was

60. Dunn, *Embodied*, 1–2.

61. See Roland Barthes work on 'The Grain of the Voice', in Roland Barthes, *Image, Music, Text* (London: Fontana Press, 1977), 179–89.

62. Dunn, *Embodied*, 1–2.

63. Anne Carson, 'The Gender of Sound', in Ann Carson, *Glass, Irony and God* (New York: New Directions Publishing Corporation, 1995), 119–39.

64. Aristotle contended that the high vocal pitch of the female was evidence of her malevolent disposition and deviance from masculine ideals of self-control. In contrast deep masculine voices denoted bravery and justice. Carson, 'The Gender', 119. Carson further notes that the female in classical literature is given to involuntary and uncontrolled sonic flows (lament, laughter, wailing etc.). She cites Euripides' view that 'it is women's inborn pleasure always to have her current emotions coming up to her mouth and out through her tongue'. Euripides, cited in Carson, 'The Gender', 126.

65. Carson, 'The Gender', 119.

66. Mary Beard likewise proposed that public speaking was the exclusive proviso of the male and 'a woman speaking in public was, in most circumstances, by definition not a woman'. Aristotle contended that the high vocal pitch of the female was evidence of her malevolent disposition and deviance from masculine ideals of self-control. See Mary Beard, 'The Public Voice of Women', *London Review of Books* 36(6) (2014), 11–14.

frequently linked to disorder and/or possession. Demonstrating such associations, Jin Young Choi, for example, points out in his recent Asian hermeneutical reading of the gospels that 'individuals [with] high pitched cries or screams are a sign of uncleanness, because these voices are related to demon-possession and the one who speaks is the unclean spirit within the person'.[67] The case of Rhoda the maid-servant in Acts 12:12-19, the only female character directly accused of madness (from μαίνομαι to be out of one's mind), in the New Testament, is 'othered to Peter in terms of gender and social status'[68] on account of her voice and (comedic) bodily performance and is accordingly censored, subdued and stigmatized:

> Peter's voice is the first in a succession of voices: Rhoda's voice announces Peter's reappearance the collective voice of the assembly declares Rhoda is mad, and Peter shares his prison ordeal in his own voice. Only the male voices count. Rhoda's voice is othered as representing madness and as unreliable … In the end it did not matter what Rhoda said.[69]

A focus on 'sonorous' elements of speech requires both the emission of sound from one body and its reception by another/others. Dunn and Jones term this encounter 'an intersubjective acoustic space', which demands the interpreter to 'reconstruct … the contexts of … hearing'.[70] Notwithstanding the fact that our only access to vocal sounds in biblical literature are through written words – 'silent texts to prompt our imagination into a "mental image" of those voices that once "nourished the ancient soundscape"'[71] – striking is the fact that both biblical women under review, as will be seen, are marked out in some way in both texts and interpretations on account of their respective vocal performances. Furthermore,

67. Jin Young Choi, *Postcolonial Discipleship of Embodiment: An Asian and Asian American Feminist Reading of the Gospel of Mark* (New York: Springer, 2015), 109–31.

68. Mitzi J. Smith, *The Literary Construction of the Other in the Acts of the Apostles: Charismatics, the Jews and Women* (Cambridge: James Clarke, 2012), 127.

69. Smith, *Literary*, 127. So too, in F. Scott Spencer's words, 'More specifically, it is Peter's voice which ultimately persuades. He not only appears alive before the confused assembly, but motions for them "to be silent" and "describe[s]" for them the details of his deliverance (12:17). In the process, Peter silences Rhoda as well and effectively usurps her role as witness. Recalling, too, that from the very start Rhoda's testimony was based on "recognizing Peter's voice" (12:14), we find her word being wholly bracketed (stifled) by Peter's in the story. The assembly's dubious reaction to Rhoda's "mad" report is closely parallel to the apostles' dismissal of the women's witness to Jesus' empty tomb in Luke 24 as an "idle tale".' F. Scott Spencer, 'Out of Mind, Out of Voice: Slave Girls and Prophetic Daughters in Luke-Acts', *Biblical Interpretation* 7(2) (1999), 133–55.

70. Dunn and Jones, 'Introduction', 2.

71. Matthew Fox, 'Review of Maurizio Bettini, *Voci: Antropologia sonora del mondo antico. Saggi, 892*. Torino: Einaudi, 2008', *Bryn Mawr Classical Review* (2008). Available online at: http://bmcr.brynmawr.edu/2008/2008-12-09.html.

their voices are frequently rendered by commentators as symptomatic of their femaleness, psychopathology and/or social disorder/madness.

Recourse to Head's madness narrative can also give insights into how these woundings and voices/vocality can be alternatively heard and/or reconfigured. Maria Wenzel in her work on Head's *A Question of Power* notes that the protagonist Elizabeth has various dialogues in her 'soul journeys' with the voices of two male characters Sello and Dan, each respectively denoting racial and gender subjugation. However, these voices are also shown to be in conflict which indicates 'the subversive quality of the discourse' and the ways in which these, and Head's own voice, stand in contention. Wenzel notes how Elizabeth initially is a bystander, the voiceless victim exposed to her covert fears, encased in Sello's and Dan's taunting and snide remarks. However, their 'mechanisms of power' are ultimately unmasked and deconstructed by her as she moves from consumer to constructor of the discourse. Furthermore, Elizabeth's voice reveals how oppressive systems ultimately entrap and wound not just the victim but also the perpetrators. Thus she claims: 'The victim is really the most flexible, the most free person on earth ... The faces of oppressed people are not ugly. They are scarred with suffering. But the torturers become more hideous day by day.'[72] Wenzel too notes how vocality, intonation, dissonance and conflict all play parts in deconstructing oppressive systems. She employs the Russian literary critic Bakhtin's view of the carnivalesque evidenced in irony and so on to show how literature is political, variously acceding, parodying, re-accenting, subverting and reformulating cultural power structures and ideologies of the discourses it narrates. Citing Patricia Yaegar, Wenzel concurs:

> The narratives that we read are filled with power struggles in which some voices rise higher than others. The business of the dialogic imagination is to elicit these forbidden vocalities and show them at work. The business of a feminist dialogics is to gender these voices and to unmask the complex, contorted play of hegemonic forms and female speech – to explore the ways in which women from a variety of temporalities, ethnicities, races, and classes initiate dialogues with their oppressions.[73]

It is attending to allied struggles and resistance within the narrative of the Canaanite Woman and the Pythian slave girl that I now turn.

Wounding, Voice and Vocality: The Canaanite Woman (Mt. 15:21–28)

The 'wounding' that is most explicit in the Canaanite woman's speech encounter involves her status as a colonized subject. Musa Dube famously identifies

72. Head, cited in Marita Wenzel, 'An Approach to Power Relations: Bessie Head and Luisa Valenzuela', *Literator* 19(1) (1998), 51–64, 53.

73. Wenzel, 'An Approach', 53.

the Canaanite woman as a 'colonized ethnic' in her postcolonial feminist interpretation[74] and posits Jesus as a neocolonial figure entering the foreign land of Tyre and Sidon (v.22) and inflicting verbal abuse on a colonized subject. Elizabeth Amoah too sees Jesus dehumanizing the woman, first by refusing to interact with her and second by analogously implying that she and her people are dogs (κυναρίοις v. 26). In Mark Nanos's words: 'Because dogs parade about naked, defecate, conduct sexual behavior, and generally carry on without regard for "human" conventions of modesty or prudence; they are characterized to be shameless.'[75] Animalistic labelling of this sort was also typically used as a cipher for human vices such as 'cowardice, modesty, and arrogance, all presumed blots of the canine species'.[76] The woman's seemingly uncritical (even normalizing) acceptance (and echoing) of this label denotes in Amoah's view 'a reaction typical of African women, some of whom go through all sorts of emotional abuse and dehumanization for the sake of children or family as a whole'.[77] Internalization of [neo]colonial rhetoric has long been recognized to be part of the mechanics of ideological oppression and is a feature that is also echoed, in part, in Head's novel. Indeed Elizabeth's 'pure' African identity is questioned by accusatory voices which characterize her biracialism in similar bestial terms: "Dog, filth, the Africans will eat you to death"[78] and she in turn is shown to understand herself, at least in part, through these categories.

The Canaanite woman's voice and vocality is also reckoned to be inflected by her 'unattachment to a male' and feminized hysteria: 'a single woman [who has] a daughter with an unclean spirit ... [and as a result is] is stigmatized, frustrated, and constantly experiencing humiliation'.[79] She is portrayed approaching Jesus 'calling out' (ἔκραζεν), or as the NRSV more forcefully translates, 'shouting' (Mt. 15:22). Interpreters have accordingly judged her to be 'exhibit[ing] a significantly

74. Musa Dube, *Postcolonial Feminist Interpretation of the Bible* (St Louis: Chalice Press, 2000), 148.

75. Mark Nanos, 'Paul's Reversal of Jews Calling Gentiles "Dogs" (Philippians 3:2): 1600 Years of an Ideological Tale Wagging an Exegetical Dog?', Blog Post (2007). Available online at: http://www.marknanos.com/Phil3Dogs-Reverse-6-27-07.pdf.

76. Sophia Menachel, 'Dogs: God's Worst Enemies?', *Society and Animals* 5(1) (1997), 23–44, 23. Mention of dogs in biblical traditions are normally cast negatively – related to carrion and carcasses (Exod. 22:31; Jer. 15:3). Proverbs attest: 'Like a dog that returns to its vomit is a fool who reverts to his folly' (Prov. 26:11). The New Testament too attests to negative canine traits: 'do not give what is holy to the dogs' (Mt. 7:56).

77. Elizabeth Amoah, 'Theological Perspective on Mutual Solidarity in the Context of Globalization: The Circle's Experience', in Mary McClintock Fulkerson and Sheila Briggs (eds), *The Oxford Handbook of Feminist Theology* (Oxford: Oxford University Press, 2012), 239–49, 246.

78. Head, *A Question*, digital version, no pages.

79. Surekha Nelavala, *Liberation beyond Borders: Dalit Feminist Hermeneutics and Four Gospel Women* (Lambert Academic Publishing, 2009), 81.

loud voice … [displaying] unacceptable behaviour in public, shouting desperately and crying after Jesus'.[80] The disciples' dismissal on account of her 'shouting after us' (NRSV) (κράζει ὄπισθεν ἡ'μῶν v.23b) further underscores the woman's vocal action as a prominent aspect of her perceived social disorder. Her performance is thus rendered contrary to expected norms regarding the social decorum of the female:

> As the woman is described in the text, she does not exhibit any sense of shame, even though she is acting differently from other women. According to the social norms of her context, women are usually confined to the private space and expected to act soberly in public space. A woman shouting in the streets and seeking help from a man does not fit the stereotype of a dignified woman. Such an action in the public sphere may be considered shameful.[81]

Others have gone further in underlining the supposed social deviancy of the woman's initiation of this encounter. Amy Richter follows others in associating the 'Canaanite'– a stereotyped code-word often laced with racialized assumptions regarding illicit sexuality[82] – with Tamar: 'Tamar and the Canaanite woman both meet in a public setting the man they believe can give them what they need; this meeting is in a public setting brings with it an association with prostitution.'[83] Could such assumptions also lie behind the frequently cited sanist psychopathological labelling of this character as a 'hysterical' woman of Canaan?[84] Ancient attitudes surrounding female 'hysteria' as symptomatic of madness often sustained and enforced women's submission and normative subordination to men through

80. Nelavala, *Liberation*, 79–80.

81. Nelavala, *Liberation*, 79–80.

82. Amy Richter, *Enoch and the Gospel of Matthew* (Oregon: Pickwick Publications, 2012), 72–3. For others on the sexual overtones of the encounter, see E. Anne Clements, *Mothers on the Margin?: The Significance of the Women in Matthew's Genealogy* (Oregon: Pickwick Publications, 2014), 215; Talvikki Mattila, *Citizens of the Kingdom: Followers in Matthew from a Feminist Perspective* (Finnish Exegetical Society, 2002), 113; Stuart L. Love, *Jesus and Marginal Women: The Gospel of Matthew in Social-Scientific Perspective* (Cambridge: Clarke, 2009), 152ff.

83. Richter, *Enoch*, 69.

84. Terence Cuneo, 'Liturgy and the Moral Life', in Christian B. Miller, R. Michael Furr, Angela Knobel and William Fleeson, *Character: New Directions from Philosophy, Psychology, and Theology* (Oxford: Oxford University Press, 2015), 572–89, 583. In feminist readings there has been a deconstruction of links between the feminine and hysteria and a reformulation of it as subversive resistance. Jane Ussher notes, for example, how 'hysteria is being reinterpreted by feminists as an expression of women's anger, women's oppression, and the power of a misogynnistic discourse to define what "woman" means, and to exert control over women's lives'. Jane Ussher, *Women's Madness: Misogony or Mental Illness?* (Amherst: University of Massachusetts Press, 1992), 75.

marriage.[85] Hysteria was linked in various ancient traditions to gender and 'curious behavioural disturbance[s] in adult women'.[86] In Greek ideas, the phenomenon of 'wandering womb' and disordered sexualities were frequently linked to hysteria. For Roman medical writers too, the association of 'hysteria exclusively with the female generative system' was common.[87] Not insignificant in this light is the frequent linkage in ancient traditions of the mouth (the organ of the voice) and female sexuality. Anne Carson states:

> It is an axiom of ancient Greek and Roman medical theory that a woman has two mouths. The orifice through which vocal activity takes place and the orifice through which sexual activity takes place are both denoted by the term stoma... Ancient medical writers note with interest ... symptoms of physiological correspondence between upper and lower mouth for example that an excess or blockage of blood in the uterus will evidence itself as strangulation or loss of voice ... that defloration causes women's neck to enlarge and her voice to deepen.[88]

Head's novel can provide insights into the deconstruction of ideologies which uncritically associate madness with social disorder; indeed madness for her becomes a means by which 'Elizabeth [can] challenge the normal way of narration and negotiation'.[89] Elizabeth encounters 'Dan' in her episodes of madness. He is described by her as a 'spectacular display of soul power', masculinity and assertiveness.[90] Like Jesus in this episode, Dan (seems to) shape Elizabeth's identity through his labels. Ultimately, however, Dan is unmasked as an unsavoury example of sexual dominance and ethnic pride who seeks to control her identity and self-opinions. Through Dan's approach and verbal abuse, Head is able to expose the ways in which such men 'have utilized their power to manipulate black women sexually, emotionally, and mentally, but also the way in which black women give their power away'.[91] The Canaanite woman's 'mixed' speech address to Jesus, 'Lord, Help me' (Κύριε βοήθει μοι. v.25) which many commentators see as an echo of a Jewish lament somewhat ironically delivered by a Canaanite, demonstrates a consuming and echoing of the colonial and patriarchal identity labels projected

85. John Read, 'A History of Madness', in John Read, Loren R. Mosher and Richard P. Bentall (eds), *Models of Madness: Psychological, Social and Biological Approaches to Schizophrenia* (Hove: Psychology Press, 2004), 9–20, 12ff.

86. Donald Capps, *Jesus the Village Psychiatrist* (Louisville: Westminster John Knox Press, 2008), 16.

87. Capps, *Jesus*, 16.

88. Carson, 'The Gender', 134.

89. Sayyed Rahim Moosavinia, 'Janus-Faced Madness in Bessie Head's *A Question of Power*', *Journal of Research in Applied Linguistics* 7(2) (2012), 135–50, 144.

90. Head, *Question*, 104.

91. Williams, 'Re-membering', 79–80.

onto her. At the same time, however, her hybrid talk also ironically exposes the supremacist power and conceit of the system that seeks to marginalize her. She uses her subordinate position for her own advantage and embodies 'the role of the trickster the person without power, the colonized subject ... the Cynic, the social critic who calls householders to accountability'.[92]

Associated with this, in Africana women's consciousness, is the claim that what is frequently rendered disorder in the colonizer's view – they are '"ill" and needing correction and cure'[93] – is often understood as altered consciousness of spirit possession in indigenous cultural contexts. In Head's work, Elizabeth embarks on a transcendental voyage through spiritual initiation. Through this, 'Elizabeth eventually accepts her "mixed blood" and moreover relishes in the insight it gives her into the idiocy of racial supremacy. She realizes that power over another, whether it is black power or white power, is "the root cause of human suffering"'.[94] Maggi Phillips sees Head's characterization of Elizabeth's breakdowns as 'comparable to shamanic election rituals. Shamans, here, are defined as all spiritual healers who employ altered states of consciousness as the main resource for their healing methods'.[95] Phillips acknowledges that objections to this hypothesis could include the fact that 'Elizabeth appears more "possessed" than in control of the forces and, in the second place, that Head never makes any reference to ideas on shamanism'. Nevertheless, she defends the connection as follows:

> My response to the former is that careful analysis will show that possession coincides with the ordeals of initiation and that once Elizabeth has been pummelled, abused and pushed to the edge by the evil forces, there is an abundance of textual evidence to show that she maintains the moral strength to wrest herself from danger and find the gift of insight which heals. On the other issue, I would reply that an experience which is intensely felt by a private human being does not have to be described under a label which connects it with similar phenomena around the world or in time. If I see a valid connection, I make it analytically to elucidate the text and to accentuate the novel's role in healing Head's own fractured sense of identity, caused by her status as a 'Coloured' person in South Africa, and her subsequent role as a narrative healer for the villagers of Serowe.[96]

92. Amy-Jill Levine, 'Matthew's Advice to a Divided Readership', in David Aune (ed.), *The Gospel of Matthew in Current Study* (Grand Rapids: William Eerdmans Company, 2001), 22–41, 39. Accordingly, the related appellation of Cynics as dogs, given to the followers of Diogenes of Sinope, indicates their specific reactionary traits: rejection of traditions, living without material goods and shamelessness. See Menachel, 'Dogs', 26.

93. Meerai, Abdillahi and Poole, 'Introduction', 24–5.

94. Williams, 'Re-membering', 82.

95. Maggi Phillips, 'Storytellers, Shamans and Clowns: Postcolonial Engagement with the Supra-Human in the Novels of R. K. Narayan, Nuriddin Farah, Bessie Head, Ben Okri and Salman Rushdie', PhD Thesis, Northern Territory University (1996), 6.

96. Phillips, 'Storytellers', 6.

In this light, could the Canaanite woman's 'crying out' also potentially be linked to indigenous cultic or shamanic practices? Carson's study of female vocality in the ancient world suggests that high-pitched female cries often happened 'at certain climactic moments in ritual practice … [yet] no man would make such a sound. No proper civic space would contain it unregulated',[97] which could also be significant in this instance. Likewise, while the Canaanite woman's daughter is silent in the text – and this silence is often understood as emblematic of the 'un-sound-ness' of her 'taboo and stigmatizing'[98] demonic possession – in the postcolonial work of Laura Donaldson, she has been refigured as shamanic, her gifts echoing the 'unofficial' religions of other outlawed women such as the medium of Endor (1 Samuel 28).[99] Thus, the Canaanite woman's daughter's madness could be representative of altered states of consciousness and indigenous spiritual traditions, which hegemonic, sanist and colonial interpretations have slighted and smeared as 'demonic' or 'out of control'.[100]

In Head's novel, also, irony is used heavily to evoke dialogism, resistance and polyphony. For Head, while colonizers assumed the African woman to be an 'incomplete human being' lacking interiority and 'psyche', Elizabeth's madness becomes for Head a means by which the colonizer's construction of the colonized is exposed as fiction. In Sayyed Rahim Moosavinia and Shahid Chamran's words: 'Through madness Bessie Head expels the centripetal system of a despotic society and adheres to dispersion and clash of ideas. It renders the novel a very complicated and writerly texture and makes the reader "rewrite" ' the text and context.'[101]

Commenting on the dissonant voices of Head's novel, Moosavinia and Chamran state that '[a]lthough Elizabeth's hybridity is inadvertent (i.e., Elizabeth's birth to which she has been doomed), *A Question of Power* is a deliberate political hybrid of different languages, strategies and ironies'.[102] As in Head's novel, so too here in the Canaanite woman's performance and her 'carnivalesque' and 'multivocal' tones (Jewish lament etc.), she resists the monolithic discourses of colonization through a cacophony of accession, irony and parody. The woman, who achieves her aims and is celebrated for her faith, ultimately emerges from the encounter as a dissident, multivocal innovator. Like Elizabeth, this Canaanite woman 'confronts a tightly structured order that is moribund and points the way to forms that will

97. Carson, 'The Gender', 125.

98. Kwok-Pui-lan, 'Reading the Christian New Testament in the Contemporary World', in Margaret Aymer, Cynthia Briggs Kittredge and David Arthur Sánchez (eds), *Fortress Commentary on the Bible: The New Testament* (Minneapolis: Fortress Press, 2014), 5–30, 10.

99. Laura Donaldson, 'Gospel Hauntings: The Postcolonial Demons of New Testament Criticism', in Fernando Segovia and Stephen Moore (eds), *Postcolonial Biblical Criticism: Interdisciplinary Intersections* (London: T&T Clark, 2007), 97–113.

100. Donaldson, 'Gospel', 97–113.

101. Moosavinia, 'Janus-Faced', 145.

102. Moosavinia, 'Janus-Faced', 144–5.

either provide an intensified cognitive dynamic for socio-cultural change or codify the new moral, ideational, and social structures that have been inarticulately developing'.[103]

Wounding, Voice and Vocality: The Pythian Slave Girl (Acts 16:16-21)

The Pythian slave girl's 'wounding' is centred on her status as a slave – 'human bondage for labor exploitation in domestic or market contexts'[104] – her femaleness, and her perceived possession and social vulnerability. Titles frequently given to the tradition indicate as such: 'The Demented Slave Girl'[105] and 'A Fortune-Teller and Her Masters'.[106] Hans-Josef Klauck's rather flat and dismal characterization aptly crystallizes such suppositions: 'Luke describes her as a pathetic specimen of humanity. She has been deprived of her freedom and must work as a fairground attraction practising her arts for tiny wages.'[107]

The context of her story is set with Paul and Silas going 'to a place of prayer' (v.16). En route they are met by a girl[108] with a 'python spirit' (πνεῦμα πύθωνα) who is presented as crying out (ἔκραζεν) after them: 'These men are slaves of the most High God, who proclaim to you a way of salvation' (v.17). The source of Paul's great annoyance (from διαπονηθεὶς) does not at first sight seem to be just the content of her speech but rather its repetitive persistence: 'she kept doing this for many days' (πολλὰς ἡμέρας v.18). While some have identified this as evidence of Paul's complicity in the systems which keep her captive – 'a delay probably intended to show Paul's deference to the legal rights of the girl's master'[109] – others offer far more pedestrian understandings – 'Paul just found her plain annoying'.[110]

Ethnically, it could be assumed that she does not share the Roman colonist's identity, for she was a slave, yet she numbers herself among Romans discursively at the close of the encounter in warning against 'customs which it is not lawful for

103. Phillips, 'Storytellers', 121.

104. Modupe Olaogun, 'Slavery and Etiological Discourse in the Writing of Ama Ata Aidoo, Bessie Head, and Buchi Emecheta', *Research in African Literatures* 33(2) (2002), 171–93, 171.

105. William Barclay, *The Acts of the Apostles* (Edinburgh: Saint Andrew Press, 1953), 144.

106. David Peterson, *The Acts of the Apostles* (Grand Rapids: Eerdmans, 2009), 462.

107. Hans-Josef Klauck, *Magic and Paganism in Early Christianity: The World of the Acts of the Apostles* (Edinburgh: T&T Clark, 2000), 68.

108. 'The slave girl was young reinforces the allusion to the mantic girl at Delphi ... in the broader milieu it might be relevant that children were also often thought more susceptible to inspiration'. Keener, *Acts*, digital version, no pages.

109. Young-Ho Park, *Paul's Ekklesia as a Civic Assembly: Understanding the People of God in their Politico-Social World* (WUNT II, 393. Tübingen: Mohr Siebeck, 2015), 188.

110. Paul Walaskay, *Acts* (Louisville: Westminster John Knox, 1998), 157.

us to observe, being Romans' (v.21). It is, however, still broadly the case that the Roman colonists practiced Roman religion, inclined to other sorts of divinatory practices, in contrast to the more Greek phenomenon of Delphic prophecy, with Pythian being the presiding priestess at Delphi's Temple of Apollo. Craig Keener thus notes, 'Romans would consult her [the Pythian slave girl] but she was probably culturally and linguistically Greek.'[111] Although her possession is not marked as demonic in the text, quite the contrary, her divination is on account of her python spirit nonetheless, due to Paul's eventual exorcism of the spirit, it is often slighted as evil, branded a source of social disorder, and through sanist strategies, 'demonised' in commentaries.[112] Despite the text itself using the term 'πνεῦμα' throughout, Mal Couch negatively inflects the phenomenon as follows:

> The fact that she followed Paul and his companions shouting that they were 'servants of the Most High God who show unto us the way of salvation' (16:17) was not because she believed this for herself. However, it proved to be spoken by the *demon* within her (16:18) attempting to arouse the anger of rulers and disrupt the ministry of Paul. This is why people became distressed and commanded the *demon* to 'come out of her'. As an apostle Paul had the gift of exorcism.'[113]

Her possession is further marginalized by its vocal associations. It was widely held that Apollo was incarnated in a serpent and initiated what Plutarch terms 'belly talkers'. Graham Twelftree reveals how Hippocrates compared the noisy breathing of a patient to the sonorous tones of 'the women called belly talkers'. In Twelfree's words,

> For Luke, the belly talking probably had strong evil connotations, as seen from the Septuagint ἐγγαστρίμυθος ('belly talker') of the witch of Endor (1 Sam 28:7) and from Luke describing her as 'soothsaying' or 'fortune telling' ... This

111. Keener, *Acts*, digital version, no pages.

112. 'Nowhere in the story is the "Python sprit" labelled unclean or evil or demonic ... here her incessant mantic activity, not the misleading nature of her message, so annoys Paul that he exorcises the spirit to get a little peace and quiet.' Mikeal C. Parsons, *Acts: Paideia Commentaries on the New Testament* (Grand Rapids: Baker Academic, 2008), 231.

113. Mal Couch (ed.), *A Bible Handbook to the Acts of the Apostles* (Grand Rapids: Kregal Publications, 1999), 97; my emphasis. Marianne Kartzow similarly notes how this character is presented as 'talkative in more than one way' but is eventually quietened and quelled through exorcism: 'First of all she is a fortune-teller. However, her fortune-telling is interpreted differently by the various characters in the story: Paul is irritated by it and her owners profit from it. The owners need this talent, regardless of whether she was possessed or out of her mind; Paul on the other hand ... interprets her talent as a possession of a competing spiritual power and heals her, just as he heals other sick or disabled people on his travels.' Marianne Bjelland Kartzow, *Destabilizing the Margins: An Intersectional Approach to Early Christian Memory* (Oregon: Wipf and Stock, 2012), 123.

> is the only time the word appears in the New Testament. Its strong negative connotations relating to false prophets in the Septuagint and its use for pagan ecstatic activity in non-Christian literature around the period show that Luke would have viewed the girl as inspired by an evil spirit and in need of exorcism.[114]

Like the body from which it originates, these 'disturbing vocalisations [are assumed to] threaten to overwhelm the "civilized" order espoused by the text'.[115] The censoring of this woman's threats are accomplished through Paul's exorcism and discursive silencing – 'containment of her utterance within a textuality identified as masculine, thus opposing her literal, embodied vocality to his metaphorical dis-embodied voice'.[116]

Many commentators have also viewed the exorcism as a release from spiritual bondage: 'Paul sets this slave priestess free from her cultic entrapment'.[117] Others see it as indicative of liberation from exploitative social shackling. As William Barclay states, it brings freedom from 'the hands of unscrupulous men who used her misfortune for their gain. When Paul cured her of her madness, these men felt not joy at her restoration to health, but fury that their source of revenue was gone'.[118] However, her change of status from slave to free is nowhere implied in the text. One can assume that she is still a slave but, now presumably without her mantic abilities, 'a worthless one'[119] to her owners.

Kathy Williams has explored the possible overtones of sexual exploitation in the label παιδίσκη (v. 16) commonly translated as slave, maid or slave girl. In her opinion, '[I]f we translate παιδίσκη as 'prostitute' (an alternate definition used by Herodotus and Plutarch) then the sexual innuendo is a possibility. This translation is supported by the fact that the servant girl has a 'lord' who could function as a "pimp"'.[120] The dissonance between this (sexualized?) enslavement and the Pythian slave's mantic gifts are jarringly underlined by the fact that her oracular function was often revered in tandem with virginity: 'Although she uttered what the god desired her to say her words were connected to the purity of her intact body. Controlled sexuality was so intrinsic to prophetic speech that it must not be compromised in any way … If it were compromised the consequences were

114. Graham H. Twelftree, *In the Name of Jesus: Exorcism among Early Christians* (Grand Rapids: Baker Academic, 2007), 146.

115. Dunn and Jones, 'Introduction', 7.

116. Dunn and Jones, 'Introduction', 7.

117. Earl F. Palmer, *Integrity: A Commentary on the Book of Philippians* (Vancouver: Regent College Publishing, 1992), 26.

118. Barclay, *Acts*, 144–5.

119. V. George Shillington, *An Introduction to the Study of Luke-Acts* (London: T&T Clark, 2006), 113.

120. Kathy Williams, 'At the Expense of Women: Humor (?) in Acts 16: 14–40', in Athalya Brenner (ed.), *Are We Amused?: Humour about Women In the Biblical World* (London: T&T Clark, 2003), 79–89, 84–5.

dire.'[121] Keener also attests to the sexual use of female slaves. He notes that slaves with special abilities were usually treated better that those without them. The loss of her gift could therefore have opened her up to further abuse and exploitation. Keener writes, 'Given the common nature of this abuse, we cannot be sure that she was not abused even when she profited them, but a male slaveholder might think twice about sleeping with a woman thought to be possessed by a deity.'[122]

The retrieval of the traditions of python soothsaying, denoting her as a servant and priestess of the Greek God Apollo, rather than 'belly breathing' or ventriloquism controlling the vocal chords of the possessed,[123] reclaims the veracity of her vocal performance. In Herbert Lockyer's terms, 'This girl is not a mere ventriloquist or sheer imposter, nor a somnambulist or lunatic as some have supposed … [she has the] power to divine and predict.'[124] However, while some have seen her pronouncement – 'These men are slaves of the Most High God who proclaim to you a way of salvation' (v.17) – as a confession of faith and/or legitimization of the Christian movement in a Roman colony due to the fact that 'external validation was necessary to counter the resistance to the movement on the part of the inhabitants of a new region',[125] others have argued that a more 'syncretistic understanding would be equally as plausible'.[126] Klauck, for instance, has noted that there is no article before the noun, so her proclamation could be understood as: 'they proclaim to you *a* way of salvation' which would imply that there was a multiplicity of paths available. Corroborating this position, Klauck notes that the salvation/redeemer trope 'was shared by the saviour God Asclepius, the divinised emperor, and many others'.[127]

Alternatively, one could see the unnamed girl initiating a somatic protest against her intersecting social oppressions. It is in her pre-exorcized state, rather than her exorcized state, in which her agency and embodied protest is most keenly displayed. Moreover, it is in her speech that she most provocatively warns others of Paul and Silas's power-based intentions. Ironically, she voices through her mouth, Paul's domineering intentions. Akin to Dube's reading of Jesus, here Paul and Silas could be constructed as neocolonial power wielders who are imposing their cult onto the Macedonians. In this light, the Pythian is a resister, who strategically reveals her possessive missionary intentions to others, though, as the narrative reveals, ultimately she is muted by them. Of direct relevance

121. Williams, 'Expense', 85.

122. Keener, *Acts*, digital version, no pages.

123. Robert L. Cate, *One Untimely Born: The Life and Ministry of the Apostle Paul* (Macon: Mercer University Press, 2006), 83.

124. Herbert Lockyer, *All the Women of the Bible* (Grand Rapids: Zondervan, 1967), 242.

125. Parsons, *Acts*, 231.

126. Hans-Josef Klauck, *Magic and Paganism in Early Christianity: The World of the Acts of the Apostles* (London: T&T Clark, 2003), 68.

127. Klauck, *Magic*, 68.

here is PhebeAnn Wolframe's study of women's madness narratives, in which she adopts Ahmed's framework of 'wilful female characters'. These are those individuals who embody 'the potential to deviate from well-trodden paths … to speak out about the injustice of what precedes; wilfulness might be required to keep going "the wrong way"'.[128] In Wolframe's view, such figures can sensitize readers to the power structures which circulate around and through them.[129] In Africana madness narratives, likewise, authors frequently rely on 'wilful characters' to seditiously expose the cracks in domineering strategies that seek to control others. In this light, as Jacqueline McDaniel reveals: 'Insanity in African Literature is often stripped of its negative connotations for satirical purpose. Here, the mad person, indeed, has the trappings of a hero, a prophet, a sage, the custodian of communal morality, the irrepressible conscience of the community or a martyr. Madness in this case becomes less of a taboo than a valorized metaphor.'[130] The experiences of Head's protagonist Elizabeth have also been read in this way. Through her madness, Elizabeth explicitly voices the oppressive conditions to which she is subject. Madness enabled her to destabilize identities projected onto her and demonstrate the senselessness of oppressive sociopolitical regimes. Indeed, she terms the apartheid regime as itself a site of 'madness'.[131] Williams, similarly, sees the Pythian slave girl exposing the intentions of Paul and Silas's approach. Ultimately, the girl does fall silent on the narrative stage, but 'through her preaching occasions [at least momentarily] the imprisonment of her attackers Paul and Silas'.[132]

Ex-centric Women

The opening vignette from Daniels's play, featuring supermarket hell populated by marginalized biblical women, sharply drew the (Western) audience's attention to the critical intersections between gender, voice, power and social constructions of madness. Daniels's main purpose was to try to imaginatively evoke the subjectivities of those long muted in interpretative history. By creatively giving these women a voice, they were also afforded a chance to 'change the master script' and partake in 'making a history different from the one the status quo would produce'.[133] Yet Daniels's 'supermarket hell' was also redolent of a specific Eurocentric and, at least in part, white privileged space. Louise Tam contends that

128. Wolframe, 'Madwoman', 46.

129. Wolframe, 'Madwoman', 47.

130. McDaniel, *Madness in Exile,* 3.

131. Elinettie Kwanjana Chabwera, 'Madness and Spirituality in Bessie Head's A Question of Power', *African Studies Bulletin* 71 (Winter 2009/10), 59–70.

132. Williams 'At the Expense', 84–5.

133. Leslie Bloom, cited in Hubert, *Questions*, 21.

> too often Mad artists and activists blame capitalism for devaluing 'unproductive' Mad bodies without calling attention to how capitalism is a global system that helps to maintain gendered and racial lines. Consequently constructions of health, including mental health are shaped by various racial projects, defined by national-states and global policy frameworks. In particular, I notice the Mad movement extolling the virtues of culturally appropriated practices such as mindfulness, mediation and shamanism, without disclosing their own relationship to Indigenous peoples, transnational or not.[134]

Here, Bessie Head's Africana perspectives were specifically employed to mitigate the Eurocentricism which often 'whitewashes' mad studies and mad advocacy discourses and perpetuates the marginalization of attention to colonization and race.[135] These areas are often perceived in non-Western madness narratives as potent locations of 'disordered states' (verbal abuse, exploitative practices etc.)[136]; moreover, 'the language of rationality and madness is commonly used to make sense of political violence'.[137]

Here, attention has purposefully been paid to the ways in which wounding, voice and vocality are implied and resisted in Head's protagonist Elizabeth's and the Canaanite woman's and Pythian slave girl's narratives. Elizabeth, like the Canaanite woman, is presented as 'the victim of racism' and, like the Pythian slave girl, 'a low-breed … a madwoman'.[138] Yet here all three have been shown not only to embody personal alienation and disintegration but also to reveal how these experiences impact on wider communities. In Williams's words:

> [They] dramatize how the failure to acknowledge problems among the collective adversely affects individuals within communities … 'collective failure' … to address adequately the psychic wounds inflicted by aggression is the breeding ground for a psychology of victimhood wherein learned helplessness … and/or feelings of overwhelming powerlessness and despair

134. Louise Tam, 'Whither Indigenizing the Mad Movement? Theorizing the Social Relations of Race and Madness through Conviviality', in LeFrançois et al. (eds), *Mad*, 281–97, 285.

135. Ameil J. Joseph, 'The Necessity of an Attention to Eurocentrism and Colonial Technologies: An Addition to Critical Mental Health Literature', *Disability & Society* 30(7) (2015), 1021–41.

136. Byron J. Good, Mary-Jo DelVecchio Good, Sandra Teresa Hyde and Sarah Pinto, 'Introduction: Postcolonial Disorders: Reflections on Subjectivity in the Contemporary World', in Mary-Jo DelVecchio Good, Sandra Teresa Hyde, Sarah Pinto and Byron J. Good (eds), *Postcolonial Disorders* (California: University of California Press, 2008), 1–40, 23.

137. Good et al., 'Postcolonial', 24.

138. Margaret E. Tucker, '"A Nice-Time Girl" Strikes Back: An Essay on Bessie Head's "A Question of Power"', *Research in African Literatures* 19(2) (1988), 170–81, 170.

> abound in the psyches … yet are not attended to in ways that empower and promote holistic states of well-being. The significance of collective identity is apparent throughout each text as is the announcement of the need for collective healing.[139]

Fanon interrogated the ways in which offensive colonial encounters destabilized not only binary oppositions of sanity and insanity but also the picture of the Western rational human. Mad 'ex-centric' characters in this respect have a key part to play in subversively unpicking not only colonized but also [neo]colonial identities:

> The theme of alienation when perceived through the anamorphic lens of madness, is magnified and charged with an excruciatingly questioning and destabilizing power, laying bare political, as well as existential and moral urges. From the ex-centric, broadly exilic position it is the ideology and practice of colonialism that demand to be rubricated under the sign of psychopathology. More broadly, in fiction the mad character's ex-centric vision is a continuous warning against the temptation to believe in those discourses that pass themselves off as reflecting the given, 'natural', order of things.[140]

While Elizabeth, the Canaanite woman and the Pythian slave girl have been subject to social 'othering' which feeds perceptions of these women's various 'non-identit[ies]' and disorder also, through their resilient and dissident strategies, somewhat ironically, they have also been rendered '*logical* guest[s] of the madhouse'.[141] For these 'ex-centric women' parody the rationality (and sanism) of the contexts and others who dismiss their testimony as madness. Through their respective experience of losing and having to remake their identities, they attain 'a hard-won independence from conventional ways of seeing the world and of using language'.[142] They speak truths about dehumanizing ideologies, structures and practices (abusive language, colonialism, servitude, exploitation), which others seem blind to.[143] Through their performances, the notion of a fixed, colonizer's rationality is disputed and madness labels are revealed as discursive tools disguising systems of social control. These characters can problematize categories of madness imposed on those at the margins from centres of ideological power. For, as Helen Kapstein evocatively illustrates, 'All dressed up in the mismatched outfit of a South African Botswanan "colored" mad woman writer, Bessie Head skirts the edge of the colonial imagination. Forced into liminality

139. Williams, 'Re-membering', 19–20.
140. Zinato and Pes, 'Introduction', 3.
141. Tucker, 'Nice-Time', 170; my emphasis.
142. Lizbeth Goodman, *Literature and Gender* (Hove: Psychology Press, 1996), 115.
143. Carson, 'The Gender', 126.

she makes the margin her center, unabashedly announcing her presence there.'[144] In this perspective, their endeavours signal Foucauldian strategies, speaking back to power. Their ex-centric identities reveal how certain modes of control are no longer dominant and, that the marginal can take, at least in 'moments of madness', centre stage.

144. Helen Kapstein, 'A Peculiar Shuttling Movement: Madness, Passing and Trespassing in Bessie Head's A Question of Power', in Helen Kapstein and Maxine Sample (eds), *Critical Essays on Bessie Head* (Westport, CT; London: Praeger Publishers, 2003), *Contributions in Afro-American and African Studies*, no. 205, 71–98, 95.

Chapter 4

Gatekeeping the Madness of Jesus and Paul: Negotiating Mythologies of Madness in an Age of Neoliberalism

A tabloid newspaper's headlines recently stated, 'Jesus Christ may have suffered mental Health Problems Claims Church of England' (*The Daily Express*).[1] Coinciding with preparations for World Mental Health Day, the Church's campaign set out to challenge the stigmatizing of such conditions, a process it openly admitted to playing an ominous part within 'having previously cast out the mentally ill as Satan's followers'.[2] The article bears witness to two significant cultural discourses surrounding madness: first the historical reluctance to link a religious 'great' such as Jesus with mental illness and second, the increasingly widespread diagnoses of mental illness within the general population in the contemporary West.

Madness is a 'grass roots construction' with significant presence in popular and cultural discourses – mediated images, forms and stereotypes.[3] In Gramscian terms 'common sense' assumptions around madness in popular thought are to be understood 'in cultural-historical terms as the accretion of sediments of knowledge laid down in the soil stratum over centuries'.[4] The media is of course an important site in which cultural knowledge of madness is constructed, circulated and negotiated. Through it one can trace how ideas develop, transform and/or change, for as Philip Cushman attests: '[E]very era has a particular configuration of the self, illness, healer, technology … They are interrelated, intertwined, interpenetrating. So, when we study a particular

1. Ted Jeory, 'Jesus Christ May Have Suffered Mental Health Problems', *Daily Express*, 28 August 2012. Available online at: http://www.express.co.uk/news/uk/341926/Jesus-Christ-may-have-suffered-from-mental-health-problems-claims-Church-of-England.

2. Jeory, 'Jesus', no pages.

3. S. Cross, *Mediating Madness: Mental Distress and Cultural Representation* (London: Palgrave Macmillan, 2010), 2.

4. Cross, *Mediating*, 10.

illness, we are also studying the conditions that shape and define that illness, and the socio-political impact of those who are responsible for healing it.'[5]

Madness stereotypes have long been recognized as important cognitive representations that function to classify our environment and social encounters and inform popularly accepted knowledge. Accordingly, speculation about the identities, motivations and presumed psychological, neurobiological and/or psychiatric states of significant figures past and present has, despite myriad problems and perils involved in such pursuits,[6] proved irresistible for many.[7] Historians, social scientists, philosophers, leadership specialists and others have variously set out to probe such elements as significant contributors to the development of movements, events and cultural transformations.[8] Psy-stereotypes however, have not solely been employed to identify and parade the alleged dysfunctionality, deviance or abnormalities of those branded tyrants or despots – madmen in power – but have also held currency within well-established Western cultural mythologies that link wholly 'positive' modes of identity with madness. Namely, the 'mad genius' stereotype, which frequently pairs creativity

5. Philip Cushman, *Constructing the Self, Constructing America: A Cultural History of Psychotherapy* (Reading, MA: Addison-Wesley, 1995), 7.

6. Beth M. Sheppard has recently noted that '[t]he intersection between psychology and history has had an extraordinarily rocky reception in the academy'. She notes how 'psychological norms of bygone eras [are] not necessarily known' and 'the ability to verify the claims made by psychohistory is frequently in question'. She pushes back on this, however, by stating, 'Truth be told though in more recent years there is growing recognition that all interpretations are subjective and objectivity in history is more elusive.' She concludes, 'Thus this argument no longer has the force which it did when psychohistory was first taking off in the 1960's.' See Beth M. Sheppard, *The Craft of History and the Study of the New Testament* RBS 60 (Atlanta: Society of Biblical Literature, 2012), 47, 148.

7. Arno Karlen, *Napoleon's Glands and Other Ventures in Biohistory* (New York: Grand Central Publishing, 1985); Bert Edward Park, *Ailing, Aging, Addicted: Studies of Compromised Leadership* (Kentucky: University of Kentucky Press, 1993); Joshua Wolf Schenk, *Lincoln's Melancholy: How Depression Challenged a President and Fueled His Greatness* (Boston: Mariner Books, 2006).

8. William McKinley Runyan reveals as much when he claims: 'It is unquestionably simplistic to claim that "History=Biography" or that history can be reduced to nothing more than the aggregation of individual biographies … It is, however, equally reductionist to claim that an understanding of individual persons and their psychological processes has nothing to contribute to an analysis of the history of groups, social movements, institutions and nations. Only a dogmatic reductionism could maintain that the personality and life of Hitler had nothing to do with the course of World War II; of Lenin, with the Russian revolution; of Gandhi, with India's struggle with the British; or of Martin Luther King, Jr. with the civil rights movement.' William McKinley Runyan, cited in Savvas Papacostas, *Madness and Leadership: From Antiquity to the New Common Era* (Northampton: Edward Elgar Publishing, 2015), 6–7.

and giftedness with psychopathology,[9] and the 'resilient sufferer' and 'crisis leader' stereotypes which view those marked by psychopathological traits as uniquely tooled to influence and direct others in contexts of uncertainty or instability and to emerge stronger (socially, emotionally, spiritually etc.) from such situations. Such representations are affiliated to the 'supra-able' or 'virtuous sufferer' stereotypes which are often propagated in relation to physical and/or sensory disabilities and 'tend to glorify and idealize' specific figures.[10]

Media and communication studies identify the management processes by which individuals are deliberately presented as 'gatekeeping'. This denotes the strategies of selecting and constructing information for others,[11] including the moulding of an audience's worldviews about an individual: 'information that gets through all the gates can become part of people's social reality, whereas information that stops at a gate generally does not'.[12] Gatekeeping with regard to psy-discourses has differed across eras in Western media which frequently serves 'agenda-setting, priming and framing functions related to what mental illness content is included and how it is presented'.[13] All manner of ideological assumptions often underpin gatekeeping processes about an individual's identity, particularly their projected psychiatric or psychological state.[14] As previous chapters in this book have shown, often psychopathological categories[15] –

9. 'Most often manic-depressive illness or related types of mood disorders.' See George Becker, 'A Socio-historical Overview of the Creativity-Pathology Connection: From Antiquity to Contemporary Times', in James C. Kaufman (ed.), *Creativity and Mental Illness* (Cambridge: Cambridge University Press, 2014), 3–24, 3.

10. S. L. Gilman, 'Book Review: Media Madness: Public Images of Mental Illness by O. F. Wahl (1995). New Brunswick, New Jersey: Rutgers University Press', *Psychiatric Services* 48(2) (1997), 247.

11. Pamela J. Shoemaker and Timothy Vos, *Gatekeeping Theory* (New York: Routledge, 2009), 1.

12. Shoemaker and Vos, *Gatekeeping*, 3.

13. Emma McGinty, 'Mental Illness and the Media', in Samuel J. Rosenberg, *Community Mental Health: Challenges for the 21st Century* (New York: Routledge, 2018), 178–99, 183.

14. Take, for example, Christopher Cook's recent characterization of Ezekiel as mystical rather than psychopathological (contra those estimations of this character outlined in my previous chapter), on account of this figure's contemporary religious significance: 'The book of Ezekiel is better understood as being an account of mystical experience than of psychopathology. More importantly, it is a text which is taken to be revelatory of spiritual and religious truth within at least two of the world's major faith traditions.' Christopher Cook, 'Psychiatry in Scripture: Sacred Texts and Psychopathology', *Psychiatry* 36(6) (2012), 225–9, 226.

15. Betty Rudd explains that '[p]sychopathology derives from two Greek words: "psyche" meaning "soul", and "pathos" meaning "suffering". Currently, "psychopathology" is understood to mean the origin of mental disorders, how they develop and their symptoms. Traditionally, those suffering from mental disorders have usually been treated by the psychiatric profession, which adheres to the DSM-IV-TR (APA, 2002) or ICD-10 (WHO,

constructions of 'abnormal experience, cognition and behaviour'[16] as disease and/or disorder, both medical and/or metaphorical – are pejoratively projected onto figures presumed deviant, errant, or tyrannical to underscore and account for their perceived social, religious, cultural and political aberrations.[17] Psychotic disorders and schizophrenia often incur the most stigmatic portrayals – 'labelling, stereotyping, separation, status loss and discrimination'[18] – and more often than not provide encapsulating 'nominative' models of identity based on pathology: 'the psychotic', 'the schizophrenic' and so on. Such projections often serve to distinguish 'negative' forms of identity from more positive modes which, at least in the West, have traditionally prized rationality, logic, sanity, control, propositional knowledge and pragmatism.[19] Other psy-discourses surrounding depression, anxiety or trauma incur far less negative associations in Western cultures. In Emma McGinty's opinion this is due to the 'audience's increased familiarity with such conditions … and/or the lower likelihood that symptoms of depression as opposed to symptoms of psychosis induces fear'.[20] Hilary Clark too notes that '[t]he effect of depression on reasoning and perceptual cognitive and communicative capabilities is often less disabling than the effects of other severe conditions: moods of despair

1992) for classifying mental disorders. It therefore follows that psychiatrists use the term "psychopathology" more than people in other professions'. Betty Rudd, *Introducing Psychopathology* (London: Sage, 2014), 2.

16. Femi Oyebode, *Sims' Symptoms in the Mind: An Introduction to Descriptive Psychopathology* (Exeter: Elsevier Limited, 2008), 3.

17. Manfred F. R. Kets de Vries, 'The Spirit of Despotism: Understanding the Tyrant within Human Relations', *Human Relations* 59(2) (2006), 195–220; see also Manfred F. R. Kets de Vries, *Lessons on Leadership by Terror: Finding Shaka Zulu in the Attic* (Cheltenham: Edward Elgar Publishing, 2004); Seth A. Rosenthal and Todd L. Pittinsky state that '[t]he pantheon of purportedly narcissistic leaders ranges from the great tyrants of recent history, including Adolf Hitler, Joseph Stalin, and Saddam Hussein, to lesser-known malevolent leaders such as the founder of the American Nazi Party, George Lincoln Rockwell and cult leader Jim Jones; great historical figures such as Alexander Hamilton; a diverse group of business leaders, including Steve Jobs, Michael Eisner, David Geffen and Kenneth Lay; and an eclectic and sometimes surprising list of current political leaders such as Benjamin Netanyahu, John McCain, George W. Bush, and both Jimmy Carter and his mother Lillian'. See Seth A. Rosenthal and Todd L. Pittinsky, 'Narcissistic Leadership', *The Leadership Quarterly* 17 (2006), 617–33.

18. Bruce Link and Jo Phelan, 'Conceptualising Stigma', *Annual Review of Sociology* 27 (2001), 363–85, 363.

19. Robert M. McManus and Gamaliel Perruci, *Understanding Leadership: An Arts and Humanities Perspective* (London: Routledge, 2015). See also Michael I. Handel and Karl-Friedrich Walling, *Strategic Logic and Political Rationality: Essays in Honor of Michael I. Handel* (Hove: Psychology Press, 2003).

20. McGinty, 'Mental', 191.

and sadness may be easier to integrate'.[21] In contextualizing the gatekeeping of madness, Harper urges interpreters to investigate how psy-discourses have burgeoned in advanced capitalist societies and how therefore madness (and its strategic gatekeeping vis-à-vis particular individuals) should be understood in relation to its broader social, political and economic contexts rather than 'a [purely] medical model of "mental illness"'.[22] The ascendency of the neoliberal project which transformed capitalism and insists that each person 'configures themselves as a resilient flexible entrepreneur of their own selves willing to adapt to changing market conditions'[23] unsurprisingly, in Ian Parker's words, 'required more psychology'.[24] Others, too, have noted how the Western cultural fascination with the figures of a mad genius and/or resilient sufferer who prevails over their difficult experiences to attain distinction and renown neatly dovetails in the contemporary era with 'the meritocratic and voluntaristic ethos of neoliberalism'.[25]

This chapter will attempt to unveil a variety of gatekeeping strategies surrounding the madness of Jesus and Paul in recent decades. Through much of the twentieth century, there has been a marked reluctance to link Jesus and Paul with any notion of 'madness' given the largely negative cultural associations such conditions often harboured. Where madness has been entertained in relation to their respective characters, often it has been linked with creativity and/or genius. Such positive madness stereotypes frequently serve to underscore their exceptional ability and/or hyper-productivity. In the neoliberal age, there has been yet another gatekeeping strategy in which certain 'psychological' conditions (most particularly depression and/or stress, which have widespread appeal in the neoliberal West) are featured in relation to Jesus and Paul. Both these figures are seen to individually triumph through these mental adversities and emerge as capable, proficient (and sane) subjects.

The management of Jesus's madness will be illustrated through analysis of two psycho-biographical commentaries on his identity: John Miller's *Jesus at Thirty: A Psychological and Historical Portrait* (1997) and Andries van Aarde's *Fatherless in Galilee: Jesus as a Child of God* (2001). It will be proposed that

21. Hilary Clark, *Depression and Narrative: Telling the Dark* (New York: SUNY Press, 2008), 23.

22. Stephen Harper, *Madness, Power and the Media: Class, Gender and Race in Popular Presentations of Mental Illness* (Basingstoke: Palgrave Macmillan, 2009), 1.

23. Ian Parker, 'Psychology Politics Resistance: Theoretical Practice in Manchester', in Bonnie Bursto et al. (eds), *Psychiatry Disrupted* (Montreal: McGill-Queen's University Press, 2014), 52–64, 54.

24. Parker, 'Psychology', 54.

25. Harper, *Madness*, 101. D. Harvey defines 'neoliberalism' as follows: 'The theory of political economic practices that proposes that human well-being can best be advanced by liberating individual entrepreneurial freedoms and skills within an institutional framework characterised by strong private property rights, free markets, and free trade.' D. Harvey, *A Brief History of Neoliberalism* (Oxford: Oxford University Press, 2005), 1–2.

psy-discourses are employed in these projects not to negatively 'other' Jesus's identity, but rather to align it as representative of more widespread experiences in the neoliberal West, and to confirm Jesus as an able and productive neoliberal subject. Second, following a broad introduction to gatekeeping constructions of Paul, two works – Richard Dormandy's *The Madness of St Paul* (2011) and Richard Ascough's and Charles Cotton's *Passionate Visionary: Leadership Lessons from the Apostle Paul* (2005) – will be scrutinized. These, it will be proposed, variously appropriate and employ elements of two positive madness mythologies – the mad genius and the tortured/creative crisis leader models – both of which also harmonize neatly with the dominating ethos of neoliberalism.[26] Brief and critical reflections on the Western mythologies surrounding madness and their perpetuation in neoliberal politics, culture and biblical studies will be offered by way of conclusion.

Cultural Epistemes of Madness

Certain conditions garner descriptive and pragmatic popularity in different cultural and historical contexts. Taylor Donnelly in 'Vogue Diagnosis: The Function of Madness in Twentieth Century American Literature'[27] sets out to trace 'cultural epistemes' (determining outlooks/worldviews) regarding the ways in which mental illnesses have been invested with meaning: 'Certain illness[es] and certain literary uses of illness[es] … tend to cluster at certain moments in time … "vogue diagnoses" reveal the complex interactions of psychiatry, cultural history and fictional representation.'[28] Donnelly notes how the twentieth-century Western history of madness can be conceptualized into three cultural epistemes: the eugenic, the psychodynamic and the psychopharmological/neurobiological.[29] The eugenic episteme (1900–40) constructed psychiatric models focused on heredity causes and degeneration and practised often invasive somatic treatments. Socially, the eugenic episteme (as its names suggests) was focused on 'mental hygiene' and the ridding of mental illness from the general population.[30] The psychodynamic episteme

26. Harper, *Madness*, 101.

27. Taylor Donnelly, 'Vogue Diagnosis: The Function of Madness in Twentieth Century American Literature', Doctoral dissertation (2012). Retrieved from University of Oregon Graduate Dissertations and Theses. Available online at: https://www.google.co.uk/url?url=https://scholarsbank.uoregon.edu/xmlui/bitstream/handle/1794/12366/Donnelly_oregon_0171A_10353.pdf%3Bsequence%3D1&rct=j&frm=1&q=&esrc=s&sa=U&ved=0ahUKEwiB7sGQpL7VAhXiCsAKHW6qCGIQFggUMAA&usg=AFQjCNGMwY228bevkvzBN6CTNPDGznaDGg.

28. Donnelly, 'Vogue', 2.

29. Donnelly, 'Vogue', 18.

30. Donnelly, 'Vogue', 19.

(1940–late 1960s) drew from experiences of treating soldiers involved in the Great War and, inspired by Freud, promoted more emotional, relational and developmental causes for madness. It practised psychoanalytic forms of psychiatry which focused on therapy around emotions and memories.[31] The psychopharmological/neurobiological episteme (1970s–present) emphasizes chemical imbalance within the brain and prescribes drugs as treatments. This model has acquired widespread domination within the contemporary West: 'most people today think of madness as a chemical imbalance requiring meds, this scientific hypothesis has permeated common sense'.[32] It has also found ready compatibility with its political and economic context of neoliberalism and an associated emphasis on individual entrepreneurial initiative in a competitive system.[33] In Joanna Moncrieff's terms, 'The chemical imbalance model promotes a coercive as well as a consumerist response to disturbance through its suggestion that there is such a thing as a "normal" brain. The idea of "normal" abolishes the tolerance of difference and diversity.'[34] Within this consumerist model, and the development of a widespread 'mental health industry',[35] individual discontent is turned away from society and rather focused on the self[36] who ideally is a reliable, responsible and accountable subject. Emotions are seen as resources to be managed: 'feelings frequently become another material foundation for market-orientated behaviour: emotions are acquired, invested, traded and speculated upon'.[37] Socially, the dominance of this model has also transformed not only psy-discourses surrounding mental

31. Donnelly, 'Vogue', 20.

32. Donnelly, 'Vogue', 21.

33. Rachel Greenwald Smith contends that '[n]eoliberalism began as a set of economic policies in the late 1970's and early 1980's aimed toward unfettering domestic and global markets, dismantling social safety nets, and privatizing previously public institutions. With the end of the Cold War and the beginning of the Clinton presidency neoliberalism began to look as if it could exist in perpetuity, uncontested from superpowers abroad or political parties at home. As a result neoliberal policy has become increasingly normalized, accompanied by a corresponding shift in the social expectations that are placed upon individuals'. Rachel Greenwald Smith, *Affect and American Literature in the Age of Neoliberalism* (Cambridge: Cambridge University Press, 2015), 1–2. Bruce Cohen likewise contends, 'Over the past 35 years scientific ideas on mental pathology from the designated experts of the mind have seeped onwards from the psychiatric institution into many spheres of life.' Bruce Cohen, *Psychiatric Hegemony: A Marxist Theory of Mental Illness* (Basingstoke: Palgrave Macmillan, 2016), 1.

34. Joanna Moncrieff, 'Neoliberalism and Psychiatry: A Marriage of Convenience', in Carl I. Cohen and Sami Timimi (eds), *Liberatory Psychiatry: Philosophy, Politics and Mental Health* (Cambridge: Cambridge University Press, 2008), 235–55, 250.

35. Cohen, *Psychiatric*, 3.

36. Moncrieff, 'Neoliberalism', 251.

37. Smith, *Affect*, 6.

health, but also their prevalence among the population.[38] The publication of the latest version of the *DSM-5* has been viewed as a useful tool in the promotion of this neoliberal facing discourse, for

> the DSM was [originally] elaborated in the USA as an answer to a number of disciplinary needs, in a Foucauldian sense. On the one hand it had military origins; a tool designed for the psychological and behavioural screening of groups … the other hand the reasons that led to its formulation are extremely rational and simple, in the sense of that organization rationality and constant optimization of processes which are the essential form and content of neoliberal reason.[39]

Neoliberal framings of mental health discourses, however, are not the sole touchstones between the politico-economic and psychopathological. Indeed many contend that neoliberalism itself promotes mental illness. As Oliver James, a clinical psychologist, contends in his provocatively entitled book *The Selfish Capitalist: Origins of Affluenza* (2008)[40] the pattern of chronic overwork, debt, anxiety and waste induced by a fixation with possessions has meant that neoliberal economies have seen rates of mental illness double in twenty years. Others too attest to a 'clear connection between socioeconomic-political system, its structures and processes and detrimental effects on mental health'.[41]

Within the current, and prevalent, psychopharmological/neurobiological cultural episteme the ways in which individuals are imaged and constructed have been transformed. The neoliberal subject expects mental distress, but also embodies resilience and creativity in the face of such pressures. Such a cultural episteme starts to make more sense in locating *The Daily Express* article about Jesus and mental illness, and its contention that '[p]erhaps we need to ask why it would be so terrible to think that some of our most inspirational forebears [like Jesus] might have experienced mental health illness … Who do we think "these people" are? Statistics show us that one in four people suffer from mental health illness during their lives'.[42] Such dynamics contribute to what Stephen Prothero would

38. 'In the UK for example, prescriptions for antidepressants rose by 235% in the 10 year up to 2002 … A larger proportion of the general population are now willing to identify themselves as needing psychiatric help and psychiatry has become a more confident and biologically inclined profession. These developments in psychiatry parallel propound economic and social changes referred to here as neoliberalism.' Moncrieff, 'Neoliberalism', 235.

39. K. W. M. Fulford, Martin Davies, Richard Gipps, George Graham, John Sadler and Tim Thornton (eds), *The Oxford Handbook of Philosophy and Psychiatry* (Oxford: Oxford University Press, 2013), 96.

40. Oliver James, *The Selfish Capitalist: Origins of Affluenza* (New York: Random House, 2008).

41. R. C. Smith, *Society and Social Pathology: A Framework for Progress* (New York: Springer International Publishing, 2017), 12.

42. Jeory, 'Jesus', no pages.

term the construction of a cultural Christ.[43] A Jesus not of his own first-century context, but rather a figure constructed (either unconsciously or by design) for a neoliberal cultural episteme.[44]

Gatekeeping the Madness of Jesus

C. S. Lewis's famed trilemma – that Jesus was either a liar, a lunatic or Lord[45] – often serves to caricature the dominant Christian impulse in the twentieth century to prove that 'Jesus' life shows no psychiatric symptoms and, therefore, his claims about himself were not delusions but fact'.[46] In biblical studies, Albert Schweitzer's classic 1913 work *The Psychiatric Study of Jesus: Exposition and Criticism*[47] undoubtedly influenced the gatekeeping of Jesus's identity from psychopathologies for much of the twentieth century. Schweitzer's own construction of Jesus as a fervent apocalyptic prophet perhaps ironically stimulated studies and diagnoses of his character by psychiatrists of his day. Yet Schweitzer took such projects to task, in particular the work of three European psychiatrists (George de Loosten [1905], William Hirsch [1912], and Charles Binet-Sanglé [1910–12]), who had independently applied psychiatric insights into Jesus's supposedly 'delusional' character and 'hallucinatory' experiences. Jesus emerged from their respective consulting rooms variously as a 'psychic degenerate', a 'paranoid psychotic' and a 'religious paranoid'.[48] Schweitzer felt compelled to respond to such constructions

43. Stephen Prothero, *American Jesus: How the Son of God Became a National Icon* (New York: Farrar, Straus and Giroux, 2003), 7–10.

44. See James Crossley, *Jesus in Age of Neoliberalism* (Durham: Acumen Publishing, 2012), 8.

45. 'A man who was merely a man and said the sort of things Jesus said would not be a great moral teacher. He would either be a lunatic – on a level with the man who says he is a poached egg – or else he would be the Devil of Hell. You must make your choice. Either this man was, and is, the Son of God: or else a madman or something worse. You can shut Him up for a fool, you can spit at Him and kill Him as a demon; or you can fall at His feet and call Him Lord and God. But let us not come with patronising nonsense about His being a great human teacher. He has not left that open to us. He did not intend to ... We are faced, then, with a frightening alternative. This man we are talking about either was (and is) just what He said or else a lunatic, or something worse. Now it seems to me obvious that He was neither a lunatic nor a fiend: and consequently, however strange or terrifying or unlikely it may seem, I have to accept the view that He was and is God.' C. S. Lewis, *Mere Christianity* (New York: MacMillan, 1952, revised edition), 55–6.

46. O. Q. Hyer, 'On the Mental Health of Jesus Christ', *Journal of Psychology and Theology* 5 (1977), 3–12.

47. A. Schweitzer, *The Psychiatric Study of Jesus: Exposition and Criticism* (Whitefish: Literary Licensing, 2011 [German original 1913]).

48. Schweitzer, discussed in Donald Capps, *Jesus the Village Psychiatrist* (Kentucky: Westminster John Knox Press, 2008), xxii.

and vehemently defend Jesus's sanity. In distancing Jesus from such diagnoses, Schweitzer located Jesus and his beliefs as typical in his own first-century environment. Power over spirits, messianic expectancy and the hope of an imminent dawning of the kingdom were all widespread Jewish hopes.[49] Jesus's apocalyptic eschatological outlook was, in Schweitzer's words, therefore, 'in no rational sense evidence of mental disease'.[50] Schweitzer's critique was incisive with regard to the uncritical use of biblical source material in the three respective works and the questioning of the psychiatric labels employed with regard to assumed 'symptoms'.[51] Specifics aside, however, it seems that Schweitzer's response was at least implicitly grounded in ideology. Writing in the era of the 'eugenic episteme', a diagnosis of degeneracy, psychosis or paranoia could literally 'annihilate' Jesus. Schweitzer's historical Jesus, albeit a fervent Jewish apocalyptic-eschatological prophet was, as George Marshall and David Poling submit in their biography of Schweitzer, still most crucially 'a sane man, well balanced and able to give direction and guidance'.[52]

Schweitzer effectively halted the use of psy-discourses in relation to Jesus's identity within the discipline, amounting to what Wayne Rollins terms 'a virtual ban on things psychological ... for the better part of the century'.[53] Rollins detects a more open posture towards psy-discourses in biblical studies beginning in the late 1960s, presumably in response to the ascendency of the psychodynamic cultural episteme, but, he admits, most of this work was in reference to Paul, rather than to Jesus.[54]

49. See Albert Schweitzer, *The Quest of the Historical Jesus*, trans. W. Montgomery (Mineola: Dover Publications, 2005 [German original 1906]).

50. Donald Capps, 'Beyond Schweitzer and the Psychiatrists: Jesus as Fictive Personality', in J. Harold Ellens and Wayne G. Rollins (eds), *Psychology and the Bible: From Christ to Jesus* (Westport: Praeger Publishers, 2004), 89–124, 93.

51. 'The only symptoms to be accepted as historical and possibly to be discussed from the psychiatric point of view – the high estimate which Jesus has of himself and perhaps also the hallucination at the baptism – fall far short of proving the existence of mental illness.' Andries G. van Aarde, *Fatherless in Galilee: Jesus as Child of God* (Atlanta: Trinity Press International, 2001), 15–16.

52. George N. Marshall and David Poling, *Schweitzer: A Biography* (Maryland: John Hopkins University Press, 2000), 79. Allan Beveridge testifies to Schweitzer's gatekeeping of the character of Jesus when he writes: 'Schweitzer drew on the psychiatric authorities of *his* time to argue that the picture Jesus presented did not meet the criteria for a diagnosis of insanity ... Schweitzer observed that hallucinations were also found in people who were not mentally ill.' Allan Beveridge, *Portrait of the Psychiatrist as a Young Man: The Early Writing and Work of R. D. Laing* (Oxford: Oxford University Press, 2011), 155.

53. Wayne Rollins, *Soul and Psyche: The Bible in Psychological Perspective* (Minneapolis: Fortress Press, 1999), 63.

54. Rollins, *Soul*, 65–87.

Jesus and Mythologies of Madness in a Neoliberal Age

At the turn of the millennium a number of works have tried once more to adopt pys-discourses and analyses within their constructions of Jesus. Contra the projection of negative psychopathologies which were so vehemently criticized by Schweitzer, those which have been applied to Jesus's character in this era tend not to 'other' him but rather mark him as representative of more common experiences/conditions within the neoliberal West, and positively inscribe these experiences/conditions as evidence of his normativity, as well as his individual creativity and resilience.[55]

John Miller, for example, in his tellingly entitled work *Jesus at Thirty* – purposefully redolent of the clichéd contemporary Western male's crisis stage[56] – proposes that Joseph's death in Jesus's youth had a profound effect on Jesus's identity. Jesus would have assumed the role of head of household following his father's death and likely did not marry due to the absence of a father who could arrange such a union. Miller here draws on a 'psychodynamic episteme', in particular Freud's insights into family relationships, sexuality and strife, and is shown as eventually achieving 'peace and wholeness recognising he had found a heavenly father'.[57]

Jesus's encounter with John the Baptist – 'one of the "great men" of his generation'[58] – offered a significant independent alternative to his domestic responsibilities. Miller identifies evidence which would seem to belie a certain rift between Jesus and his biological kin (Mk 3:32). He surmises that 'Jesus saw life's ultimate loyalties as potentially discordant with the claims of biological family'.[59] Moreover, his teaching predominantly featured men as 'dominant figures',[60] a dimension that Miller sees as crucial for men navigating change within their lives. Mentors are identified as important direction-setters, and men who can negotiate this crisis point productively often exhibit renewed resourcefulness.

55. See Bas Van Os, *Psychological Analysis and the Historical Jesus* (London: T&T Clark, 2011).

56. 'Mid-life crisis' was coined in 1965 by Elliot Jacques, a Canadian psychologist. Interestingly the *DSM-IV* accounts mid-life crisis as a kind of adjustment disorder, in particular defining it as a 'maladaptive response or reaction to an identifiable psychological stressor or stressors'. See http://midlifeclub.com/age-gracefully-dealing-with-your-mid-life-crisis.htm.

57. James H. Charlesworth, 'Should Specialists in Jesus Research Include Psychobiography?', in James H. Charlesworth, Brian Rhea and Petr Pokorn (eds), *Jesus Research: New Methodologies and Perceptions* (Grand Rapids: Eerdmans Publishing Company, 2014), 436–67, 454.

58. John Miller, *Jesus at Thirty: A Psychological and Historical Portrait* (Minneapolis: Fortress Press, 1997), 19.

59. Miller, *Jesus at Thirty*, 16.

60. Miller, *Jesus at Thirty*, 49.

Miller's indebtedness to the psychosocial theorist Daniel Levinson's 1978 work, *The Seasons of a Man's Life*, is explicit. This study was centred on interviews with forty working men in America, aged 35–45 years (ten novelists, ten biologists, ten factory workers and ten business executives). It pinpoints 30 as an age of transition, where anxiety and self-doubt arise, though also one where self-recognition and sufficiency are developed.[61] Levinson's theory placed the neoliberal male body (productive, effective and profitable)[62] within a cycle of wider events in the individual's life. As a theory, therefore, 'it emphasises the psychology of the individual and the internal subjective career rather than its outward manifestations … in American men in the 1970's'.[63] From a clinical perspective, Levinson's model has been used to 'identify transitional periods that were often times of internal conflict and thus motivation for seeking treatment'.[64] *DSM-IV* names such conditions as 'adjustment disorders' (symptoms in response to stress) and early adult and midlife transitions.

Critics of Miller's project have, of course, pointed out the anachronism of a thesis predicated on modern identities and life spans projected onto an ancient figure. James Charlesworth avers that the age of 30 documented by Luke was more probably indicative of ancient ideas of wisdom and maturity (Lk. 2:52).[65] Such criticisms are undoubtedly justified. What is more interesting for present purposes, however, are the ways in which a model of age-related crisis, predicated on a neoliberal vision of the body and mind, is so overtly plotted onto Jesus. Jesus, inflected in this framework, becomes representative of 'common' human psychological experiences in able(ist) neoliberal bodies and minds. Most crucially, Jesus ultimately does not succumb to psychopathology: rather, he triumphs as a functioning, neoliberal ideal male, emerging from his crisis point as a much stronger individual.

To take another example, Andries van Aarde's study *Fatherless in Galilee* explores the social stigma and psychological fallout and alienation of being illegitimate and fatherless. Through a social-scientific lens van Aarde shows that these social and psychological experiences became a potent stimulus for Jesus's vision and message. He also questions 'Why would Jesus want to be baptized?' and submits that 'the unfortunate relationship with his family and his critique against the patriarchal family as such provide the probable clue'.[66] He sees the baptism as

61. Daniel Levinson, *The Seasons of a Man's Life* (New York: Ballantine Books, 1978).

62. Hannele Harjunen, *Neoliberal Bodies and the Gendered Fat Body* (London: Routledge, 2016), 6.

63. Kerr Inkson, *Understanding Careers: The Metaphors of Working Lives* (Thousand Oaks: Sage Publications, 2006), 59–60.

64. Katherine M. Fortinash and Patricia A. Holoday Worret, *Psychiatric Mental Health Nursing* (St Louis: Mosby Incorporated, 1996), 122.

65. Charlesworth, 'Should Specialists', 455.

66. van Aarde, *Fatherless*, 47.

a ceremonial ritual through which '"sinful sickness" [e.g. the stigma of being a fatherless son] was addressed and healed'.[67]

Contra those who want to situate Jesus as unique or exceptional in kind and/or experience, van Aarde is keen to show that 'as a first-century Israelite from Galilee should be studied like other historical persons and should not be regarded as absolutely unique'.[68] As such, the psychological alienation proposed for his identity is not used to 'other' Jesus's character but rather to a certain extent 'normalize' it as expressive of widespread experiences of ruptured family systems. van Aarde is explicit in connecting this trope to his own contemporary Western cultural experience when he writes:

> One of the most urgent social problems of our time is the fact that millions of children are growing up fatherless – as can be seen in the title of David Blankenhorn's (1995) book *Fatherless America: Confronting our most urgent social problem.* On the wrapper of this book Don Browning, Professor of Ethics and the Social Sciences at the Divinity School of the University of Chicago, writes: 'Fatherless America is the strongest possible refutation to a thesis widely held in our society – that fathers are not really important. David Blankenhorn exposes the multiple ways our culture has convinced itself of this falsehood and shows how to reconstitute fatherhood for the future.'[69]

Blankenhorn's thesis has not been uncontroversial vis-à-vis madness discourses. He flatly constructs (and pathologizes) fatherless children as a greater risk for drug and alcohol abuse, mental illness, suicide, poor educational performance, teen pregnancy and criminality. Niobe Way notes that such portrayals reflect a seemingly ineradicable stereotype, the urban teen: 'pregnant, drug-addicted, violent, fatherless, welfare dependent, poor, black and uneducated'.[70] And as this converts such subjects into the 'ungovernable by neo-liberal governments … [t]hey are considered to be jeopardizing the good life by constructing pathological biographies beyond the limits of what is responsible or accountable'.[71]

67. van Aarde, *Fatherless*, 47.

68. van Aarde, *Fatherless*, 38.

69. Andries van Aarde, 'Fatherlessness in First-Century Mediterranean Culture: The Historical Jesus Seen from the Perspective of Cross-Cultural Anthropology and Cultural Psychology', *HTS* 55(1) (1999), 97–119, 97. Available online at: http://www.hts.org.za/index.php/HTS/article/viewFile/1526/2819.

70. Niobe Way, *Every Day Courage: The Lives and Stories of Urban Teenagers* (New York: New York University Press, 1998), 1.

71. Richard Lakes, 'Unemployed Youth and Vocational Pathways: Opportunity Structures in the New Economy', in Liv Mjelde and Richard Daly (eds), *Working Knowledge in a Globalizing World: From Work to Learning, from Learning to Work* (Bern: Peter Lang, 2006), 255–66, 263.

Loïc Wacquant similarly notes how moral individualism (so central to neoliberal discourses) structure a national ethos and gender ideology in which fatherless children are converted 'into abnormal, truncated, suspect beings who threaten the moral order and whom the state must therefore place under harsh tutelage'.[72] Crucially for van Aarde, of course, Jesus is ultimately saved (gate-kept) from such 'mentalism': for he is ultimately rendered a 'fathered subject' by his trust in God as his father, and as such ultimately emerges as a governable neoliberal individual. His mission is to a certain extent individualized in this neoliberal framework too. Reviewing van Aarde's project, Allan Boesak, for instance, bemoans that Jesus is crucified after an 'outburst of emotion' in the temple which completely 'ignor[es] the political fact that Jesus was executed by a Roman governor'.[73] As such 'this revolutionary [van Aarde's Jesus] comes to us almost exclusively by way of Jesus' fatherlessness and the consequences of context-specific patriarchy thereof in Judean society. The political significance of this is lost'.[74] van Aarde's project could (like Miller's) be chastised for its anachronism – unlike contemporary Western fatherlessness, largely patterned on family breakdown, fatherless in antiquity was more normally rooted in paternal death 'which was pervasive and endemic, not merely the occasional or exceptional by-product of environmental catastrophe or war'[75] – and lack of evidence – 'it is impossible to write a definitive psychobiography of Jesus from the perspective of his childhood experiences'.[76] However, it is through a quest for a cultural Christ that such moves are legitimated. As van Aarde himself attests: '[M]y own sense of fatherlessness propelled me toward my present Jesus studies. A friend suggested that I tell my life story along with my interpretation of the Jesus story'.[77]

For both Miller and van Aarde, Jesus ultimately emerges as a 'normate' neoliberal subject with regard to his mental disposition. The ready acceptance of psy-discourses and models as givens bear witness, as Peter Homans attests, to the dominance of psy-discourses as 'a guiding set of ideas woven into the fabric of institutional life' figuring a new subject: 'psychological man'.[78] James Crossley in

72. Loïc Wacquant, *Punishing the Poor: The Neoliberal Government of Social Insecurity* (Durham: Duke University Press, 2009), 81.

73. Allan Aubrey Boesak, *Pharaohs on Both Sides of the Blood-Red Waters: Prophetic Critique on Empire, Resistance, Justice and the Power of the Hopeful Sizwe – A Transatlantic Conversation* (Oregon: Wipf and Stock, 2017), 100.

74. Boesak, *Pharaohs*, 99.

75. Sabine R. Hübner and David M. Ratzan, 'Fatherless Antiquity? Perspectives on Fatherlessness in the Ancient Mediterranean', in Sabine R. Hübner and David M. Ratzan (eds), *Growing Up Fatherless in Antiquity* (Cambridge: Cambridge University Press, 2009), 3–28, 9.

76. Bas Van Os, *Psychological*, 3.

77. van Aarde, *Fatherless*, 6.

78. Peter Homans, *Jung in Context: Modernity and the Making of a Psychology* (Chicago: University of Chicago Press, 1979), 1–5.

his important work *Jesus in an Age of Neoliberalism* (2012) forcefully argued that the conception of Jesus within a 'great man' tradition (seeing the individual as a central mover in historical situations over and above social and political processes) likewise works in accord with a 'dominant capitalist understanding of causality, particularly the importance of a freely acting autonomous individual with little concern for material conditions as a historical mover'.[79]

It is also not incidental that the frequent characterization of Jesus as healer or therapist also denotes a certain gatekeeping of his character from those 'others' within biblical traditions perceived more negatively through negative stereotypes of madness and/or mental illness. Donald Capps's work is perhaps most overt in its attempt to locate Jesus 'not as a mental patient but as a forerunner of the modern psychiatric profession'.[80] Adopting insights from the 'psychodynamic episteme' Capps sees therapies involving dynamics of transference and empowering words between therapist and patient characterizing the ministry of Jesus. In taking Jairus's daughter's hand and commanding her 'Little girl, get up' (Mk 5:41) Jesus 'transferred his faith to her' and '[gave] her faith in the future'.[81] The bleeding woman touching Jesus's cloak (Mk 5:25–34) likewise functioned as 'a powerful illustration of the importance of the role of transference in the curative process'.[82] Capps concludes that he wants to explicitly provide an alliance between those ministering to and living alongside those experiencing mental illness in the contemporary world and the ministry of Jesus. He writes:

> The purpose of this book is not to encourage readers to replicate what Jesus did, and it is certainly not intended to persuade them to oppose the curative methods of Jesus to the curative methods of professional psychiatrists and psychotherapists today. Instead, what I hope to show is that the methods Jesus employed are congruent with many of the methods that have been demonstrably effective in the treatment of the mentally ill today.[83]

Ultimately, Capps's major 'gatekeeping' provocation, as laid down in the title of the piece, is casting Jesus as the 'Village Psychiatrist'. One of the most sure-fire ways to 'protect' Jesus from madness and psychiatric labelling is to cast him as a healer of such conditions. Moreover, by using this psychiatric discourse to separate Jesus from those he 'cured' Capps is enabled both to 'talk about [eradication of] madness' as a means to ultimately 'reinforce idea[ls] of normalcy'.[84]

79. Crossley, *Jesus*, 68.

80. Donald Capps, *Jesus the Village Psychiatrist* (Louisville: Westminster John Knox Press, 2008), xxiii.

81. Capps, *Village*, 124.

82. Capps, *Village*, 124.

83. Capps, *Village*, xxv.

84. Luke Heighton, 'Reason Dazzled: Klimt, Krakauer and the Eyes of Medusa', in Gemma Blackshaw and Sabine Wieber (eds), *Journeys into Madness: Mapping Mental Illness in the Austro-Hungarian Empire* (New York: Berghahn, 2012), 145–61, 145.

Whether through attempts to 'normalize' Jesus's mental state as more representative of common experiences of the neoliberal West, or to present a portrait of Jesus as one who 'overcame psychological problems and emerged as a relatively healthy male'[85] or by constructing him as psychiatrist or therapist, various gatekeeping strategies surrounding madness, in reference to his identity, are, I contend, observable.[86]

Gatekeeping the Madness of Paul

Another significant leadership figure within early Christianity, who has often been assumed to offer some insights into his own sentiments, experiences and 'alleged personal conflicts and idiosyncrasies'[87] and who has also, it will be submitted here, been frequently defined in relation to rationalist and positive mythologies of madness, is Paul. His correspondence to early Christian communities now constitutes a substantial portion of the New Testament canon and, as apostle to the Gentiles, he is frequently credited with founding a mixed and intellectually coherent community. 2 Corinthians especially evokes Paul as both a masterful teacher who experiences ecstatic visionary and auditory encounters (2 Cor. 12:2–4) but at the same time one who could be exacting, foolish and acutely aware of his own subjection to weakness, most notably a certain 'thorn in the flesh' (2 Cor. 12:7). These features have of course been the source of much dispute and debate within biblical scholarship but for the most part such discussions have been marked by a hermeneutical tendency

85. Charlesworth, 'Should Specialists', 459.

86. Sociological models of madness have been used in reference to Jesus's characterization as mad in biblical studies. Often these understand such instances as forms of deviance labelling or symptomatic of social conflict, rather than actual mental/experiential diversity. Justin Meggitt's work on the 'Madness of King Jesus', for example, firmly locates Jesus's assumed lunacy within the social perception of the Roman authorities. The Romans did not pursue his followers in the wake of his death for they considered Jesus an erratic and deluded madman whose cause would be dissipated with his death. Meggitt thus writes: 'If this Jesus is not one that resembles the historical Jesus' own self-understanding or the Jesus proclaimed by his followers, that is to be expected and supports, rather than undermines, the plausibility of this thesis. For ultimately power and madness are inextricably linked, and the gulf between the visions of the world held by those labelled mad, and who suffer the consequences, and those who successfully label others mad, is unbridgeable. Although the historical Jesus probably would not have called for his enemies' damnation, as with Nathaniel Lee, so with Jesus of Nazareth: "They called me mad, and I called them mad, and damn them, they out voted me."' Justin J. Meggitt, 'The Madness of King Jesus: Why was Jesus Put to Death, but His Followers Were Not?', *JSNT* 29(4) (2007), 379–413, 417.

87. Richard Hughes, 'The Cain Complex and the Apostle Paul', *Soundings: An Interdisciplinary Journal* 65(1) (1982), 5–22.

to ring fence the 'sanity' of Paul largely on account of the cognicentrism of Western interpreters – 'prejudice against a concept of non-ordinary reality ... the analogue in consciousness of ethnocentrism'[88] and cultural preferences for rationality, logic and systems. As Robert Jewett submits, this '"drive towards system building" inclined European scholars to think of Paul as a systematician'.[89] Paul is thus cast predominantly in the role of 'enlightenment reasoner'.[90] Moreover, it is his reason which is often cited as the wellspring and guarantor of his intellectual and discursive power and legacy rather than his 'alternative' auditory and visionary experiences.[91]

In Pauline studies, there has of course been a general resistance to conjecturing about the interiority of Paul since Krister Stendahl's important 1963 article 'The Apostle Paul and the Introspective Conscience of the West'. This differentiated Paul's anxiety from centuries of individualizing, psychologizing and spiritualizing interpretations with what Douglas Harnick termed 'the audacious claim that a great deal of Paul's theology is about Gentiles and Jews rather than about guilt-ridden individuals seeking to escape the punishment of an angry God'.[92] Latterly, Bruce Malina and Jerome Neyrey have correspondingly submitted that ancient Mediterranean persons were anti-introspective: 'What counted was on the outside of a person ... [because] they were collectivistic persons.' 'One constantly reads about the tensions, psychological struggles or personality traits of Paul, Jesus and others. We suggest that such statements are ethnocentric and anachronistic projections without the slightest basis outside the imagination of the modern writer. Modern psychology is rooted in individualist culture. And there simply were no individualist cultures before the sixteenth century.'[93] Despite such warnings, selected interpreters have variously persisted not only to infer details about Paul's presumed state of mind, but also more broadly (even when avoiding experimental 'diagnoses' of Paul) to employ ideological tropes and

88. M. Harner, *The Way of the Shaman* (San Francisco: Harper, 1980), xvii.

89. Robert Jewett, *Paul the Apostle to America: Cultural Trends and Pauline Scholarship* (Louisville: Westminster John Knox Press, 1994), 4.

90. Colleen Shantz, *Paul in Ecstasy: The Neurobiology of Paul's Life and Thought* (Cambridge: Cambridge University Press, 2009), 27.

91. In one recent commentator's words: 'Of all the apostles he alone was an intellectual, and this was to prove of great significance in the progress of the new faith. For Christianity to make an intellectual as well as a moral and spiritual conquest of the world it needed someone of Paul's mental calibre to explain and enforce the significance of Christ's death and resurrection and other related doctrines.' J. Oswald Sanders, *Dynamic Spiritual Leadership: Leading Like Paul* (Grand Rapids: Discovery House Publishers, 1999), chapter 2, no pages, digital version.

92. Douglas Harnick, *Paul among the Post-Liberals: Pauline Theology beyond Christendom and Modernity* (Grand Rapids: Brazos Press, 2003), 14.

93. Bruce Malina and Jerome Neyrey, *Portraits of Paul: An Archaeology of Ancient Personality* (Louisville: Westminster John Knox, 1996), 13.

language reflective of certain assumptions concerning psychopathology and madness.[94]

In the Acts of the Apostles, Festus is famously depicted accusing Paul of being out of his mind (μαίνῃ) on account of too much learning which is driving Paul insane (εἰς μανίαν περιτρέπει; Acts 26:24), to which Paul responds: 'I am not out of my mind, most excellent Festus, but I am speaking the sober truth' (Acts 26:25). Commentators have variously asserted that this episode not only underscores Festus's profound misunderstanding of Paul's message, but also exhibits Luke's concern to assure his readers of Paul's sanity (defined in relation to normative ancient cultural ideals and virtues) post-conversion. John Lenz is representative of such a position:

> Paul, who 'sees the light' at his conversion is changed into a man of truth and self-control. Festus' response is full of ironic import, for Festus could not be more incorrect. Paul has been converted not to madness but sanity. In recognising Christ, Paul has become a man of true virtue corresponding to the natural advantages of a good pedigree, wealth, high social status, as described by Luke.[95]

Madness here is primarily understood as a deviance label and Paul is ideologically distanced and protected from it.[96] Margaret Mitchell, commenting on patristic understandings of Paul's conversion in Acts, similarly points out how Paul's Christian leadership is safeguarded and secured by these early commentators (according to ancient cultural ideals and virtues) who contrast the responses of Paul's pre-conversion leadership with his more measured post-conversion performances:

> When he [John Chrysostom] wishes to construct a then-and-now argument to accent the magnificent divinely inspired turnabout made by Paul, John even heightens the viciousness of the famous, vivid Lukan picture of Paul 'breathing threats and murder'. In these portraits Paul the persecutor of Christians was a madman, one in the grip of an ungovernable insanity, a crazed lion running

94. C. H. Dodd, for example, saw Paul as 'highly-strung – sensitive to conditions, a man of moods, with emotions readily roused. The emotional temperament is reflected in his literary style. At its best it is elevated, moving and impassioned, at its worst, involved and incoherent. It is seldom or never level, cool or tame'. C. H. Dodd, 'The Mind of Paul: I', *NTS* (1953), 67–82, 68.

95. John Clayton Lentz, *Luke's Portrait of Paul* (Cambridge: Cambridge University Press, 1993), 83.

96. Corroborating this position, Lentz notes, 'P. W. Walaskay's comment that Festus called Paul mad because he wanted to release him for "reasons of insanity" is hardly an appropriate interpretation. Walaskay not only presses his interest in stressing the fairness of the Roman authorities to the extreme but he also misses the literary intention of the narrative.' Lentz, *Luke's*, 83.

> about, a murderer with a thousand malefacting hands. The then and now contrast moves to the predictable result, as the meteoric metamorphosis of Paul's conversion recast him as gentle as a lamb or, in an equally uncanny reversal, the wolf becomes a shepherd.[97]

In Paul's own writings too, references to madness (1 Cor. 14:23; 2 Cor. 5:13; 11:23) have often been understood as discursive tools to defend and corroborate Paul's (and the early Christian communities') sanity. Reason and rationality are understood by many commentators to be preferred by Paul over ecstatic experiences which could be misconceived as madness to outsiders. Thus Ian Scott writes:

> The whole body of the Apostle's writings attests to Paul's view that human reason is central to achieving all religious knowledge. Just as we found in 1 Cor 1:17–2:16 evidence that the Spirit-led believer continues to employ reason in understanding the world, so elsewhere we see the expectation that believers must think rationally. In 1 Corinthians 14, for example, Paul clearly favours prophetic speech over glossolalia, precisely because it is rationally comprehensible. It engages the mind and allows the message to be understood. Why is such comprehensible speech better? Because it is such speech which 'builds up' the hearers. While incomprehensible speech remains ineffective (14:3–5, 12, 17). The implication is that moral edification of the believers takes place through intellectual activity, as they comprehend the truth with their reason.[98]

Commenting on such references, David Garland has similarly projected rationalistic ideals onto this ancient context:

> Ecstasy is the opposite of self-control and can refer to all kinds of behaviour that may seem irrational. Someone, such as his Jewish opponents, may be accusing him of some kind of mental instability – he has gone mad. Or those in Corinth 'who thought highly and confidently about themselves and their outward status and show could have regarded Paul as abnormal'. He was perhaps too eccentric for their tastes ... 'If we are in our right mind, it is for you'. 'Right mind' refers to 'mental sobriety'. They should know him well enough to realize that whatever he does is for God or them and not for himself. His previous letter was not written from personal pique at the one who offended him or to cause them grief. It was to bring them back to God.[99]

97. Margaret Mary Mitchell, *The Heavenly Trumpet: John Chrysostom and the Art of Pauline Interpretation* (Louisville: Westminster John Knox, 2002), 251.

98. Ian W. Scott, *Paul's Way of Knowing: Story, Experience, and the Spirit* (Grand Rapids: Baker Academic, 2008), 51.

99. David E. Garland, *Second Corinthians* (Nashville: Broadman and Holman, 1999), 277.

Colleen Shantz would classify such references as cognicentric. She has drawn on the anthropologist Michael Harner's work on shamanism to identify this particular bias, which seeks to 'arbitrate what counts as acceptable knowledge as well as what counts as acceptable ways of coming to know'.[100] Shantz reveals how cognicentrism has negatively judged intelligence and ecstasy. She notes how 'ASC's [Altered states of consciousness] particularly in religious contexts' are yet another 'victim of this [cognicentric] prejudice. Although ASC's are tolerated in Western therapeutic contexts, such as hypnosis where they are controlled by a professional and even in some meditative practices, their use in virtually every other context is seen as mental weakness at best and pathology at worst'.[101] As a result of viewing ecstasy as 'psychologically and socially deviant' Paul's experiences, Shantz contends, in Western scholarship are schematized as rational. Moreover, due to Protestantism's bias against sacramental and mystical forms, Paul is hailed as 'the patron saint of thought in Christianity'. As a result, in Shantz's opinion, 'The scholarly imagination is understandably, though unnecessarily, limited by its own cultural parameters . . . Despite Paul's references to multiple ecstatic religious experiences, Enlightenment sensibilities continue explicitly and tacitly to bracket out such experiences as a contributing factor in Paul's writing.'[102] Written words in Western culture (or in oral environments ordered speech as opposed to disordered speech) have often been seen to give an epistemological privilege and 'rational' claim to power. Sheldon Pollock writes that '[t]he authorization to write . . . is no natural entitlement, like the ability to speak, but is typically related to social and political and even epistemological privileges'.[103] The interpretations of Paul's words in scholarship also belie 'expressions of power manifest in social hierarchy . . . based on the possession of specific, constructed knowledge'.[104] The model of prophet, the medium of divine knowledge, testifies to this. As John Ashton writes, '[I]f we are to do justice to the riches of Paul's religious heritage

100. Shantz, *Ecstasy*, 26.

101. Shantz, *Ecstasy*, 26.

102. Shantz, *Ecstasy*, 33. Note though Dunn's more moderate position: 'Not least of interest is the fact that both terms were thought to be necessary – even though the range of usage of each overlapped with the other. In other words, it was important, for Paul as well, that the human being was not just rational and not just a bundle of feelings, but both . . . It would probably not be straining the evidence too much to say that Paul thus in effect refused to reduce the wholeness of the personal to rationality, but sought rather to maintain a balance between the rational, emotional and volitional. In which case, here too Paul provides some precedent for a western European culture which holds the heritage of the Enlightenment and of the Romantic Revival in uneasy tension.' James D. G. Dunn, *The Theology of Paul the Apostle* (Grand Rapids: William Eerdmans, 2006), 75.

103. Sheldon Pollock, *The Language of the Gods in the World of Men: Sanskrit, Culture, and Power in Premodern India* (California: University of California Press, 2009), 4.

104. Pollock, *Language*, 25.

we must be prepared to bestow on him the grand title of prophet that he was too modest to claim for himself.'[105]

The importance of order and rationality, in relation to rhetoric and words, is also seen within commentators' various estimations of Paul's so-called fool's speech in 1 Corinthians 1–4. Laurence Welborn proposes that rather than the proclamation of the crucified Christ being considered as 'an absurdity to the people of the ancient world'[106] actually the folly of the cross is better comprehended in light of popular theatre, in particular the fool's function in mime. Either way, each interpretation is aligned with subversive intellect, reason and veracity:

> The term 'folly' was generally understood as a designation of the attitude and behavior of a particular social type, the lower class buffoon. As a source of amusement, these lower class types were widely represented on the stage in the vulgar and realistic comedy known as the mime … Paul's Corinthian detractors labeled him as a 'fool', in contrast to the eloquent and sophisticated Apollos. Paul's acceptance of the role of the fool mirrors *the strategy of a number of intellectuals in the early Empire*, who exploited the paradoxical freedom which the role permitted for the utterance of a *dangerous truth*.[107]

Gatekeeping has also in part been observable within reflections on Paul's mysterious 'thorn in the flesh' which, he declares, was given him to keep him from commending himself too much (2 Cor. 12:7). This phrase is now frequently used as a colloquialism in Western culture to express a variety of illnesses (physical and mental), irritation, distresses or problems. Arthur Bellinzoni notes that speculations surrounding the nature of the thorn in the flesh have offered three main responses: first, persecution, torture and opponents; second, personal anxiety and spiritual torment (by demons or a malevolent angel)[108]; and third, physical or mental illness.[109] Bellinzoni, along with many other commentators,

105. Alonzo Huntsman, 'Authoring Authority: The Apostle Paul and the Prophet Joseph Smith – A Critical Comparison of Texts and Power in the Generation of Religious Community', *CGU Theses & Dissertations*. Paper 28 (2012), 246. Available online at: http://scholarship.claremont.edu/cgu_etd/28.

106. Laurence L. Welborn, 'Paul's Appropriation of the Role of the Fool in 1 Corinthians 1–4', *Biblical Interpretation* 10(4) (2002), 420–35.

107. Welborn, 'Paul's', 420–35.

108. David Abernathy states: 'Satan, through a demonic agent, was determined to oppose and punish him in order to discourage and hinder his ministry in every possible way. Paul was convinced that an evil force followed and opposed him wherever he went, but he was determined never to succumb to the pressure to give up or slack off. By God's grace he was enabled to stay at his task, even with an angel of Satan beating him, and as with Job, it was God's grace that enabled Paul to endure.' David Abernathy, 'Paul's Thorn in the Flesh: A Messenger of Satan?', *Neotestamentica* 35(1/2) (2001), 70, 69–79.

109. Arthur J. Bellinzoni, *The New Testament: An Introduction to Biblical Scholarship* (Eugene: Wipf and Stock, 2016), 279. For a review of scholarship which assumed the thorn

favours the latter explanation, and while noting that one cannot firmly 'diagnose' a mental or physical illness even when the patient is at hand, leave alone when they are a historical figure only known through written texts, commentators have continued to offer judgements concerning the condition, including visual defects on account of cerebral haemorrhage[110] and temporal lobe epilepsy.[111] What is interesting is the ways in which such medical diagnoses are also often accompanied by strategies to defend and manage Paul's 'madness' and underscore his ability and sanity. Alan Hisey and James Beck, for example, state the following:

> There was no loss of articulate speech; Paul was clearly understood ... There was no deterioration in the formation of ideas, in the use of logic, or in the judgment of values; Paul's writings testify to acuity in all of these ... There was no loss of memory and no apparent defect in it; his opponents would have used this against him, and there is no record that they did. Paul's writings make plain that he was in no way disoriented ... When this extreme condition was overcome, Paul was, nevertheless, left with the 'thorn in the flesh' that was to plague him for the remainder of his life. The perception of light is made possible by an anatomic visual mechanism consisting of the eyes, the pathway of nerve tissue that leads from the eyes, and the visual cortex in the hind part of the brain which is the terminus for the pathway.[112]

Another common sanist strategy employed by interpreters is, while acknowledging the fear and shame involved in proposed diagnoses of Paul's condition in his first-century context, to reinscribe hypothesized conditions with supra-abilities. Thus, Adela Yarbro Collins submits that visions and auditory phenomena when understood as manifestations of epilepsy would normally be hidden by the individual subject to them within Paul's context. In contrast, she notes, Paul openly discusses these experiences and 'associate[s] the "sacred disease" with his role as messenger of God'.[113] Other commentators speculating around psychopathological

represented a physical disability (including Bultmann, Deissmann, Knox, Lietzmann, Lightfoot, Ramsay and Schweitzer), see Terence Y. Mullins, 'Paul's Thorn in the Flesh', *Journal of Biblical Literature* 76(4) (1957), 299–303. Margaret Thrall also lists possible 'psychological conditions' potentially represented by the 'thorn in flesh' reference. See Margaret Thrall, *ICC Commentary, II Corinthians 8–13* (London: T&T Clark, 2000), 809ff.

110. 'On the basis of the available evidence and the lack of reference to any other condition, the only tenable hypothesis seems to be that the "thorn in the flesh" was a defect of vision.' Alan Hisey and James S. P. Beck, 'Paul's "Thorn in the Flesh": A Paragnosis', *Journal of Bible and Religion* 29(2) (1961), 125–9.

111. See Louwai Muhammed, 'A Retrospective Diagnosis of Epilepsy in Three Historical Figures: St Paul, Joan of Arc and Socrates', *Journal of Medical Biography* 21(4) (2013), 208–11.

112. Hisey and Beck, 'Paul's', 125–9.

113. Adela Yarbro Collins, 'Paul's Disability: The Thorn in his Flesh', in C. Moss and J. Schipper (eds), *Disability Studies and Biblical Literature* (Waco: Baylor University Press, 2006), 169–80, 174.

diagnoses also frequently provide a defence of Paul's abilities, thus implying an association between psychiatric conditions and exceptional capabilities, insights, talents and originality. Arthur Bellinzoni thus avers that 'Paul's propensity for ... revelations and auditory experiences suggest the possibility that Paul may have suffered from schizophrenia'[114] and psychiatrists Evan Murray, Miles Cunningham and Bruce Price cite Paul as an example in their tellingly titled article 'The Role of Psychotic Disorders in Religious History'.[115] This work attempts to analyse Abraham, Moses, Jesus and Paul from behavioural, neurological and psychiatric perspectives. Accordingly, they declare:

> St Paul's mood in his letters ranged from ecstatic to tears of sorrow, suggesting marked mood swings. He endorsed an abundance of sublime auditory and visual perceptual experiences (2 Corinthians 12:2–9) that resemble grandiose hallucinations with delusional thought content. He manifested increased religiosity and fears of evil spirits, which resembles paranoia. These features may occur together, in association with primary and mood disorder-associated psychotic conditions.[116]

However, this psychopathology is ultimately used to bolster Paul's distinction and eminence. Their argument ultimately, in their words, 'supports[s] the possibility that persons with primary and mood disorder-associated psychotic symptoms have had a *monumental influence on the shaping of Western civilization*. It is hoped that these findings will translate into increased compassion and understanding for persons living with mental illness'.[117] A related strategy employed by commentators is to view physical and mental conditions as sources of redemptive suffering. Thus Ronald Russell views Paul's thorn in the flesh as inducing 'suffering from both physical pain (the chronic illness) and spiritual pain (the challenge this produced to his personhood). He sought to relieve his suffering and to restore an unhampered sense of meaningfulness that came from pursuing his divine vocation'.[118]

In short, Western scholarship has through a variety of means worked to strategically gatekeep 'madness' within Paul's identity and accordingly protect and preserve the sanity of the post-conversion Paul. Elements often associated with negative conceptions of madness (violence, unrestrained emotion etc.) are projected

114. Arthur Bellinzoni, *The New Testament: An Introduction to Biblical Scholarship* (Oregon: Wipf and Stock, 2016), 279.

115. Evan D. Murray, Miles G. Cunningham and Bruce H. Price, 'The Role of Psychotic Disorders in Religious History Considered', *Journal of Neuropsychiatry Clinical Neuroscience* 24(4) (2012); my emphasis. Available online at: http://neuro.psychiatryonline.org.

116. Murray, Cunningham and Price, 'Role'.

117. Murray, Cunningham and Price, 'Role'; my emphasis.

118. Ronald Russell, 'Redemptive Suffering and Paul's Thorn in the Flesh', *JETS* 39(4) (1996), 559–70. Available online at: http://www.etsjets.org/files/JETS-PDFs/39/39-4/39-4-pp559-570_JETS.pdf.

onto the pre-conversion Paul to serve as foils for his post-conversion identity. When psychological/psychiatric labels are hypothetically discussed in reference to Paul, for example, in connection with his ecstatic experiences and his thorn in the flesh, often commentators link such conditions with supra-abilities: privileged insights, heroic suffering and so on. Perhaps this is unsurprising, for these traits, as will be seen, are also frequently inscribed within Western mythologies of madness and neoliberal contexts. It is to the elucidation of these, and their influence on specific constructions of Paul, that we now turn.

Paul and Positive Mythologies of Madness

The association between madness, creativity, genius and psychopathology is deep-rooted in, though not entirely limited to, Western cultural traditions.[119] Perpetuated via a number of social, cultural, metaphorical and (latterly) medical constructions, 'the [mad] creative genius' in Anna Lavin's words, 'like madness, [should be taken] as socially constructed, tantamount to "the mystery surrounding [the artist/hero/leader], and the magic emanating from him"'.[120] This mythology can be traced back to ancient Greece.[121] Aristotle famously enquired, 'Why is it that all those who have become eminent in philosophy or politics or poetry or the arts are clearly melancholic and some of them to such an extent as to be affected by diseases caused by black bile?'[122] This citation would be later adapted by Seneca the Younger as 'No great genius has existed without a strain of madness'.[123] Connections between divine inspiration and altered mental state was common, inducing Plato to state, 'Madness, provided it comes as the gift of heaven, is the channel by which we receive the greatest blessings ... Madness comes from God, whereas sober sense is merely human.'[124] Crucially, then, ancient conceptions of madness distinguished between divine and human madness, a distinction which would persist into Renaissance times and views of the melancholic temperaments of artists ('eccentricity, sensitivity, moodiness and, to some extent, solitariness'[125])

119. See Russell R. Monroe, *Creative Brainstorms: The Relationship between Madness and Genius* (New Hampshire: Irvington Publishers, 2002).

120. Anna Lavis, '"La Muse Malade", "The Fool's Perceptions" & "Il Furore dell'Arte": An Examination of the Socio-cultural Construction of Genius through Madness', *Anthropology & Medicine* 12(2) (2005), 151–163, 151.

121. Becker, 'Socio-historical', 5–6.

122. Aristotle, cited in Becker, 'Socio-historical', 5–6.

123. Cited in Simon Kyaga, *Creativity and Mental Illness The Mad Genius in Question* (London: Palgrave Macmillan, 2015), 1. Plato saw philosophy and poetry in conflict, the latter 'possessing a "frenzy" that defied reason'. See Lavis, 'La Muse Malade', 151.

124. Plato cited in Adrienne Sussman, 'Mental Illness and Creativity: A Neurological View of the "Tortured Artist"', *Stanford Journal of Neuroscience* 1 (2007), 21–4.

125. Kyaga, *Creativity*, 1.

as linked to gifts akin to divine madness. The age of enlightenment, with its emphasis on rationality, refigured the genius (and consequently distanced him from madness) as someone who 'displayed ground-breaking novelty and originality'. In Simon Kyaga's words:

> The emphasis was now on rational thought, and the genius was seen as someone who could wisely balance mental forces into harmony. True genius was ... the consequence of a synthesis of a) imagination, b) judgement, c) sense, and d) memory. While the creativity was born out of an active imagination, this imagination had to be tempered and subjected to established laws ... Thus, ideas on genius during the Enlightenment accepted sub-rational components reflected in creative imagination, yet established judgement, or reason, as an important counterbalance to this faculty. This emphasis on rational judgement made it essentially impossible to accept *madness* – clinical or divine – as concurrent with genius.[126]

In the time of the Romantics, however, 'imagination' was once more at the heart of the creative process, and 'any attempt to temper imagination by rationality would only obstruct its potential'.[127] This had the consequence of distancing the creative genius from those qualities most readily connected to sanity and in part paved the way for the rebirth of cultural connections of genius with madness. This was to be later undergirded by scientific developments and research in creativity, 'clinical madness' and psychopathology. Many clinicians and academics have since proposed general associations between creativity and psychopathology as an advantageous evolutionary trait[128] and 'between bipolar disorder and creativity' in particular.[129] However science and popular culture do not occupy entirely separate domains and each influences the other in particular ways. Indeed Katie Rose identifies what she terms 'the creativity mystique' as a 'rhetorical romanticization' which shows how 'a particular group of psychiatric disabilities – mood disorders – has been influenced by popular characterizations of mental illness and creativity'.[130] In her

126. Kyaga, *Creativity*, 14–21; my emphasis.

127. Kyaga, *Creativity*, 14–21.

128. Andrew Robinson, *Genius and Madness: A Very Short Introduction* (Oxford: Oxford University Press, 2011), 14.

129. 'Referencing prominent historical individuals thus serves an important part of providing credibility to the proposed association between genius and madness. However, as poignantly put by George Becker, the leading scholar on the historical background of the mad genius link, while the anecdotes affirming an association for genius with *divine madness* have been historically abundant, the idea of creativity being associated with *clinical madness* seems to be a modern invention not predating the 1830s.' Kyaga, *Creativity*, 14–21.

130. Katie Rose Guest Pryal, 'The Creativity Mystique and the Rhetoric of Mood Disorders', *Disability Studies Quarterly* 31(3) (2011), no pages. Available online at: http://dsq-sds.org/article/view/1671/1600.

opinion, this assumption is often rehearsed in both the selection and retrojective diagnoses of both actual patients and historical and literary persons selected as 'creative' by scientists. She writes:

> When performing a retroactive diagnosis, a researcher gives a diagnosis such as 'major depression' to a person who died long before the psychiatric diagnoses currently in use were drafted by the American Psychiatric Association. In her various works, for example, psychologist Kay Redfield Jamison retroactively diagnoses Tennessee Williams, Virginia Woolf, Edgar Allan Poe, and many others. In one article, psychiatrist Nancy C. Andreasen relies upon retroactive diagnoses of Vincent Van Gogh, Sylvia Plath, Martin Luther, and Ernest Hemingway, among others.[131]

Reflecting, I contend, both the tortured genius trope and creativity mystique is Richard Dormandy's provocatively entitled work *The Madness of St Paul* (2011). He seeks to offer a close reading of 2 Corinthians and question the predominant 'heroic trouble-shooter'[132] view of Paul to instead focus on him as a figure 'emerging from one of the most stressful periods of his life',[133] what could be termed 'a mid-ministry crisis'. In Dormandy's words:

> The aim … is to study Paul's mental anguish as revealed in the imagery, argument and style of his letter; to highlight some of the life-saving theological and spiritual treasures he discovered in places of deep darkness; to consider the pattern of Paul's life and ministry in the light of this dark period; and to see how this can reflect on ministry and mission today.[134]

The suffering and turbulence involved in Paul's encounters with the Corinthian church are explicitly compared with what Dorothy Rowe coined as 'the prison of depression'.[135] Paul's statement in 2 Cor. 7:5, 'Even when we came to Macedonia, this body of ours had not rest, but we were harassed at every turn – conflicts on the outside and fears within' is seen as a 'classic expression of the depressive state, his anger turns in on himself, blaming "this body of ours"'.[136] Similarly, 2 Cor. 11:28 is read not as informing pastoral confidence but rather as 'dripping with self-absorbed anxiety'.[137] In 2 Corinthians for Dormandy, 'we see his [Paul's]

131. Pryal, 'Creativity', no pages.

132. Richard Dormandy, *The Madness of St Paul* (Alton: Redemptorist Publications, 2011), 13.

133. Dormandy, *Madness*, 14.

134. Dormandy, *Madness*, 14.

135. Dorothy Rowe, *Depression: The Way Out of Your Prison* (New York: Routledge, 2003).

136. Dormandy, *Madness*, 49.

137. Dormandy, *Madness*, 48.

wounded soul laid bare'[138]: 'The imagery of the first five chapters of 2 Corinthians is unremittingly dark. Whenever Paul pushed his gaze in a heavenward direction he sinks back down to earth. This is no deliberate or diplomatic theoretical style. It is the unstoppable unconscious process of a deeply troubled man.'[139] Implicitly linking emotion and violence with such mindsets, Dormandy also contends that the tone and style of Paul's writings is 'wild and angry'[140] and 'full of extremes',[141] signifying an individual 'not fully in control of either the content or style of what he penned'.[142] He cites the argument regularly rehearsed by commentators that such hardships frequently featured as literary foils in Graeco-Roman depictions of the serenity of the sage, for 'to endure adversity with sangfroid was universally taken as a mark of real character'. Yet, Dormandy contends, 'Paul's "sang" is far from "froid" in this letter'[143]:

> Time and again Paul's language gives him away, demonstrating the fragility of internal equilibrium and the sensitivity of his emotional state. How easily he could lose his composure, and as one emerging from darkness, how fragile and previous that composure was ... He claims that God alone is the source of his competence as a minister, repudiating human accreditation, yet he desperately challenges the Corinthians to act as his authentication. His defensiveness in 2 Corinthians is powerful and pertinent, but it is forced defiance borne out of extreme personal isolation. Little wonder that Paul sees his true home as being in heaven.[144]

Dormandy further chastises commentators of 2 Corinthians for failing to take account of 'the emotional temperature' of the letter. In contrast he submits that 'Paul's attempt to win over, to goad, to chasten, or to provoke his readers are anything but emotionally neutral. They reveal a man in deep relationship trouble, becoming more and more isolated, backing himself further and further into a lonely corner'.[145] Anna Lavis, tracing stereotypical identities of the 'madman' throughout the ages, has shown how such figures were often perceived as marginal in the ancient world, inhabiting '"primitive" peripheries as opposed to the "civilised" centres'.[146] She goes on to demonstrate how this image of seclusion was modified, however, in contemporary culture to the tortured genius type: 'the cultural construction of

138. Robin Parry, discussing Dormandy in Parry, *Lamentations* (THOTC) (Cambridge: William Eerdmans Publishing Company, 2010), 25.

139. Dormandy, *Madness*, 25.

140. Dormandy, *Madness*, 39.

141. Dormandy, *Madness*, 37.

142. Dormandy, *Madness*, 14.

143. Dormandy, *Madness*, 37.

144. Dormandy, *Madness*, 40, 47.

145. Dormandy, *Madness*, 26.

146. Lavis, 'La Muse Malade', 151.

the artist struggling alone in the garret or attic, a space hitherto associated with closeted madness. This solitary artist also adopted the role previously attributed to the madman, as the marginalized social commentator'.[147] Lavis also points out how both madness and genius are deemed to contravene boundaries. She links this with the construction of the 'fool'; 'a jester more intelligent than the king'; 'the servant more savant than the master'. In such carnivalesque constructions, the world is frequently turned upside down and 'social and political boundaries are contravened', so much so that the fool transiently can become the hero.[148] In correspondence to the tortured genius motif, Paul's depressive turmoil in 2 Corinthians is also cited as the wellspring of his theological genius. 'His victorious outbursts should not be read as glib triumphalism, but rather as transcendent moments of grace, pathways of spiritual energy through which he managed to rise above the day-to-day struggle.'[149] Moreover, Dormandy invokes the heroic sufferer's passage from despair to strength; he notes that 'in 2 Corinthians the journeying motif surfaces more often than in any other'.[150] The status of the tortured genius mythology and its ideological value is, in Dormandy's project, not contextualized primarily in Paul's time but rather the neoliberal West. His book is designed for contemporary readers 'who struggle to trust in hard times'.[151] It is applied and practical in nature. However, this framework also indelibly inflects Paul and his writings with Western assumptions and cultural discourses surrounding mental illness. G. Thomas Couser identifies depression as the 'the paradigmatic illness of the postmodern period' – one which is widespread, but crucially emotionally not mentally disturbing.[152] Harper too notes how 'narratives about individuals who struggle through adversity uphold a particularly American tradition of voluntarism … heroic mental distress … [and] seem to support and extend neo-liberal discourses of meritocracy and competitive individualism'.[153] In Harper's view,

> Such narratives doubtless carry particular appeal for audiences in post-traditional societies, in which subjects increasingly abandon long-established lifestyle scripts structured by class or kinship affiliations in favour of individualised modes of self-fashioning. [The] Mad genius [trope] spectacularly

147. Lavis, 'La Muse Malade', 152.

148. Lavis, 'La Muse Malade', 152.

149. Dormandy, *Madness*, 90. Lennard Davis warns against the narrative structure of depression stories which inevitably include an overcoming story or triumphant resolution. Lennard Davis, *The End of Normal: Identity in a Biocultural Era* (Michigan: University of Michigan Press, 2013), 66.

150. Dormandy, *Madness*, 87.

151. Dormandy, backcover.

152. G. Thomas Couser, *Signifying Bodies: Disability in Contemporary Life Writing* (Michigan: University of Michigan Press, 2009), 5.

153. Harper, *Madness*, 76.

> dramatise[s] the inherent psychological risks of artistic self-construction while reassuring audiences that, far from being a barrier to 'success' madness may in some sense constitute a rite of passage leading ultimately to social and/or professional recognition. Mania in particular is undergoing just such a cultural revelation in modern American culture; the much lauded creativity of manic artists is now often compared to the creativity of 'manic' CEOs reinforcing the ideology of meritocracy.[154]

Harper also notes how this meritocratic message is often sustained by social class. For the characters selected to carry the 'tortured genius' stereotype are 'typically petty bourgeois celebrities: writers, musicians and artists (indeed, the term genius itself is generally reserved for artists and intellectuals and seldom applied to bus drivers or refuse collectors)'[155] or those, such as Paul, whose legacy history have deemed noteworthy. Thus, while trying to no doubt 'humanize' Paul to a certain extent, ironically through the employment of the tortured genius type, Paul's difference and supra-ability is here further inscribed.

Dormandy's project situates itself amid others which seek out 'uncommon people . . . creators and leaders whose impact on their own and later times has been so great that they deserve the label "genius" '[156] and have frequently been linked with 'dispositional attributes' akin to psychopathology.[157] Such retrospective diagnoses of those considered 'great' in different fields have also contributed to the mad genius type/creativity mystique increasingly being featured within leadership studies. This is a transdisciplinary field spanning social-scientific, humanities, professional and applied domains. Leadership studies has probed history for models of leadership through a variety of theoretical lenses (trait and behavioural leadership, transformational leadership, servant leadership etc.). Such examinations of exemplary leaders (both past and present) are an important part of the discipline, for 'without examples and case studies, an argument lacks credibility with an audience starved of leadership secrets'.[158] While 'leaders [from a Western viewpoint] are expected to be rational, efficient and results orientated',[159] Savvas Papacostas in his recent study of *Madness and Leadership: From Antiquity to the New Common Era* (2015) has proposed that madness coupled with leadership can augment innovation, resourcefulness, change and unity within movements. Leadership figures who demonstrate personality traits and 'mild

154. Harper, *Madness*, 76.

155. Harper, *Madness*, 76.

156. Dean Keith Simonton, *Genius, Creativity, and Leadership: Historiometric Inquiries* (Cambridge: Harvard University Press, 2013), 2.

157. Sophie von Stumm and Adrian Furnham, *The Wiley-Blackwell Handbook of Individual Differences* (New Jersey: Wiley Blackwell, 2011), 646.

158. Richard Ascough and Charles Cotton, *Passionate Visionary: Leadership Lessons from the Apostle Paul* (Peabody: Hendrickson Publishers, 2005), 9.

159. McManus and Perruci, *Understanding*, xxii.

psychopathologies' consolidate their potential for unique leadership status over others. Thus, Papacostas submits that 'to be successful, a leader must have a degree of paranoia in his personality'.[160] Not insignificantly, Papacostas explicitly cites the apostle Paul (and a largely unsupported retrospective diagnosis of his mental condition) as an example in this regard:

> The Pauline version of Christianity becomes dominant and takes on the world. His fervent enthusiasm, extensive travel, copious writings, and overbearing personality helped shape the way this new religion would evolve. Paul's personality with elements of manic psychosis on the one hand and depression on the other was certainly instrumental in the establishment of Christian orthodoxy. He remains one of the most instrumental leaders that history has known.[161]

Nassir Ghaemi, director of the Mood Disorders Program at Tufts Medical Center in Boston and author of *A First-Rate Madness: Uncovering the Links between Leadership and Mental Illness* (2011) has likewise posited a correlation between madness (or more specifically depression and mania) and leadership. Accordingly, in his opinion, leaders with psychopathological traits are better equipped to lead others in times of crisis than those who are 'sane'. Those elements endemic to mood disorders – realism, empathy, resilience, creativity and spirituality – are the same highly valued traits for leadership in uncertain times – the so-called inverse law of sanity.[162] In Ghaemi's words:

> I don't claim that depression invariably leads to realism, nor that mania always enhances creativity, nor that depression on every occasion increases empathy nor that hyperthymia inevitably promotes resilience. Rather, I argue on the whole, more often than not, those mental illnesses enhance or promote those qualities more frequently than is the case in the absence of those mental illnesses. Some people with manic-depressive illness are unrealistic (even psychotic), unempathetic, and unresilient... We will see that our greatest crisis leaders toil in sadness when society is happy, seeking help from friends and family and doctors. Sometimes they are up, sometimes they are down, but they are never quite well. Yet, when calamity occurs, if they are in a position to act, they can lift up the rest of us, then can give us the courage we may have temporarily lost, the fortitude that steadies us. Their weakness is, in short, the secret of their strength.[163]

160. Savvas Papacostas, *Madness and Leadership: From Antiquity to the New Common Era* (Northampton: Edward Elgar Publishing, 2015), 16.

161. Papacostas, *Madness*, 72.

162. Nassir Ghaemi, 'Depression in Command: In Times of Crisis, Mentally Ill Leaders Can See What Others Don't', *Wallstreet Journal* (2011), no pages. Available online at: http://www.wsj.com/articles/SB10001424053111904800304576474451102761640.

163. Nassir Ghaemi, *A First-Rate Madness: Uncovering the Links between Leadership and Mental Illness* (London: Penguin, 2011), no pages, digital version.

Reflecting such trends is Richard Ascough and Charles Cotton's work, *Passionate Visionary: Leadership Lessons from the Apostle Paul* (2005), an interdisciplinary and collaborative project by a biblical scholar and organizational leadership specialist. Contemporary leadership studies[164] has distinguished Paul as 'one of those colossal figures who impress themselves indelibly on history'[165] and while paying lip service to him as a 'vulnerable "man of passion" '[166] he is, on account of his historical legacy, also predominantly seen as embodying 'legacy spiritual leadership'[167] and 'transformational leadership'[168] models. Paul is accordingly numbered by Ascough and Cotton among 'the pantheon of leadership icons'[169] and celebrated for his 'transformational genius' … in both 'sacred and secular domains'.[170] They submit: 'Paul was a complex human being, driven to engage others in conversations that have transformed human history again and again. We may not always like him as an individual, but his leadership gifts and the lessons he offers for today, merit our continuing attention.'[171] Ascough and Cotton's project (like Dormandy's) is framed within twenty-first-century, neoliberal context. Here, creativity is very much seen as the 'expression of a unique individual' that is valued for 'innovation and breaking conventions'.[172] Paul's success is measured through Western neoliberal and capitalist categories of hyper-productivity.[173] He is seen to 'take a new and struggling faith product out in the tough marketplace of his times' and effectively distribute it: 'He started with virtually nothing except faith and passion, yet he built and sustained a fragile network across the known world, one where he coached, cajoled and inspired hesitant followers.'[174] Moreover, his reason and logic was underscored by his pragmatism and clear vision: 'Paul is a profoundly

164. Cheryl Patton, 'Asoka and Paul: Transformations That Led to Effective Transformational Leadership', *Leadership and the Humanities* (2015), 133–44.

165. J. Oswald Sanders, *Dynamic Spiritual Leadership: Leading Like Paul* (Michigan: Discovery House Publishers, 1999), no pages, digital version.

166. Sanders, *Dynamic*, no pages.

167. Lee Whittington et al., 'Legacy Leadership: The Leadership Wisdom of the Apostle Paul', *The Leadership Quarterly* 16(5) (2005), 749–70.

168. Michael Cooper, 'The Transformational Leadership of the Apostle Paul: A Contextual and Biblical Leadership for Contemporary Ministry', *Christian Education Journal* 2(1) (2005), 48–61.

169. Ascough and Cotton, *Passionate*, 12.

170. Ascough and Cotton, *Passionate*, 12.

171. Ascough and Cotton, *Passionate*, 151.

172. Keith Sawyer, 'The Western Cultural Model of Creativity: It's Influence on Intellectual Property Law', *Notre Dame Law Review* (2011), 2053–54.

173. Akemi Nishida, 'Neoliberal Academia and a Critique from Disability Studies', in Pamela Block, Devva Kasnitz, Akemi Nishida and Nick Pollard (eds), *Occupying Disability: Critical Approaches to Community, Justice, and Decolonising Disability* (New York: Springer, 2016), 159–74.

174. Ascough and Cotton, *Passionate*, 10.

normative leader who always teaches and offers guidance to his followers with a vision of community uppermost in his mind. Winning individual souls is not his only market niche as an apostle; he is unequivocally an intentional community builder.'[175] Despite this emphasis on able normativity, the major premise of the book is that Paul is a 'chaordic leader'. 'Chaordic' – a term combining both chaos and order – was coined by Dee Hock to describe 'any self-organizing, self-governing, adaptive, non-linear, complex organism, organization, community or system, whether physical, biological or social, the behaviour of which harmoniously combines characteristics of both chaos and order'.[176] In contrast to a Newtonian, mechanistic model where order is imposed from above, in chaordic movements order coexists with disorder and disequilibrium (elements often assumed to be allied to madness, when defined as other to normativity) and power is dispersed. Through such chaos and dynamism, transformation, it is argued, can occur. Chaos, often a term used in conjunction with madness, is given a firmer relationship with madness mythologies through association with violence and struggle (again elements often constitutive of negatively framed madness stereotypes). Ascough and Cotton underscore that 'the potential for physical violence is always part of the transformational process'[177] and 'the personal costs – to health and reputation – are high: "People who lead frequently bear scars from their efforts to bring about adaptive change"'.[178] In this sense, the 'virtues of disorder' within leadership are seen as a wellspring of creative potential and subversion of established orders.[179] It is no coincidence, therefore, that throughout Ascough and Cotton's work Paul is repeatedly referred to as a 'creative genius'[180] and a leader uniquely tooled to lead in times of crisis for, in their words, 'in times of change we want transformational leaders rather than transactional managers'.[181] They submit,

> Certainly he does not fit the stereotype of a compliant, politically correct, eternally polite, please-person that we might associate with a good team player. But such people rarely make significant contributions in the turbulent world of complex change, where resources are limited, goals are diffuse, cohesion is problematic and meaning are constantly under negotiation. Transformational change is never smooth, and is rarely accomplished by people who devote most of their energy and time to being 'nice'.[182]

175. Ascough and Cotton, *Passionate*, 97.

176. Dee Hock, 'The Art of Chaordic Leadership'. Available online at: http://www.meadowlark.co/the_art_of_chaordic_leadership_hock.pdf.

177. Ascough and Cotton, *Passionate*, 48.

178. Ascough and Cotton, *Passionate*, 49.

179. Heinrich V. Pierer and Bolko V. Oetinger, *A Passion for Ideas: How Innovators Create the New and Shape Our World* (Indiana: Purdue University Press, 2001), 111.

180. The 'leadership genius of this passionate apostle' is also celebrated. Ascough and Cotton, *Passionate*, 12, 15.

181. Ascough and Cotton, *Passionate*, 26.

182. Ascough and Cotton, *Passionate*, 89.

Emotion, a category so often aligned with madness, is also seen as a crucial dimension of chaordic identity. Paul is a '*passionate* visionary' and while, in Ascough and Cotton's words, '[w]e may be afraid of passionate leaders, preferring cold, rational less "chaordic" types ... this fear exhibits the natural human tendency to think in stereotypes and neglect the evidence of our experience ... Leaders require emotional intelligence because change itself is an emotional process'.[183] 2 Cor. 1–2:4 is cited as evidence of Paul 'wearing his heart on his sleeve' and talking from the heart rather than the 'cool, analytical talk of a dispassionate, detached leader'.[184] Moreover, the fool's speech in 2 Corinthians is seen to be an ironic self-parody where the status quo is subversively transformed.[185] Perhaps most telling, however, about the implicit use of the 'creativity mystique' – '[a] commonplace assumption in Western society ... [t]hat profound creativity has an intimate connection to psychopathology'[186] – is the direct analogy drawn by Ascough and Cotton between Paul and the wartime British prime minister, Winston Churchill. They write:

> If Paul has a kindred spirit, a brother-in-arms in facing adversity, in 20th century history, it would be Sir Winston Churchill. Like Paul, Churchill's career as leader had many ups and downs, and countless moments that demanded decisive, courageous actions. He was no stranger to adversity and to the personal costs associated with adaptive leadership ... Paul [too] could have acquiesced to his opponents, but he knew that some things are worth continuing, whatever the cost.[187]

Within leadership studies, Churchill is a character who is seldom discussed without some reference to his supposed depression (as shown through his now almost proverbial 'black dog' metaphor).[188] Papacostas goes further and sees in Churchill a 'paranoid personality' which he identifies as 'the key ingredient that enabled him to see the nation through the vicissitudes and dangers of what followed'.[189] Illustrating the socially constructed nature of both positive and negative stereotypes of the 'irrational', Papacostas goes on to claim that

> [h]e [Churchill] was unquestionably the right man for the job. In his case his personality helped him take such stances against the Germans that eventually led to allied victory. The same cannot be said of Hitler, whose paranoid personality

183. Ascough and Cotton, *Passionate*, 35, 67.

184. Ascough and Cotton, *Passionate*, 73.

185. Ascough and Cotton, *Passionate*, 47.

186. Becker, 'Socio-historical', 45.

187. Ascough and Cotton, *Passionate*, 51.

188. See discussion of Churchill's despair in Philip Sadler, *Leadership* (London: Kogan Page Publishers, 2003), 38. See also Anthony Storr, *Churchill's Black Dog* (New York City: Harper Collins, 2011).

189. Papacostas, *Madness*, 99.

> led to the destruction and defeat of Germany. Two men and two countries; one rises and becomes a hero, the other loathed as a madman.[190]

Paul is ultimately judged by Ascough and Cotton as analogous to the Churchillian 'hero' for, in their opinion, while battling dark feelings, he 'does not display the dysfunctional hallmarks of a narcissist'.[191] This assumption, coupled with his projected chaordic identity, serves to mitigate (and gatekeep the unleashing of) unrestrained madness onto his character. He is mad, but not *that* mad; ordered, but not *that* ordered. The creative crisis leader trope aids them in holding together such tensions.

In both Dormandy's and Ascough and Cotton's projects, Paul's disposition is ultimately rendered normative. Elizabeth Castelli is vocal in her suspicion of such interpretative moves, when she states that 'there appears to be a persistent psychologising aspect to some reconstructions in which some rhetorical move on Paul's part, for example, is explained in terms of a kind of "natural response to a difficult situation" implying both a unified human nature and a singular mode of experience'.[192] The Western capitalist context of many of the positive mythologies of the mad individual are also reflective of an aristocratic legacy which conceives of heroes of the past as 'great men'. Bobby Loubser notes that the modernist idea of the individual as the agent of history set the groundwork for the conception of Paul as an individual genius:

> Such a type of treatment has a long history in Western scholarship, exemplified by Nietzsche's idea of Paul as 'the inventor of Christianity'. George Bernard Shaw could say with much certainty that, '[t]hough in Acts he [Paul] is only a vulgar revivalist, he comes out in his own epistles as a genuine poet ... He does nothing that Jesus would have done, and says nothing that Jesus would have said ...' For Adolph von Harnack he is 'the founder of Christian civilisation'.[193]

Loubser demonstrates through media-critical analysis that the epistles themselves had corporate authorship, and therefore should not be understood as a product of an individualistic subject: '[I]t is not the dominating voice of the singular apostle portrayed as "disembodied brain" that has to be listened to, but also the many voices of his co-workers.'[194] This refocuses attention on the collective, rather than the solitary individual, and in turn also invites Western interpreters to recognize the ways in which the cultural scripts of neoliberal economic policies in the West

190. Papacostas, *Madness*, 99.

191. Ascough and Cotton, *Passionate*, 141.

192. Elizabeth Castelli, *Imitating Paul: A Discourse of Power* (Louisville: Westminster John Knox Press, 1991), 17–18.

193. J. A. (Bobby) Loubser, 'Media Criticism and the Myth of Paul: The Creative Genius and His Forgotten Co-workers', *Neotestamentica* 34(2) (2000), 329–45, 343.

194. Loubser, 'Media', 329.

have increasingly focused attention on the resilient individual[195] as a competitive consumer[196] in a chaotic world.

Negotiating Mythologies of Madness

Judith Scheslinger in her provocatively entitled *The Insanity Hoax* (2012) is sceptical of the retrospective diagnoses often given to historical characters without sufficient evidence. Moreover, she underscores the contextual, shifting and fluid nature of conceptions of madness throughout history. That said, Scheslinger is despondent about overcoming the 'insanity hoax' for the mythologies surrounding creativity and psychopathology are so deep and prevalent in Western society – the proverbial 'fine line between genius and madness' is an example of this – that such constructions are regularly and often unconsciously incorporated into interpretations with or without firm evidence. In her words, 'The doctrine that great talent exacts a great price is so popular that few people think to question its validity; … "the price of greatness" confirms that genius is psychologically expensive … the jury is in, sentence has been pronounced, and we can all go home.'[197] If she is right, no matter how questionable the historical or scientific basis of the pathology and genius/crisis leader stereotypes are, nor how complicit they are with neoliberal statecraft in its celebration of individual creativity and resilience, these tropes' resonances continue to be commanding and widespread in a number of disciplinary fields. Yet Harper sees such positive modes of madness mythologies being equally as damaging as negative stigmatizing stereotypes, not least because they tend ironically to reinscribe a certain 'normativity' to those who are considered 'genius' rather than the deviant and/or pitiable 'insane'.

> Even when contemporary cultural representations of madness are 'positive' they are never simply or uniformly 'glorifying'; on the contrary, they also reinforce discriminations of social class, race and gender … whatever lustre does attach to madness is mainly reserved for white middle-class males, while women and visible minorities are often presented as tragic victims of mental distress or simply ignored.[198]

The multiple pictures of Jesus and Paul surveyed here (all imagined, all culturally determined) are involved in performing 'certain discourses' and neoliberal 'regimes

195. Katrina Kathleen Tierney, 'Resilience and the Neoliberal Project: Discourses, Critiques, Practices', *American Behavioural Scientist* 59(10) (2015), 1327–42.

196. Moncrieff, 'Neoliberalism', 235–56.

197. Judith Scheslinger, *The Insanity Hoax: Exposing the Myth of the Mad Genius* (New York: Shrinktunes Media, 2012), 64.

198. Harper, *Madness*, 9.

of truth'[199] with regard to madness. Each project, in albeit quite different ways, is involved in strategic gatekeeping to ensure their respective Jesus and Paul emerges as representative of a normative (and able) ideal of their neoliberal cultural episteme.

Donnelly evocatively asks whether disability and mad studies could iterate a new 'mad cultural episteme' which could 'incorporate modern disability ideas including a deauthorizing of universal claims and an appreciation of diversity and of situated subjectivity'.[200] Disability scholars Anne Wilson and Peter Beresford, similarly, have proposed an alternative to the pathological models of the eugenic, psychodynamic and psychopharmological/neurobiological epistemes, in their notion of a 'continuum of distress' which would dissolve the binaries of sanity and insanity and its associated exclusions of certain bodies and minds (on account of either their innate evil or supra-brilliance): 'a continuum upon which all people would place themselves, in different positions and at different times in their lives … The world does not consist of "normal" and the "mentally ill" it consists of people, all of whom may experience mental and emotional distress.'[201] Dan Goodley, too, has defied the widespread medicalizing of human experiences. He proposes 'a debility politics' which accepts rather than pathologizes 'the inability of any of us to match the neoliberal imperative'.[202] Inspired by Jasbir Puar's work on deconstruction of the 'adequately-abled-body',[203] he asks: 'Where will our debility take us in terms of contesting dis/ability. Could we become dis/abled together? What forms of humanity are demanded by human debility?'[204] Such mad cultural epistemes would presumably prompt quite different responses to the eye-catching tabloid feature 'Jesus Christ may have suffered from mental health problems' which opened this chapter. Indeed, it may defiantly obviate the occasion for such a sensationalized headline at all.

199. Fatima Tofighi, *Paul's Letters and the Construction of the European Self* (New York: Bloomsbury T&T Clark, 2017), 12.

200. Donnelly, *Vogue*, 23.

201. Donnelly, *Vogue*, 23.

202. Dan Goodley, *Dis/ability Studies: Theorising Disablism and Ableism* (New York: Routledge, 2014), 96.

203. Jasbir Puar, 'Rethinking Homonationalism', *International Journal of Middle East Studies* 45 (2013), 336–9.

204. Goodley, *Dis/ability*, 96.

Chapter 5

Madness, the Affect Alien and the Gospel of Mark: Critically Probing a Happiness Turn in Biblical Studies

The American artist Norman Rockwell's famed painting *Freedom from Want* (1942),[1] depicting a white family, sat orderly (and hierarchically) around a dinner table, with a smiling grandma serving roast turkey on a platter, has attained the status of 'national icon or archetype'.[2] Recognizable across the world as a 'nostalgic, family-centred vision' of happiness, it represents a 'distinctly American consciousness and culture'.[3] Behind the ideal, however, lies a more complex personal story: 'You paint your happiness', Norman Rockwell's psychoanalyst is said to have once told him, 'but you don't live it.'[4] Fifty years later, and parodying the original, Frank Moore's 1994 work *Freedom to Share*, depicts a multiracial cast at the table, some diverted looking towards the viewer, with grandma's platter now serving syringes, pills, medicines and vials.[5] Moore, a famous gay activist who died of AIDS in 2002, problematizes and exposes the disabling effects of the 'compulsory happiness'[6] often perpetuated by the pharmaceutical industry, industrial food system and heteronormative family models.[7] From a mad studies

1. Norman Rockwell's *Freedom from Want* is one of four artworks based on Franklin D. Roosevelt's 1941 State of the Union Address, Four Freedoms. See Richard Halpern, *Norman Rockwell: The Underside of Innocence* (Chicago: University of Chicago Press, 2006), 159.

2. Halpern, *Norman*, 159.

3. Halpern, *Norman*, 159.

4. Mark Hudon, 'Norman Rockwell: Lost America Captured in Kitsch', *The Telegraph*, 2 December 2010. Available online at: http://www.telegraph.co.uk/culture/art/art-features/8177324/Norman-Rockwell-lost-America-captured-in-Kitsch.html.

5. Halpern, *Norman*, 160.

6. Carl Elliott, 'The Tyranny of Happiness', in Erik Parens (ed.), *Enhancing Human Traits: Ethical and Social Implications* (Washington: Georgetown University Press, 1998), 177–88, 187.

7. Kim Q. Hall, 'Cripping Sustainability, Realizing Food Justice', in Sarah Jaquette Ray and Jay Sibara (eds), *Disability Studies and the Environmental Humanities: Toward an Eco-Crip Theory* (Nebraska: University of Nebraska Press, 2017), chapter 15, digital version, no pages.

perspective, madness is obliterated (through the medical props in the painting) so that social and cultural order, and the normative conception of happiness it respectively constructs, can be maintained. Those seen to fall outside of normative scripts are silenced, corrected and/or cured; forgoing compulsory mental health or happiness is presumed inconceivable.

Sara Ahmed, in her provocative book *The Promise of Happiness* (2010), submits that orientation to certain objects (marriage, family, heterosexuality and one could add 'mental health', 'wellbeing' and 'sanity') are rendered 'happy'; they delineate the pattern of life that should be one's goal. Unhappiness as a result is anything which departs from this standard. Individuals and groups who do not follow the culturally affective script of happiness, or find happiness in unexpected objects, are marked as deviant: 'the feminist killjoy', 'unhappy queer', 'melancholic migrant' and what is termed here the 'mad affect alien'.[8] Ahmed powerfully invites her readers to dissociate conceptions of happiness from what is normatively presumed as 'good', and unlock the 'unhappy archives' of those deviant figures as a means by which alternative cultural forms and identities can be elucidated.

In illustrating and critically responding to these trends, my aims here are threefold. First, I will seek to outline the so-called happiness turn (a cultural focus on happiness as virtue and its related affiliate mental well-being) and critically assess ways in which it has been taken up in biblical studies through selected recent studies focused on this theme. Following Sara Ahmed's important cultural deconstruction of the North Atlantic cultural imperative to 'be happy' and her work on the cultural affects and orientations of 'happiness' (exploring not what it *is*, but rather what it *does*[9]) it will be argued that such projects often exemplify (albeit unconsciously) ableist and sanist impulses. Such impulses employ happiness as an instrument of normative regulation and exclusion of 'non-normative' mad and/or distressed bodies or minds, rendering them, in Ahmed's terms, 'affect aliens': 'one[s] [who] do not experience the appropriate affective response to the objects valued in one's community'.[10]

Second, and in response to Ahmed's incisive critique, I will introduce two projects which have produced readings of the Gospel of Mark among readers who could be understood as 'mad affect aliens'. First, Simon Mainwaring's work *Mark, Mutuality and Mental Health* (2014), the only book-length study in biblical studies hitherto which initiates a series of dialogue-based Bible studies with those

8. Mari Rutis's recent work *The Ethics of Opting Out: Queer Theory's Defiant Subjects* (New York: Columbia University Press, 2017) offers a description of queer theories' various rejections of neoliberal scripts of achievement, happiness and self-actualization. She demonstrates how many queer theorists have opted out of normative social goals, questioned future-orientated teleological norms and refigured ethics and praxis as a result.

9. 'I want to attend to how happiness is spoken, lived, practiced; Happiness for me is what it does.' Sara Ahmed, *The Promise of Happiness* (Durham: Duke University Press, 2010), 15.

10. Sara Ahmed, 'Happy Objects', in Melissa Gregg and Gregory J. Seigworth (eds), *The Affect Theory Reader* (Durham: Duke University Press, 2010), 29–51, 37.

identified by Mainwaring as 'persons with poor mental health'. And second, my own contextual Bible studies on the Gospel of Mark with a local *Hearing Voices Network* (HVN) group. This is an anti-psychiatric user group which attempts to provide a space and 'foreground[s] practices of self/other compassion',[11] within which 'people can adopt different relations to their voices, producing very different ways of thinking, being and acting'.[12] Resisting psy-discourses of disease and disorder, the HVN begin from the premise that 'hearing voices is a normal variant of behaviour, much like left-handedness and is not merely a sign of disease'.[13] As such, in Lisa Blackman's terms: "There is an inversion from the "psy-" ethical system which defines the experience, to an expression of acceptance, where voice-hearers are invited to focus on the voices, recount what they are saying, to record them, document them, and integrate them into their lives.'[14] These group readings do *not* espouse a 'curative' or 'therapeutic' consciousness – 'an understanding of disability [/mental illness] that not only *expects* and *assumes* intervention but also cannot imagine or comprehend anything other than intervention'.[15] Rather, these readings engage the 'affect[ive] aliens' – and in so doing, in Shayda Kafai's opinion, can transgressively set out to challenge and undo the absoluteness of the categories of sane/mad, normal/abnormal[16] – when posing direct challenges to cultural constructions of happiness which exclude or dismiss their complex experiences and relationships as 'other'.[17]

Third, and finally, the Gospel of Mark's own affective economy encircled by grief and distress will itself be proposed as an 'affec[tive] alien' which troubles the need for a 'happy' resolution so often pursued by exegetes. Such a text disrupts

11. Helen Spandler and Meg-John Barker, 'Mad and Queer Studies: Interconnections and Tensions', guest blog. Available online at: https://madstudies2014.wordpress.com/.

12. Lisa Blackman, *Hearing Voices: Embodiment and Experience* (London: Free Association Press, 2001), 189.

13. Blackman, *Hearing*, 189. Blackman elsewhere notes that 'a phenomenon [like voice hearing] has largely been specified, understood and acted upon within the psychological and psychiatric disciplines and approached largely as a singular if irrational perception … in the early 1990's in the UK the view held by psychiatric professionals which seemed absolutely intractable at the time was that voices were simply signs of disease and if you talk to the voice hearer about their voices you will simply be reinforcing their diseased and troubled reality'. Lisa Blackman, *Immaterial Bodies: Affect, Embodiment, Mediation* (Thousand Oaks: Sage Publications, 2012), xxi.

14. Lisa Blackman, 'Ethics, Embodiment and the Voice-Hearing Experience', *Theory, Culture and Society* 17(5) (2000), 55–74, 60.

15. Alison Kafer, *Feminist, Queer, Crip* (Indiana: Indiana University Press, 2013), 27; emphases original.

16. Kafai, 'Mad Border', no pages.

17. James O. Pawelski, 'Today, Tomorrow, and the Day After Tomorrow: A Case Study for the Theology of Joy Project'. Available online at: http://faith.yale.edu/sites/default/files/pawelski_today_tomorrow_and_the_day_after_tomorrow.pdf, 2.

the North Atlantic cultural obsession with happiness and well-being – what Carl Elliot has referred to as 'the tyranny of happiness'[18] – which is assumed at times, to be not just a right, but a duty: 'As our founding fathers instructed us, pursue it [happiness] aggressively. And if that means taking Prozac so be it. This kind of thinking amounts to a kind of tyranny of happiness, which I think is especially pronounced in American life. It also gives cosmetic Prozac a kind of status that it doesn't have elsewhere.'[19]

A Happiness Turn

Ahmed has dated the so-called Happiness Turn to the mid-2000s, where it received critical stimulation from Martin Seligman's constructions of 'positive psychology – a new science of human strengths'. This sought to 'improve quality of life and prevent pathologies that arise when life is barren and meaningless'.[20] Seligman's work also provided, in part, the inspiration for scholars from a variety of disciplinary perspectives to sustained study of 'what causes individuals to flourish and communities to thrive'.[21] Jeremy Clifton heralds such projects as illustrative of an emergent zeitgeist in literary studies and the wider Western academy[22] in which readers are encouraged 'to see value in a text and derive "sustenance" from it'.[23] In James Pawelski's and D. J. Moores' words, '[P]ositive emotions [such as happiness and/or well-being] are just as real as negative emotions and are not just the relief from or transformation of negative emotions.'[24] Accordingly, Adam Potkay shows how happiness is appropriately directed orientations to certain goals: 'the ability not necessarily to get what you want, but to know what you should want, which is the same thing as what you would want were your soul ordered properly'.[25] Ellen Charry's work *God and the Art of Happiness* (2010) is cited by Pawelski and Moores

18. Elliott, 'Tyranny', 187.

19. Elliott, 'Tyranny', 187.

20. M. Seligman and M. Csikszentmihalyi, 'Positive Psychology: An Introduction', *American Psychologist* 55 (2000), 5–14, 5.

21. James Pawelski and D. J. Moores, 'What Is the Eudaimonic Turn?', in James Pawelski and D. J. Moores (eds), *The Eudaimonic Turn: Well-Being in Literary Studies* (Madison: Fairleigh Dickinson University Press, 2013), 1–63, 2.

22. See Jack Bauer et al., 'Narrative Identity and Eudaimonic Wellbeing', *Journal of Happiness Studies* 9 (2008), 81–104. Also R. M. Ryan and E. L. Deci, 'On Happiness and Human Potentials: A Review of Research on Hedonic and Eudaimonic Well-Being', *Annual Review of Psychology* 52 (2001), 141–66.

23. Pawelski and Moores, 'What Is', 29.

24. Pawelski and Moores, 'What Is', 7.

25. Adam Potkay, 'Foreword', in Pawelski and Moores, *Eudaimonic*, xi–xiv, xii. Note the use of the language of reason here to manufacture consent for the construction of a conforming notion of what is, and is not, to be desired by the subject.

as a recent example of a happiness turn in the discipline of biblical studies and theology. Charry notes that historically Western theology has been 'skittish' about happiness and instead has been overly preoccupied with the presumed fallen nature of the world. As such, there has been a certain resistance to forging individual and community flourishing in the present. Where happiness has been forefronted, it has largely been in reference to future eschatological hope. In response, Charry attempts to develop an '*asherim*' perspective (from *ashrey* a Hebrew term often translated as 'happy' or 'blessed') which she identifies as the Hebrew equivalent of eudaimonia.[26] This is centred in the quest for collective happiness (also central to the covenant) through virtue. This is purposefully contrasted with *smḥ* which is more subjective and centred in pleasure.[27] Asherist themes are then traced throughout the Pentateuch, Psalms, Proverbs and Gospel of John. Charry claims happiness to be central to the 'collectivist soteriology' of the Hebrew Bible:

> The covenant grounds the biblical doctrine of happiness, Israel's responsibility to live the divinely authorized way of life shaped by divine commands that construct and maintain civil society. They structure personal and family life in terms of Israel's corporate well-being, from which all benefit. Reverent obedience to God promotes self-mastery, values, and skills that promote personal well-being and the common good.[28]

The selected biblical books surveyed variously exhibit, in Charry's opinion, an affirmation of flourishing which complements deference to the divine. A curative (/normalizing?) mindset undergirds the whole project, as illustrated in the arresting adoption of the biomedical image, which furnishes Charry's conclusions: 'Loving effectively is delightfully reinforcing. The power of Christ's love, being absorbed into the spiritual bloodstream, as it were, can eat away at ingrained temperamental and dysfunctional character traits that retard flourishing until maladroit behaviours wear thin and functional behaviours and attitudes replace them'.[29] In a related vein, Brent Strawn's edited collection, *The Bible and the Pursuit of Happiness* (2012), could also be seen as significant evidence for an emergent happiness turn in the discipline.[30] Drawing on positive psychology, Strawn and his collaborators show how biblical authors establish orientations to happiness in their constructions of collective thriving. Nathan Macdonald, for example, notes that while Torah

26. Pawelski and Moores, 'What Is', 26. Charry herself declares: 'Ashrey is a masculine intensive plural noun ... Ashrey identifies people who are privileged, fortunate, honoured or blessed.' See Ellen Charry, *God and the Art of Happiness* (Grand Rapids: William Eerdmans Publishing Company, 2010), 198.

27. See Charry, *God*, 199.

28. Charry, *God*, 193.

29. Charry, *God*, 263.

30. Brent Strawn (ed.), *The Bible and the Pursuit of Happiness: What the Old and New Testaments Teach Us about the Good Life* (Oxford: Oxford University Press, 2012).

seemingly documents happiness at the expense of others – Abraham becoming rich at Pharaoh's cost, Leah's happiness being wrought at Rachel's cost, Israel's happiness being secured at the Canaanites' cost – it also seems to posit rest (at table in the Promised Land or at the close of life) as a locus of well-being.[31] Joel Green probes the rhetoric of reversal in Luke's gospel, which is shown to be the key to happiness despite being countercultural: hospitality should be offered to those unable to reciprocate it etc.[32] Similarly Colleen Shantz submits that the contented life is Paul's overriding purpose.[33] Greg Carey focuses on the experiences of suffering and trauma that apocalyptic literature frequently responds to and the ways in which it carves out avenues for survival, hope, well-being and future happiness.[34] Strawn concludes that the biblical books do not offer simple equations between happiness and an easy life.[35]

Both Charry's and Strawn et al.'s thematic projects on biblical conceptions of happiness focus on covenantal, collective, other-regarding and virtuous habits, and neither make simplistic links between well-being and pain-free living. In so doing, both projects join Vivasvan Soni in critiquing the 'impoverished nature of the modern [Western] version of happiness' which, since the Enlightenment, has been 'hopelessly and inescapably private', the implications of which also imply 'a radical impoverishment in the horizon of our political possibilities'.[36] Philip Fisher's questioning of the Western notion of 'dispassionate knowledge' by focusing on affects is also important here. The biblical texts surveyed by Charry and Strawn et al. do not deny strong affective embodied responses (shame, sorrow, acceptance, hope etc.). On the contrary, they concur with Fisher that 'particular strong passions such as love, righteous anger, and others, are essential not only to knowing the world (and thus being able to change it) but also to self-knowledge, and by implication to being well'.[37] On a more fundamental level, however, these

31. Nathan Macdonald, 'Is There Happiness in the Torah?', in Strawn (ed.), *Pursuit*, 57–74.

32. Joel Green, '"We Had to Celebrate and Rejoice!" Happiness in the Topsy-Turvy World of Luke-Acts', in Strawn (ed.), *Pursuit*, 169–86.

33. Colleen Shantz, '"I Have Learned to be Content?" Happiness According to St Paul', in Strawn (ed.), *Pursuit*, 187–202.

34. Greg Carey, 'Finding Happiness in Apocalyptic Literature', in Strawn (ed.), *Pursuit*, 203–23.

35. Another project which could be seen as representative of a eudaimonic turn in biblical studies is Barbara Green's book *Jeremiah and God's Plan of Wellbeing* (Columbia: University of South Carolina Press, 2013). Her purposes, though literary, are also attuned to well-being in the present. Green 'constructs rather than retrieves' a Jeremiah 'deeply affected by the circumstances of his life' and accordingly offers insights to present interpreters 'struggling with analogous issues'. Green's thesis is that Jeremiah, though vulnerable and weak, must present to Judah divine plans for well-being, which involve sometimes unwelcome prophecies in times of doubt and calamity.

36. Soni, cited in Pawelski and Moores, 'What Is', 33.

37. Pawelski and Moores, 'What Is', 33.

projects which focus thematically on happiness or well-being as a lens through which to filter biblical traditions are undeniably inflected by wider contemporary Western cultural trends inherent in the happiness turn. Ahmed contends that, unlike any other affect, happiness is commonly accepted in the West as 'the object of human desire … as being what gives purpose, meaning and order to human life'.[38] Yet Ahmed's work has also destabilized the assumption that happiness is a social good per se. Rather, she shows how it is not only culturally relative and contingent (as Charry and Strawn et al. also show in its myriad conceptions within biblical traditions), but also how it is frequently located in specific normative performances, behaviours, objects and scripts. It is in short a 'world-making device' for 'bringing a certain world "happily" into existence, in which the line between good and bad [normal and abnormal, sane and insane] is clearly drawn'.[39] As such happiness resides 'in some lives [those who are perceived to adhere to and fulfil normative expectations] and not others'.[40] Moreover, the hierarchies of happiness that are drawn often correspond to social hierarchies. Even within classical models, Ahmed contends, 'the forms of happiness that are higher are linked to the mind, and those that are lower [weaker/thinner] are linked to the body [or mere enjoyment]'.[41] As such, 'if higher forms of happiness are what you get for being a certain kind of being, then the being of happiness would certainly be recognizable as bourgeois'.[42]

Heeding Ahmed's warning that certain constructions of happiness exclude and marginalize other bodies, minds and ways of being, it becomes clear that certain exclusionary dynamics are detectable within both Charry's and Strawn's respective works. Charry's adoption of the word 'flourishing' provides an important touchstone with the positive psychology movement and its related underbelly, with the latter concentrating on the deficits of 'disabled' bodies and disordered minds.[43] Indeed, in an earlier work, Charry tellingly utilizes a medical analogy to denote salvation: 'Christianity is medicine for the soul'[44]; 'the theme of Christianity as therapy runs throughout Christian theology'.[45] Charry thus explicitly connects happiness with healing and implicitly presumes a curative mindset in which 'othered' bodies and minds will be normalized. In her words, 'Asherism works out that healing process in a life of reverent obedience to divine commands that shape character and bring moral-psychological flourishing.'[46] Strawn's collection likewise

38. Ahmed, *Promise*, 1.

39. Sara Ahmed, 'The Happiness Turn', *New Formations* 63 (2007), 7–11, 11.

40. Ahmed, *Promise*, 17.

41. Ahmed, *Promise*, 12.

42. Ahmed, *Promise*, 12.

43. Nadia Marais, 'Happy? A Critical Analysis of Salvation in Ellen Charry That Portrays Human Flourishing as Healing, Beauty and Pleasure', *Verbum et Ecclesia* 36(1) (2015). Available online at: http://dx.doi.org/10.4102/ve.v36i1.1359.

44. Ellen Charry, *God and the Art of Happiness* (Grand Rapids: Eerdmans, 1997), 11.

45. Charry, *God*, 11.

46. Charry, *God*, xi.

insists on the centrality and innate value of happiness (however that is defined), even when the biblical documents are shown to work against dominant cultural conceptions of happiness, reversing status hierarchies and so on. In Ahmed's terms, the Bible for Strawn is undeniably presumed to be a 'happy object'; 'such objects are passed around, accumulating positive affective value as a social good.'[47] Strawn does acknowledge that the 'thick description' of happiness in the Bible does not shy away from suffering or pain and is aware that happiness within his project has been filtered into particular types of biblical literatures and not others. He concludes that 'only a deeply transformed understanding of "happiness" – a term so carelessly used, so poorly defined, and so deeply polluted in our context – can make sense of Job and James [two books tellingly absent, along with the Gospel of Mark, from his edited collection]'.[48] However, those caveats notwithstanding, the centrality of 'happiness' as a goal is never questioned. Strawn's epilogue to the volume sums up a biblical theology of happiness as encompassed in 'the theme of the triumph of life' and its associated normative assumptions regarding kin, fertility, embodiment, flourishing and sound-mindedness and so on.

> That true, original language of happiness is, according to several of the essays in this volume, God's mother tongue. God is happy, Fretheim says, and necessarily so, Charry adds. Divine happiness, moreover, is directly related to the happiness – the flourishing – of the human and nonhuman worlds. The biblical authors knew this, even without the insights of positive psychology, though we can be very happy that the insights of the latter are helping us, with fresh eyes and a new hermeneutical lens, to begin to recapture the full language of happiness found in those ancient writings.[49]

[Un]Happiness Archives

Ahmed, largely critical of projects foregrounded in the Western assumption that orientation to happiness is a self-evident good, subversively turns her attention to unhappiness and 'unhappy archives' – 'alternative histor[ies] of happiness … [crafted by] those who are banished from it, or who enter history only as troublemakers, dissenters, killers of joy'[50]– written by feminist, queers, anti-racists and other 'affect aliens' (including those labelled disabled or mentally ill) who have been excluded from normative assumptions of happiness.[51] She provocatively asks:

47. Ahmed, *Promise*, 21.

48. Brent Strawn, 'The Triumph of Life: Towards a Biblical Theology of Happiness', in Strawn (ed.), *Pursuit*, 287–322, 312.

49. Strawn, *Bible*, 315.

50. Ahmed, *Promise*, 17.

51. In Ahmed's words: 'An unhappy archive, is one assembled around the struggle against happiness … these archives do not simply supplement philosophy and its happiness archive.

> Can we rewrite the history of happiness from the point of the view of the wretch? If we listen to those who are cast as wretched perhaps their wretchedness would no longer belong to them. The sorrow of the stranger might give us a different angle on happiness, not because it teaches us what it is like or must be like to be a stranger but because it might estrange us from the very happiness of the familiar.[52]

She cites mythologies such as the 'happy family' (often inflected in biblical traditions with covenantal kin patterns), which acts as 'a powerful legislative device, a way of distributing time, energy and resources'[53] and 'the happy [heterosexual] marriage' on which it is built, as examples of normative ideals of happiness. In tracing queer 'affect alienation' to these two normative structures she purposefully contrasts what she terms 'a happy queer' with 'happily queer'. The former involves an individual masking their queerness so as to appear to act appropriately in regard to established happiness models.[54] In contrast, the latter provocatively subverts traditional transcripts of happiness. Ahmed's deconstructive analysis of the ways in which happiness plays into and perpetuates the 'pathology of normalcy'[55] persuasively demonstrates how the current Western preoccupation with happiness is not liberating but oppressive.[56]

Happiness studies, ironically, yield most attention to [un]happy images of human beings. Of course, 'consciousness of well-being is often at its highest when threatened, triggering desperate attempts to find protection against its losses'.[57] D. J. Moores noted that much identity politics focuses on struggle and oppression: 'well-being manifests, at least in much literary discourse, as a preoccupation with its absence; in other words, it is really a concern with ill-being'.[58] This is never truer than in relation to presumed mental states. For while the positive psychology movement proclaimed itself a corrective to a predominant 'illness ideology', Ashley Frawley claims that it 'simply provides its own ostensibly objective "standard of sanity" to which individuals are meant to aspire but are similarly unlikely to achieve'.[59] Kathryn Ecclestone and Dennis Hayes have been key voices in this area, showing how 'therapeutic' interventions for 'happiness' or 'wellbeing' likewise

They challenge it. My aim is to follow the weave of unhappiness, as a kind of unravelling of happiness, and the threads of its appeal'. Ahmed, *Promise*, 18.

52. Ahmed, *Promise*, 17.

53. Ahmed, *Promise*, 45.

54. Ahmed, *Promise*, 112.

55. Ahmed, discussed in David Pilgrim, *Understanding Mental Health: A Critical Realist Exploration* (London: Routledge, 2014), 110.

56. Ahmed, discussed in Pilgrim, *Understanding*, 111.

57. Pawelski and Moores, 'What Is', 1.

58. Pawelski and Moores, 'What Is', 27.

59. Ashley Frawley, 'Happiness Research: A Review of Critiques', *Sociology Compass* 9(1) (2015), 62–77, 64.

perpetuate a dominant ethos of 'diminished subjectivity' of those presumed to be 'unhappy'[60] including, most particularly, those deemed by medical models to suffer 'poor mental health' or those experiencing phenomena that the medical model would variously label 'psychotic', 'delusional' or 'hallucinatory'.

In challenging the orientation to happiness as a 'substantive thing' or end goal, Ahmed instead argues for a 'politics of the hap'[61] (recovering the etymology of happiness derived from the 'Middle English word hap, meaning chance'[62]) which, ironically, often uses unhappiness as a prompt for action. In order to access Ahmed's [un]happiness archives, one needs to hear the voices of those 'affect aliens' who disrupt normative cultural constructions of happiness or well-being. In biblical studies, initiating encounters between biblical texts, readers and/or contexts that society would deem 'detached' from happiness or well-being are potentially important spaces to encounter the 'hap'. Crucially, these voices need to be taken seriously on their own terms within the encounter. They should not be enforced to conform to certain cultural ideals of normalcy, or indeed be involved as passive recipients of a 'therapeutic' reading.

Encountering [Un]Happiness Archives

Simon Mainwaring in his book *Mark, Mutuality and Mental Health* (2014) initiated a series of studies on the Gospel of Mark with readers identified as marked by 'poor mental health'. While rooted in liberation biblical hermeneutics, which privilege voices from below, Mainwaring is largely critical of the essentializing binaries which often undergird such pursuits – marginalized/centre, oppression/liberation and so on – with limited analyses of power dynamics, and 'un/happiness' inherent in such divisions. In contrast, the voices in this project are multiple, hybrid fusions, for, as the opening words of the book starkly testify, 'Conversations matter. Connections matter. How people relate to one another matters.'[63] The ordinary readers in his project were those 'suffering poor mental health' – a term Mainwaring himself adopts with the recognition that 'whilst still being a label of sorts, [it] is at least an attempt to describe a lived reality rather than an attempt to categorize persons as essentially different'.[64] It is a label, however, which inevitably distances them from dominant cultural norms of happiness and well-being. Groups were variously drawn from mental health drop-in-centres, day treatment centres and residential projects for mental health and substance abuse. Not all participants identified as Christian. For Mainwaring, these group reader-responses to gospel traditions

60. Cited in Frawley, 'Happiness', 63.

61. Ahmed, *Promise*, 223.

62. Ahmed, *Promise*, 22.

63. Simon Mainwaring, *Mark, Mutuality and Mental Health* (Atlanta: SBL Press, 2014), 1; my emphasis.

64. Mainwaring, *Mark*, 1.

became sites where 'relational dynamics of identity, agency and dialogue' could be negotiated. Foucault's analysis of power in relational encounters is used as an interpretative framework to expose 'hegemonic relational dynamics' within mental health settings. The contextual Bible studies, through their close attention to character interactions, are accordingly seen to foreground 'mutuality' as 'an effective form of resistive and transformative postcolonial praxis' – a conception which, Mainwaring submits, has important contributions to make not only to mental health but also disability theologies. Mutuality is for Mainwaring, primarily 'a way of conceiving of power within relational encounters'.[65] Largely influenced by Homi Bhaba's postcolonial theorizing, Mainwaring sees mutuality working across and within other strategies of mimicry, hybridity, sly civility and so on; most importantly, however, mutuality enables one to hear, in postcolonial terms, the subaltern speak.

Many readers in the project self-identified with the affective stigma, prejudice, alienation and discrimination of particular characters encountered in the gospels (including Jesus). This sort of correlation is unsurprising, given, as Mainwaring asserts, 'even in this age of inclusion, of antidiscrimination legislation, and of altered nomenclature, fear and stereotypical representation of poor mental health and the denigration of persons with poor mental health are still common place in North Atlantic societies'.[66] Moreover, in Mainwaring's opinion, their responses 'did not overlook, [but] rather probed as an important aspect of biblical interpretation, the profundity of human struggle when set within contexts where mutual relating is deficient'.[67] The story of Legion in Mk 5:1-20 is an illustration of where 'mutuality' was perceived to function vulnerably within the dynamics of power. Legion is one who lives among tombs, and, according to the group responses, the story 'narrates only the partial transformation of what binds the man – his "unclean spirits"'. Crucially, the narrative implies that the people of the town had shackled him ('denied his own power for self-survival and mutual relationship') and, at the end of the narrative, persist as 'troubling purveyors of power', to whom the man is sent back. Likewise, in the case of the man with the withered hand (Mk 3:1-6), even following the healing, the group realized that relational dynamics were not resolved. The Pharisees 'displace the seemingly liberatory nature of the space by their gathering of Herodians outside the synagogue who seek ways to destroy Jesus'; as one group reader put it, '[T]hey might cut off his head'.[68] Similarly, Jesus's silence in the trial before Pilate (Mk 15:1-5) was variously read as 'a [victim's] loss from the outset' and/or for others, a dialogical engagement with Pilate through silence. This is framed by Mainwaring as a 'composite axis of silence and mutuality … a way of opening up the thin space of relational dynamics Jesus is faced with for others to enter into mutual relating'.[69] The ideological assumptions and methodology

65. Mainwaring, *Mark*, 4.
66. Mainwaring, *Mark*, 1–2.
67. Mainwaring, *Mark*, 276.
68. Mainwaring, *Mark*, 265.
69. Mainwaring, *Mark*, 12.

of Mainwaring's project, in its purposeful engagement with muted voices of the 'mad-distressed', enables an experience-centred response to both the biblical text and contemporary reflections on their experiences. His informants issue a call to a much wider readership to never simplify the gospel narratives endings (by flatly casting their respective resolutions as positive) or eliding the complex webs of power inherent in contemporary discourses surrounding mental health. His hope is ultimately that, '[t]hrough the interpretation of the relational dynamics narrated in ancient biblical stories the current pattern of relational dynamics vis-a-vis poor mental health as much as they diminish human value, might be resisted and perhaps even incrementally transformed'.[70] By adopting the contextual Bible study model, one is enabled to hear in Mainwaring's project the cultural or minority voices of those occupying such spheres and also move beyond simplistic understandings of the power dynamics that often haunt such interactions. Foucault was all too aware of how the policing and confinement of 'madness' robbed the mad of their ability to speak for themselves and 'chained [them] by silence'.[71] The contextual Bible studies themselves, therefore, in encouraging these voices to speak, could well be conceived as a means to powerfully question and disrupt happiness archives by what Ahmed would understand as a position of affective alienation. As one participant in the study defiantly noted: 'I'm tired of being talked about, treated as a statistic, pushed to the margins of human conversation, I want someone who will have time for me.'[72]

To take another example, the stigma, fear and prejudice surrounding voice-hearing or other non-normative perceptions or experiences frequently mark such individuals out, in Ahmed's terms, as 'affect aliens'. Presumed to be estranged from a happy 'normal personhood' which is 'organised and lived as unified, autonomous and clearly bounded, where the person is able to make such distinctions as the grounds and foundation of psychic health and normality',[73] such individuals are frequently excluded and marked as sites of despair. Challenging such perceptions, the HVN is a pioneering and powerful grass-roots organization which explicitly pits itself against dominant (and domineering) psychiatric models and understandings of 'non-normative' sensory experiences, including voice-hearing. HVN, as a 'post-psychiatric organization', petitions for voice-hearing to be more appropriately understood as a form of human variation 'rather than a symptom of mental disease'.[74] HVN's user-led position thus advocates for the ascendancy of 'expertise by experience'.[75] In Jacqui Dillon and Eleanor Longden's words,

70. Mainwaring, *Mark*, 3.

71. Foucault, cited in Mainwaring, *Mark*, 46.

72. Mainwaring, *Mark*, 262.

73. Lisa Blackman, 'Affective Politics, Debility and Hearing Voices: Towards a Feminist Politics of Ordinary Suffering', *Feminist Review* (2015), 25–41.

74. Jacqui Dillon and Eleanor Longden, 'Hearing Voices Group: Creating Safe Spaces to Share Taboo Experiences', in Marius Romme and Sandra Escher (eds), *Psychosis as a Personal Crisis: An Experience-Based Approach* (London: Routledge, 2011), 130.

75. Dillon and Longden, 'Hearing', 129.

'Rather than a meaningless aberrant symptom of disease requiring eradication or "cure" voice hearing is deemed significant, decipherable and intimately entwined to a person's life story … if banishing voices is psychiatry's "cure" response, understanding, accepting and integrating their emotional meaning is deemed the [HVN] response.'[76] Throughout spring 2015, I conducted a series of contextual Bible studies (readings which prioritize responses 'in front' of a text) on sections of the Gospel of Mark with a local HVN group.[77] One of the main insights gained from these sessions was the ways in which members of the group identified with the voice-hearing of Jesus at the baptism and transfiguration and so on and documented how their similar experiences had moved from a valued, socially prized phenomenon (as demonstrated in the reception of Mark's Jesus's experiences) to a pathologized and disparaged one. This is a shift that others have traced as 'a process that arises when a minority perspective is at variance with dominant social beliefs and norms'.[78] One participant claimed that his voices would render him insightful as a shaman or prophet in some cultures where their content would be interrogated, whereas in the industrialized West the voices were pathologically obliterated and he was exiled as 'mentally ill'. Another questioned the predominant assumption that voices which were demonic were necessarily evil or false. He stated: 'Socrates had a demon. This was a positive experience which told him what to do or not to do. The word demon has many different connotations. It is something other to my thoughts, very definitely other, but it need not be harmful and it can give great insight.'[79] Another declared again in identification with Jesus's voice-hearing experiences: 'One of my voices keeps saying to me: "Stop putting words into our mouths." Empty and purify the vehicle. Christ seems to be such a pure vehicle. He has no ego-engagement at all. Prophets who hear voices are pre-occupied with cleansing themselves to keep their words pure.'[80] In response to the Stilling of the Storm and the Exorcism of Legion narratives (Mk 4:35–5:20) and the question 'how do these texts connect with your experiences?', both the negative effects of social stigma and more affirmative reactions to voice hearing experiences were displayed. One participant railed against the assumption given in the text that the demonic invoked fear in others and demanded cure: 'There are different status relationships in each story. The interesting thing to me seems to be the status of Jesus as healer. The representation of mental health as a danger strikes a chord with wider popular images of mental health.' Another saw that the 'swine, unclean spirits and drowning – all seem connected. The sea may represent the need for an ending'. Someone challenged 'the text which characterizes Legion as schizophrenic and evil' and noted that

76. Dillon and Longden, 'Hearing', 129.

77. Louise Lawrence, 'Transcript of Conversations with Bridge Collective', 7 May 2015. All group participants' comments, with permission, were recorded and transcribed.

78. Dillon and Longden, 'Hearing', 131.

79. Lawrence, 'Transcript', no pages.

80. Lawrence, 'Transcript', no pages.

fear was what united the community in their rejection of the figure. Another warned, however, that there were 'lots of variables in the text regarding meanings. Schizophrenic was not explicitly used in the story. People who supply the supposed meaning are in a position of huge power, just as in culture today. It is like computer programming. You can manipulate people by filling words with meanings'. Others demonstrated more confirmatory receptions of the stories and identified their voice hearing as a hugely positive aspect of their identity: 'I find it [the text] very attractive. The stilling of the storm is very inspiring, clinging on to a beam of light, just one speck of light in a sea of darkness. This provides comfort. My experiences also bring me to a spiritual state.' The encounter between biblical texts and the HVN group brought out explicit challenges to culturally accepted orientations to happiness and well-being. Rather than performing a 'facade of normality' – a culturally accepted version of happiness or 'mental health' – the HVN participants purposefully articulated and owned their various feelings of alterity. In the articulation of these 'alternative' experiences, and the group's stubborn 'attachment to difference'[81] (as Ahmed would put it) an alternative context not inscribed by societal prejudice or fear[82] is created. As the group's advertising literature puts it, 'Power Journeys' were created.[83] Ahmed submits that it is the bringing to light unhappy affects that is confirmatory, that offers different orientations to what may constitute a better life. Affect aliens in this way snub any simple dismissal of alternative feelings or experiences (including those which the medical model would name as hallucinatory, delusional or psychotic) in the name of 'just getting along'. And as such powerfully attest that '[a] concern with histories of hurt is not then a backward orientation: to move on you must make this return. If anything we might want to read melancholic subjects the ones who refuse to let go of suffering, who are even prepared to kill some forms of joy, as an alternative model of the social good'.[84] Jijian Voronka similarly notes that affect theory and mad studies that connect with (and transgressively transform) those so-called negative states of being holds promise to think in fresh ways about how distress is formed, mediated and made sense of. The HVN offers such a space in its critique of a reified normative conception of the 'singly bounded psychological subject as focus' and, rather, opens up ways of employing an 'affect theory that moves madness beyond individually confined deficit models [and] offers new promises for mad futurities'.[85]

81. Ahmed, 'Happy', 48.

82. Dilon and Longden, 'Hearing', 131.

83. 'Members describe how the sense of acknowledgment justice, solidarity and lightness of being the group provided rekindled their love.' Special issue: The Joan of Arc Project 2006. Available online at: http://www.recoverydevon.co.uk/edocman/Bridge_Joan_Of_Arc_Special_Issue_-_Hearing_Voices.pdf.

84. Ahmed, 'Happy', 50.

85. Jijian Voronka, 'Turning Mad Knowledge into Affective Labor: The Case of the Peer Support Worker', *American Quarterly* 69 (2017), 333–8, 333.

In different ways, these 'mad' readers themselves each plot what Ahmed would term an 'unhappiness archive', a purposeful deconstruction of dominant normative (and normalizing) transcripts of happiness in their encounters with the Gospel of Mark. While (seemingly) living outside 'normative ideals of happiness', nevertheless the readers engaged here purposefully destabilize any straightforward link between healing, therapy and happiness, and contest cultural constructions of happiness which exclude or marginalize their own lived experiences and perceptions.[86] In so doing, they contribute to what Ahmed provocatively terms 'the freedom to be unhappy'[87] (non-conformity to prevailing cultural scripts) and redraw dominant assumptions regarding well-being.

Mad Grief and Distress, and the Gospel of Mark

If certain readers of biblical texts can challenge prevailing cultural scripts surrounding happiness and well-being, can biblical texts themselves also be reappropriated as affective aliens who disrupt and question Western happiness archives? Notable by its absence in both Charry and Strawn's happiness projects discussed above is the Gospel of Mark. This particular εὐαγγέλιον did not, it seems, make the cut for their selection of canonical 'happy' (/good news?) objects. In some ways, it does sit uneasily as an 'affect alien' among its compatriots – a pithy, unrefined passion narrative, a text racked in cultural turmoil and anticolonial distress – a biography of 'a saviour who doesn't get saved'.[88]

Alexis Waller accordingly posits Mark as a work which queers the public sphere and posits 'rival modes of publicness' constructing 'a new sociability and solidarity'.[89] The Gospel of Mark's cast of distressed and disenfranchised characters, various affective responses of trance, attraction, upset, misunderstanding, insult and terror provoked by the central character – even Jesus's family fear that 'he is beside himself ["/out of his mind"] (ἐξέστη)' (3:21) – and the political authorities who wish to subdue and/or annihilate him, all contribute to good news translated within a state of anxiety. 'Mark's finale presents a social space in which authority resides in unreliable female characters and divine claims are laid on a humiliated, crucified man whose predicted triumph cannot yet be concretely realized. Mark's failure to provide conclusiveness at 16:8 might be read as a queerly productive (if unnerving) gap.'[90] Eschatological descriptions of distress are intense throughout

86. Pawelski, 'Today'.

87. Ahmed, *Promise*, 22.

88. Alexis Waller, 'Violent Spectacles and Public Feelings: Trauma and Affect in The Gospel of Mark and The Thunder: Perfect Mind', *Biblical Interpretation* 22 (2014), 473–502, 453.

89. Waller, 'Violent', 454.

90. Waller, 'Violent', 463.

(Mark 13), and Mark 'affectively alienates' triumphal understandings of its resolution, or those which are couched in 'vocabularies of transformation and wholeness'.[91] In contrast, it foregrounds grief and distress as central carriers of its message.[92]

Mai Kotrosits and Hal Taussig likewise note how 'Mark stays with loss [and thus departs from normative scripts of happiness] in ways that do not allow initial responses [of triumph] to prevail'.[93] Drawing on the work of Judith Butler they submit that loss and trauma 'haunts, dispossess and disorients us. It creates in us a sense of unknowing'[94]; in Ahmed's terms, it produces affect aliens. Moreover, against the 'fantasy of individualism' so often celebrated in the West, pain as an 'associative quality'[95] inevitably underscores and necessitates social networks and relationships. Accordingly, Kotrosits and Taussig draw together a host of troublesome and unsettling features of a gospel which radically circles loss: a healer who dies in 'angry protest' and closes with no resurrection appearances but only a few women so paralysed by fear that they say 'say nothing to anyone' (Mk 16:8). Provocatively, Kotrosits and Taussig juxtapose the 'broken, bleeding, beaten and murdered figures'[96] in Mark with sculptures of Louise Bourgeois, an artist who also focused on experiential and embodied dimensions of distress, grief and pain in her work. The rationale of such an interpretative move is described as follows:

> By placing Bourgeois' work beside Mark's gospel, we wish to surface some new meaning around these figures in Mark, meanings that step to the side of the

91. Mai Kotrosits and Hal Taussig, *Re-reading the Gospel of Mark amidst Loss and Trauma* (New York: Palgrave Macmillan, 2013).

92. Holly Toensig in her essay 'Living among the Tombs: Society, Mental Illness and Self-Destruction', for example, uses the exorcism of Legion narrative to articulate her own feelings about 'guarding the tomb' and memory of her brother who committed suicide due to paranoid schizophrenia. Legion in her reading therefore primarily represents not as perhaps expected by her schizoid brother but rather herself. She jarringly claims: 'I am the demoniac living among the tombs, shrieking in personal mourning, unwilling to give my brother into hands so bent on delivering him to hell.' Through critically contextualizing the biblical character in her own experiences she feels that 'Mark 5 provides a means to "visit that place" so often avoided'. She contends that 'viewing the text only through this lens [historical] at the exclusion or denigration of other perspectives threatens the idea that biblical texts are living traditions that are challenged and renewed by lived experience.' She sees narrative as a central tool in which people can variously listen, tell and share stories of struggle and more importantly 'find and name the numerous commonalities between people'. Holly Toensing, 'Living among the Tombs: Society Mental Illness and Self-Destruction in Mark 5:1–20', in Hector Avalos, Sarah Melcher and Jeremy Schipper (eds), *This Abled Body: Rethinking Disabilities in Biblical Studies* (Atlanta: Society of Biblical Literature, 2007), 131–43, 143.

93. Kotrosits and Taussig, *Re-reading*, 4.

94. Kotrosits and Taussig, *Re-reading*, 7.

95. Kotrosits and Taussig, *Re-reading*, 5.

96. Kotrosits and Taussig, *Re-reading*, 41.

> modern tendency towards moralizing readings that try to recoup the losses of such painful experiences, or imagine pain as ultimately serving a higher purpose. Similarly in attending to Jesus as one of a number of hurting characters in Mark, we hope to counter many readings that treat Jesus as the answer to, or at least the subject of, every question raised by the gospel.[97]

Taking Bourgeois's piece *Three Horizontals*, Kotrosits and Taussig note that themes of incompleteness, infantalization and incapacity collide, denoting 'the way women are often discussed and treated like dolls or children, as incapacitated objects, and the way their bodies [and minds] are regularly carved up and analyzed as parts and pieces'.[98] This is then put alongside Mark's account of Jairus's daughter and the bleeding woman (Mark 5) to note how, even in the wake of the healings, Jesus is also seen to experience a loss of power. Thus, figures within the narrative are 'bound to one another not only by miraculous moments, but also by desperation, blood, loss and even shame'.[99] This informs Kotrosits and Taussig's main thesis that 'Mark's insistence on experiences of trauma, conflict and loss alongside and sewn into, those of healing, beauty and connection provides a new lens through which to think about individuals in the wake of painful experiences'.[100] This is perhaps never more explicit than in Mark's portrayal of a Jesus demonstrating unfettered emotional affective responses to particular experiences and circumstances. Perhaps the most forceful instance of such distress is in Gethsemane (Mk 14:32-42), where Jesus, faced with the prospect of his imminent and violent death, is pictured as 'distressed' (ἐκθαμβεῖσθαι) and troubled (ἀδημονεῖν) (or, as the NRSV dramatically translates, 'agitated'). He declares, 'I am deeply grieved (Περίλυπ ός) even to death (ἕως θανάτου)' (Mk 14:34). Exegetes underscore the fact that emotions such as grief carried particular overtones of femininity and weakness in the ancient world. Indeed, for Hellenistic philosophy, it was among the classic passions. Grief in such contexts could denote retreat from approaching conflict or function as a symbol of retribution for wrongdoing or guilt.[101] Uncontrolled emotional responses implied, for males, a 'loss of control of the physical body', and often inferred a person's moral character as feeble.[102] Roman literature attests that males strategically monitored excessive manifestations of emotion. Seneca censured an affiliate's performance of grief at his child's death as feminine and disproportionate: 'You are like a woman in the way you take your son's

97. Kotrosits and Taussig, *Re-reading*, 43.

98. Kotrosits and Taussig, *Re-reading*, 44.

99. Kotrosits and Taussig, *Re-reading*, 48.

100. Kotrosits and Taussig, *Re-reading*, 159.

101. Donald Senior, *The Passion of Jesus in the Gospel of Luke* (Collegeville: Liturgical Press, 1989), 86–7.

102. Anthony Corbeill, *Nature Embodied: Gesture in Ancient Rome* (Princeton: Princeton University Press, 2006), 68, 76.

death.'[103] Dietmar Neufeld corroborates such dynamics in stating: 'This valorisation of constructing an external stoic facade over family grief was expressed in a related way by males taking responsibility for properly maintaining the cult of the dead – including the cult of the ancestors in Rome. Such a responsibility dictates that they did not parade their emotions of grief openly.'[104] As a result of grief's status within ancient contexts, many commentators on the Gethsemane episode are keen to differentiate this instance as a-typical of Jesus's character and demeanour in the wider gospel. Laura Sweat does not deny that 'Jesus is utterly distraught in Gethsemane' but also is keen to ensure that this outburst is unique in character 'take[ing] Mark's readers by surprise.'[105] Susan Garrett, in a similar vein, deflects distress and emotion from Jesus's broader identity, and sees this instance as a peculiar experience of passions of the flesh: 'Although in his spirit he desired to obey God, his fleshly desire was to avoid treading the path that he knew God had laid out for him. Thus with respect to his resolve, Jesus was momentarily divided.'[106]

Such calculated censoring of emotional responses of grief and distress can be allied with the contemporary Western preferences for the policing of inappropriate affective responses. Jennifer Poole and Jennifer Ward, in their provocative essay 'Breaking Open the Bone: Storying, Sanism and Mad Grief', note that in Western contexts good grief (normative grief) is 'quiet, tamed, dry and controlled … It has a time limit and a limit on the range and intensity of goods … [it is] gendered, staged, linear, white and bound by privilege and reason.'[107] In light of such cultural preferences, it is perhaps little surprise that *DSM-5* now includes 'Complicated Grief Disorder', which can be pathologized and medicated immediately following a loved one's death.[108] Such processes bolster the picture of normal grief as something which 'does not make a scene, it does not scream, it does not soil its pants in shock … It does not resist the pathology of naming, it does not resist "expert" information and referral.'[109] Poole and Ward, in response to such pathologizing interventions, posit what they term 'mad grief': 'a resistance practice that allows, speaks, names, affords, welcomes and stories the

103. Seneca, *Ep* 99.2, cited in Dietmar Neufeld, *Mockery and Secretism in the Social World of Mark's Gospel* (London: Bloomsbury T&T Clark, 2014), 163.

104. Neufeld, *Mockery*, 163.

105. Laura Sweat, *The Theological Role of Paradox in the Gospel of Mark* (London: Bloomsbury T&T Clark, 2013), 124.

106. Susan R. Garrett, *The Temptations of Jesus in Mark's Gospel* (Grand Rapids: Eerdmans Publishing, 1998), 96.

107. Jennifer Poole and Jennifer Ward, 'Breaking Open the Bone: Storying, Sanism and Mad Grief', in LeFrançois et al. (eds), *Mad*, 94–104, 95.

108. Virginia Hughes, 'Shades of Grief: When Does Mourning Become a Mental Illness?' *Scientific American*, 1 June 2011. Available online at: https://www.scientificamerican.com/article/shades-of-grief/.

109. Poole and Ward, 'Breaking', 95.

subjugated sense of less that comes to us all'. And, in this 'Mad turn', they 'seek to start a conversation not about how to progress, recover and "get over" pain and loss, but how to "get under" it, feel it, and claim it as it comes'.[110] No more affective, in this sense, is Mark's way of discipleship imaged as a literal 'getting under' an instrument of torture (Mk 8:34-35). In short, the Gospel of Mark, in Ahmed's terms, could be perceived as a 'kill-joy' text. It disrupts the Bible's status as a 'happy object' and the 'glory language of conventional Christianity'.[111] This affective alienation is crucial in reframing those 'scenes in contemporary America' in which, as Kotrosits and Taussig submit,

> the Bible is literally waved over losses and trauma as a kind of magic wand. Even when this does not happen explicitly, for most of us a subtext remains that the Bible is the answer to everything. This untenable proposal is clear and dangerous. Even if the Bible contains support of slavery, women's subservience, overblown claims of righteousness and truth, and many other damaging texts nevertheless returning to it will be good for everyone.[112]

Conclusion

In recent years, and largely in response to moves in positive psychology, a happiness turn has captured Western imaginations. Constructed views of 'happiness', however, often perpetuate normative scripts, and so-called affect aliens who do not fit these patterns are displaced and stigmatized as 'other'. Inspired by Ahmed's important work on the cultural affects of 'unhappiness archives' – histories written by the 'wretch' – those exiled from normative models of happiness and well-being (including the mad-distressed) – I went on to introduce projects which have, in different ways, initiated conversations between the Gospel of Mark and contemporary contexts indexed by what medical or social models would variously designate as 'poor mental health' or as experiencing phenomena labelled 'hallucinatory', 'delusional' or 'psychotic'. These projects did not adopt a 'therapeutic' reading strategy (which marked the readers out as 'other' in need of healing or recovery). On the contrary, these readings purposefully positioned themselves as subversions of those maps of well-being or happiness which excluded or marginalized readers' diverse embodiments and lived experiences.[113] They deconstructed ideas of happiness and well-being that the dominant culture preserved as normative and forefronted the voices of lived experience of what Kafai terms 'mad border bodies'. Such moves are vital in repositioning individuals not as objects of pathology, but rather phenomenologically as 'vehicle[s] of seeing'

110. Poole and Ward, 'Breaking', 95.
111. Kotrosits and Taussig, *Re-reading*, 169.
112. Kotrosits and Taussig, *Re-reading*, 171.
113. Pawelski, 'Today', no pages.

who 'engage in activism from the muscles and bones outward'[114] and in so doing defy the rigid dichotomies frequently constructed between sanity and madness.

The Gospel of Mark was itself constructed as an 'affective alien': capable of challenging normative scripts of distress and grief, not only in its own time, but also in contemporary Western cultures. An affect alien can generate uneasiness, it can queer and construct 'rival modes of publicness', and disconcert and unsettle the conformity, agreement and orientation towards so-called happy objects. These could be variously models of the normative family, models of normative subjectivity which do not tolerate 'other' modes of experience and label them as 'psychotic' or normative, personal, social, cultural and political preferences for certain versions of happiness and 'well-being'. While affect aliens are often 'unseated at the tables of happiness'[115] as Ashley Frawley contends, they can also radically expose, akin to Moore's satirical distortion of Rockwell's happy American family, 'social[ly] conformist feeling[s]' and transcend 'pressures upon subject[s] to conform to culturally sanctioned ideals of behaviour and disposition'.[116] In this sense, the 'affect alien' has a crucial role to play in critically interrogating broad cultural scripts surrounding happiness, well-being, distress and madness in North Atlantic contexts.

114. Kafai, 'Mad Border', no pages.
115. Ahmed, *Promise*, 20.
116. Stephen Frosh, *Feelings* (Oxford: Taylor and Francis, 2011), 53.

CONCLUSION: BEYOND BEDLAM? KEEPING OPEN[ING] MINDS IN BIBLICAL INTERPRETATION

This book has *not* been a study of those deemed 'mad' – voyeuristically parading the spectacles of those marked by their (perceived) strangeness, disorder and/or peculiarity. On the contrary, it has more directly been an interrogation of the 'sane', and the processes by which sanity is preserved and protected from madness and its supposed threats of chaos and confusion.[1] Western professional biblical studies is, I contend, subject to dominant (and dominating) political, social and cultural forces which have absorbed certain discursive frameworks, and which have indelibly shaped its conceptions of, and commentaries on, madness.[2] Regularly these represent extremes of social perception: revulsion or magnetic awe, loathing or veneration – and have accordingly played largely unacknowledged roles in the perpetuation of stereotypes of madness, and its strategic gatekeeping, within the discipline.

Psy-discourses, in particular, have leaked into the discipline's public and academic consciousness and have bolstered pathological constructions of the

1. Lucy Costa likewise notes: 'Perhaps it's time to flip the scope. Let's stop studying mentally ill people and start studying sane people, normals, well-adjusted, balanced and secure people. What do their brains look like? Why do they get the kinds of haircuts that they do? How do they behave in workplaces, at cottages in the banks? What's it like to be really rich and debt free? Let's not talk about this newly popularised notion of, "patients as teachers" and instead, discuss, "psychiatrists as bad learners." Flip the questions. Question the questioners. How many times have you been asked to participate or give your feedback on how to make the system better? Flip the scope – maybe it's time we stop answering *those* questions and have Mad Studies develop our *own* questions and research agendas' (original emphasis). Lucy Costa, 'Mad Studies – What It Is and Why You Should Care?' Blog post. Available online at: https://madstudies2014.wordpress.com/2014/10/15/mad-studies-what-it-is-and-why-you-should-care-2/.

2. Alexandra Bacopoulos-Viau and Aude Fauvel, 'The Patient's Turn Roy Porter and Psychiatry's Tales, Thirty Years On', *Medical History* 60(1) (2016), 1–18, 1.

'mad', marked by deficiency, disorder and loss of control.[3] Neoliberal policies which have understood the individual as a competitive economic unit have also dovetailed with medical models of mental illness (and their associated coercive and consumerist dimensions) in the construction of a 'normal' which seeks to close down the tolerance of difference and diversity.[4] Through the adoption of a mad studies lens within this project, I have sought to name, disturb and disrupt some of these unspoken givens[5] and expose the means by which they persist in Western biblical studies. This discipline and the broader Western academy are 'clogged in sanism'[6] and have engineered '[the] othering of unreason … resulting in it being treated in two quite divergent ways: either persecuted or lionised … [For] madness has always been a complex and ambiguous formation towards which many contradictory responses are possible, ranging from stigmatisation and horror to admiration and awe'.[7] Such viewpoints, in the words of one survivor activist, can, however, only exist 'through consensus and only persist by convention'.[8] In challenging these trends, David Wallace calls for transgressions of the 'presumption of normativity', which engage alternative perspectives and which inevitably reveal that no one holds a truly normative position. He also emphasizes the importance of 'continual reminders' of the dissolution of the normal, which he later expounds to denote 'ongoing practice'[9] within a discipline. By conceiving of madness in an alternative framework within this book, as an expressly political act and one which seeks to 'invert the language of oppression, reclaim disparaged identities and restore dignity and pride to difference',[10] I have aimed to challenge

3. Sander L. Gilman, *Difference and Pathology: Stereotypes of Sexuality, Race, and Madness* (New York: Cornell University Press, 1985), 24.

4. Moncrieff, 'Neoliberalism', 251.

5. Richard Ingram notes that '[t]he ultimate horizon that I would hope for would therefore be that if Mad Studies does enter academia that it unsettles *all* academic disciplines: That is what it should do, because universities are the place of reason. If Mad Studies achieves its objectives, it needs to have as part of its end goal the shaking up, the disturbing, of all forms of academic knowledge'. Richard Ingram, 'Doing Mad Studies: Making (Non)Sense Together', *Intersectionalities: A Global Journal of Social Work Analysis, Research, Polity, and Practice* 5(3) (2006), 11–17, 14.

6. Alex Gillis, 'The Rise of Mad Studies: A New Academic Discipline Challenges Our Ideas of What It Means to Be "Sane."' Available online at: http://www.universityaffairs.ca/features/feature-article/mad-studies/.

7. Harper, *Madness*, 9.

8. Nabbali cited by Helen Spadler and Jill Anderson, 'Unreasonable Adjustments? Applying Disability Policy to Madness and Distress', in Helen Spadler, Jill Anderson and Bob Sapey (eds), *Madness, Distress and the Politics of Disablement* (Bristol: Policy Press, 2015), 13–25, 14.

9. David Wallace, cited in Price, *Mad*, 45.

10. LeFrançois et al., 'Introducing', 10.

the normative presumption of sanity and subvert certain languages, practices and systems within the discipline in which I primarily work.[11] I have purposely deployed counter-knowledge and subjugated muted perspectives as key sites for 'contesting regimes of truth'.[12] I have joined those purveyors of radical mad studies perspectives as what the non-conformist psychiatrist Basaglia termed 'academic negative workers'[13]; consciousness-raising voices which alert others to systemic oppression. Mad-identified and m/Mad-positive academics should be highly critical of simplistic binaries of rationality/irrationality, 'dominant/subordinate, good/bad, up/down, superior/inferior'[14] and keen to 'bridge long-standing divides between scholarship and activism, theory and practice',[15] owning madness as a 'potentially rich source of knowledge'.[16] It is also my hope that m/Mad-identified scholars within the academy will also feel able to 'open up' more directly about their own experiences, rather than feel compelled to 'pass' according to discipline-endorsed norms of rationality.[17]

With this in mind, Chapter 1 attempted to outline the ways in which the ivory towers of Western academia have variously castigated, censored and exiled those perceived as 'mad' and/or 'other'. Psy-discourses and pathologizing labels have variously been projected onto certain biblical characters and scholars to either consolidate their assumed deviance or discredit their position or viewpoint. Sane privilege assumed the rational, reasonable and dispassionate individual as the 'unmarked' norm, and sanist discourses of exclusion provided ready tools by which discursive expulsions (/sectionings?) of those deemed to fall short of this norm could be accomplished.

Chapter 2 adopted a neurodiverse lens through which to approach the discourse of Jn 3:1–15. The processes by which neurotypical culture fashions and propagates narratives about an autistic 'other' (marked by deficits concerning isolation and communication etc.) were directly challenged. While Nicodemus is often labelled

11. LeFrançois et al., 'Introducing', 13.

12. LeFrançois, 'Introducing', 14.

13. Franco Basaglia, cited and discussed in LeFrançois, 'Introducing', 15.

14. LeFrançois, 'Introducing', 17.

15. LeFrançois, 'Introducing', 17.

16. Price, *Mad*, 234.

17. Jasna Russo and Peter Beresford claim that '[t]he omnipresent psychiatric narrative of mental illness has always had its counter-narrative – the life stories of people labelled mad. The relationship between these two accounts has always been one of domination: mad voices have been – and continue to be – not heard, overwritten, silenced or even erased in the course of psychiatric treatment. As survivor researchers who have had these kinds of experiences, we wish to discuss parallels between this tradition and some contemporary academic efforts that claim to disrupt it'. Jasna Russo and Peter Beresford, 'Between Exclusion and Colonisation: Seeking a Place for Mad People's Knowledge in Academia', *Disability and Society* 30 (2015), 153–7, 153.

as autistic on accounts of perceived deficits, by adopting autistic presences, and by listening to autobiographical testimonies within the interpretative process, it was submitted that the Johannine Jesus and community themselves echo many positive constructions of autistic experiences. Fluid boundaries between subject and object, characters and hearers thus demand a more participatory and neurodiverse reception of the Johannine account.

Chapter 3 sought to bring Bessie Head's semi-autobiographical 'madness narratives' into direct encounter with the stories of the Canaanite Woman and the Pythian slave girl. Head's Africana perspective moderated the whiteness and Eurocentricity of mad studies, which often overlook attention to colonization and race. All three were rendered mad 'ex-centrics', subversively troubling and disentangling not only colonial but also (neo)colonial identities. All three women were presented as wounded by racism, but also capable of performing and communicating how their breakdown was impacted by their wider context.

Chapter 4 probed the gatekeeping strategies surrounding the 'madness' of Jesus and Paul respectively. Scholarly constructions of both these 'great men' echoed stereotypical positive pictures of madness and creativity, and were also seen to rehearse neoliberal regimes of truth surrounding madness. Respectively Jesus and Paul emerged in the constructions reviewed as able agents of contemporary neoliberal cultural environments.

Chapter 5 sought to critically evaluate a 'happiness turn' within biblical studies and its associated displacements of those deemed 'affect aliens' – including the mad-distressed. [Un]happiness archives were sought through readings of biblical texts with an HVN group among others. Such groups, which intentionally separate from medical treatments of their experiences, in many ways disrupt normative cultural scripts surrounding mental health and well-being. Reflecting this stance, these readings did not adopt a therapeutic reading strategy, but rather a subversion of those maps of well-being which excluded and exiled their voices and experiences. The Gospel of Mark was then itself proposed as a 'killjoy' affect alien, challenging normative scripts of distress and grief both within its first-century context and the contemporary neoliberal West.

It is my hope that this project can stimulate the development of a certain 'transmindedness' within the discipline of Western biblical studies. This was a term coined by Anne Dalke and Clare Mullaney in their challenging article 'On Being Transminded: Disabling Achievement, Enabling Exchange'.[18] Transmindedness invites recognition of the fact that the bounded identities frequently adopted and utilized – rational/sane//irrational/mad – are conditioned by particular actions and processes – 'rationalizing'//

18. Anne Dalke and Clare Mullaney, 'On Being Transminded: Disabling Achievement, Enabling Exchange', *Disability Studies Quarterly* 34 (2014), no pages. Available online at: http://dsq-sds.org/article/view/4247/3599.

'maddening'.[19] They sought to propose ways in which 'madness' and 'sanity' long ensnared in binary frameworks might more appropriately be conceived of as interconnected, changeable and dynamic performances: 'a hybrid state that yields novel connections and perspectives'. In their words:

> 'Transminded' encompasses the inherent stretchiness of mental dis/ability, and suggests the ways in which its shape willfully molds both to and against others. We hope that this new term – not situated in psychiatry, more pliable than 'neurodiversity'– works to queer the trope of madness: 'transminded' is defined by expansion, rather than lack or impairment. It evokes multiplicity and diversity.[20]

Also challenging strict boundaries between sanity and madness, and proposing more interconnected cultures of reciprocity and inclusion, are artists and advocates The Vacuum Cleaner[21] and Hannah Hull. Their project, Madlove – A Designer Asylum, was the final exhibit in the Wellcome Collection's 2016 exhibition, *Bedlam: The Asylum and Beyond*. This sought to imagine, based on testimonies garnered from over 432 people with lived experience of mental distress in a range of settings (from high security psychiatric hospitals to activist groups), a vision of an ideal 'sanctuary' – 'a safe place to go mad'.[22] The project identified dynamics central to such a space: most fundamentally it would engage and build upon the testimonies of 'experts by experience'; it would stimulate imagination; it would consider emotional qualities; it would evoke a sensory palette; it would seek to discover what activities and facilities would work best and it would help build a team to perform and embody such a place.[23] In the artists' own words, rather than stigmatizing and censoring those considered other, 'Mad-love' can actually 'begin to [critically] understand [and interrogate] the power relations between patient and staff, lived expert and academic expert, artist and audience, neuro-diverse and neuro-typical … and start making positive change'.[24] The artists see their collaboration with 'Mad-identified' individuals as 'attempting to create a unique space where mutual care blossoms, stigma and discrimination are actively

19. Even though Dalke and Mullaney are inspired by Judith Halberstam's work *In a Queer Time and Place: Transgender Bodies, Subcultural Lives* (New York: New York University Press, 2005), it is worth noting, as Susannah Cornwall helpfully pointed out to me, that the term 'transminded' might be critiqued as an appropriation or even caricature of transgender experience: they don't seem to acknowledge this, or fully contextualize what they are doing in the context of Halberstam's broader project.

20. Dalke and Mullaney, 'On Being', no pages.

21. http://www.thevacuumcleaner.co.uk/madloveasylum.

22. 'Madlove', available online at: http://www.madlove.org.uk/.

23. 'Madlove', available online at: http://www.madlove.org.uk/.

24. 'Madlove', available online at: http://www.madlove.org.uk/.

challenged, divisions understood, and madness can be experienced in a less painful way. This temporary structure will be a reflexive and responsive space for exploring and redesigning madness'.[25] It is my hope that this book could play a part in carving such a space within Western biblical studies. In designing and embodying such a disciplinary sanctuary, all of us will need to keep open[ing] minds . . .

25. Madlove', available online at: http://www.madlove.org.uk/.

BIBLIOGRAPHY

Abernathy, David, 'Paul's Thorn in the Flesh: A Messenger of Satan?' *Neotestamentica*, Vol. 35, No. 1/2 (2001), 69–79.

Adam, A. K. M. et al., *Reading Scripture with the Church: Toward a Hermeneutic for Theological Interpretation* (Grand Rapids: Baker Academic, 2006).

Adam, A. K. M., Ascough, Richard, Gravett, Sandra, Hunt, Alice, Martin, Dale, Wimberly, Edward and Ai Yang, Seung, 'Should We Be Teaching the Historical Critical Method?' *Teaching Theology and Religion*, Vol. 12 (2009), 162–87.

Ahmed, Sara, 'The Happiness Turn', *New Formations*, Vol. 63 (2007), 7–11.

Ahmed, Sara, 'Happy Objects', in Melissa Gregg and Gregory J. Seigworth (eds), *The Affect Theory Reader* (Durham: Duke University Press, 2010), 29–51.

Ahmed, Sara, *The Promise of Happiness* (Durham: Duke University Press, 2010).

American Psychiatric Association, *Diagnostic and Statistical Manual of Mental Disorders* (3rd, 4th and 5th editions) (Washington: American Psychological Press, 1980; 2000; 2013).

Amoah, Elizabeth, 'Theological Perspective on Mutual Solidarity in the Context of Globalization: The Circle's Experience', in Mary McClintock Fulkerson and Sheila Briggs (eds), *The Oxford Handbook of Feminist Theology* (Oxford: Oxford University Press, 2012), 239–49.

Andrews, Jonathan, 'Bedlam Revisited: A History of Bethlem Hospital 1634–1770', PhD Thesis, Queen Mary, London University (1991). Available online at: https://qmro.qmul.ac.uk/xmlui/bitstream/handle/123456789/1365/ANDREWSBedlamRevisited1991.pdf?sequence=1.

Arendell, Telory Davies, *The Autistic Stage: How Cognitive Disability Changed 20th-Century Performance* (Netherlands: Sense Publishers, 2015).

Arnold, Bradley, *Christ as the Telos of Life: Moral Philosophy, Athletic Imagery, and the Aim of Philippians* (Tübingen: Mohr Siebeck, 2013).

Ascough, Richard and Cotton, Charles, *Passionate Visionary: Leadership Lessons from the Apostle Paul* (Peabody: Hendrickson Publishers, 2006).

Avalos, Hector, Melcher, Sarah, and Schipper, Jeremy (eds), *This Abled Body: Rethinking Disabilities in Biblical Studies* (Atlanta: Society of Biblical Literature, 2007).

Bacopoulos-Viau, Alexandra and Fauvel, Aude, 'The Patient's Turn Roy Porter and Psychiatry's Tales, Thirty Years On', *Medical History*, Vol. 60, No. 1 (2016), 1–18.

Bakker, Pamela, 'A Critical Analysis of the Plays of Sarah Daniels', PhD Thesis, University of Sheffield (1996). Available online at: https://core.ac.uk/download/files/139/9554313.pdf.

Banana, Canaan, *Come and Share: An Introduction to Christian Theology* (Gweru: Mambo Press, 1991).

Barclay, William, *The Acts of the Apostles* (Edinburgh: Saint Andrew Press, 1953).

Barthes, Roland, *Image, Music, Text* (London: Fontana Press, 1977).

Bartleet, Carina, 'Eve's Side of It: Sarah Daniels' Biblical Revision', in Colette Rayment and Mark Levon Byrne (eds), *Seeking the Centre: 2001 International Religion, Literature and the Arts Conference Proceedings* (Sydney: RLA Press, 2002), 191–203.

Bassler, Jouette M., 'Mixed Signals: Nicodemus in the Fourth Gospel', *Journal of Biblical Literature*, Vol. 108, No. 4 (1989), 635–46.

Bauer, Jack et al. 'Narrative Identity and Eudaimonic Wellbeing', *Journal of Happiness Studies*, Vol. 9 (2008), 81–104.

Baumgarten, Albert I., *Elias Bickerman as a Historian of the Jews: A Twentieth Century Tale* (Tübingen: Mohr Siebeck, 2010).

Beard, Mary, 'The Public Voice of Women', *London Review of Books*, Vol. 36, No. 6 (2014), 11–14.

Bell, Matthew, *Melancholia: The Western Malady* (Cambridge: Cambridge University Press, 2014).

Bellinzoni, Arthur J., *The New Testament: An Introduction to Biblical Scholarship* (Oregon: Wipf and Stock, 2016).

Beresford, Peter, 'Foreword', in Brenda LeFrançois et al. (eds), *Mad Matters* (Ontario: Canadian Scholars Press, 2013), ix–xii.

Beresford, Peter, 'Social Work and a Social Model of Madness and Distress: Developing a Viable Role for the Future', *Social Work & Social Sciences Review*, Vol. 12, No. 2 (2005), 59–73.

Beveridge, Allan, *Portrait of the Psychiatrist as a Young Man: The Early Writing and Work of R. D. Laing* (Oxford: Oxford University Press, 2011).

Biklen, Douglas, *Autism and the Myth of the Person Alone* (New York: New York University Press, 2005).

Biklen, Douglas, 'Review of Representing Autism: Culture, Narrative, Fascination', *Journal of Literary & Cultural Disability Studies*, Vol. 3, No. 1 (2009), 107–109. Available online at: http://muse.jhu.edu/journals/jlc/summary/v003/3.1.biklen.html.

Blackman, Lisa, 'Affective Politics, Debility and Hearing Voices: Towards a Feminist Politics of Ordinary Suffering', *Feminist Review* (2015), 25–41.

Blackman, Lisa, *Hearing Voices: Embodiment and Experience* (London: Free Association Press, 2001).

Blackman, Lisa, *Immaterial Bodies: Affect, Embodiment, Mediation* (Thousand Oaks: Sage Publications, 2012).

Blomberg, Craig, 'The Globalization of Biblical Interpretation: A Test Case John 3–4', *Bulletin for Biblical Research*, Vol. 5 (1995), 1–15.

Bloomquist, L. Gregory, 'Eyes Wide Open, Seeing Nothing: The Challenge of the Gospel of John's Non-vizualizable Texture for Readings Using Visual Texture', Saint Paul University Faculty of Theology. Available online at: http://www.religion.emory.edu/faculty/robbins/Pdfs/Bloomquist%20Sawyer%20presentation.pdf.

Boesak, Allan Aubrey, *Pharaohs on Both Sides of the Blood-Red Waters: Prophetic Critique on Empire, Resistance, Justice and the Power of the Hopeful Sizwe – A Transatlantic Conversation* (Oregon: Wipf and Stock, 2017).

Braidotti, Rosi, *The Posthuman* (London: Polity Press, 2013).

Brant, Jo-Ann, *John* (Grand Rapids: Baker Academic, 2011).

Brown, Robyn Lewis, 'The Absence of Psychiatric C/S/X Perspectives in Academic Discourse: Consequences and Implications', *Disability Studies Quarterly*, Vol. 33 (2013). Available online at: http://dsq-sds.org/article/view/3433/3198.

Brown, Scott G., 'Review, The Secret Gospel of Mark Unveiled: Imagined Rituals of Sex, Death, and Madness in a Biblical Forgery', *RBL* (15 September 2007). Available online at: http://www.bookreviews.org/pdf/5627_5944.pdf.

Browning, W. R., *A Dictionary of the Bible* (Oxford: Oxford University Press, 2009). Available online at: http://www.oxfordbiblicalstudies.com/article/opr/t94/e1180.

Burke, Tony (ed.), *Ancient Gospel or Modern Forgery?: The Secret Gospel of Mark in Debate* (Oregon: Wipf and Stock, 2011).

Burstow, Bonnie, 'A Rose by Any Other Name: Naming and the Battle against Psychiatry', in Brenda LeFrançois et al. (eds), *Mad Matters* (Ontario: Canadian Scholars Press, 2013), 79–90.

Butler, Shane and Purves, Alex, *Synaesthesia and the Ancient Senses* (London: Routledge, 2014).

Campbell, Fiona, *Contours of Ableism: The Production of Disability and Ableness* (London: Palgrave Macmillan, 2009).

Campion, Jane, 'Writing in the Margins: Exploring the Borderland in the Work of Janet Frame and Anna Ball', *eSharp* 5, Borders and Boundaries, 1–18. Available online at: http://www.gla.ac.uk/media/media_41163_en.pdf.

Capps, Donald, 'Beyond Schweitzer and the Psychiatrists: Jesus as Fictive Personality', in J. Harold Ellens and Wayne G. Rollins (eds), *Psychology and the Bible: From Christ to Jesus* (Westport: Praeger Publishers, 2004), 89–124.

Capps, Donald, *Jesus the Village Psychiatrist* (Louisville: Westminster John Knox Press, 2008).

Carey, Greg, 'Finding Happiness in Apocalyptic Literature', in Brent Strawn (ed.), *The Bible and the Pursuit of Happiness: What the Old and New Testaments Teach Us about the Good Life* (Oxford: Oxford University Press, 2012), 203–23.

Carson, Anne, 'The Gender of Sound', in Ann Carson, *Glass, Irony and God* (New York: New Directions Publishing Corporation, 1995), 119–39.

Carson, D. A., *The Gospel According to John* (Downers Grove: IVP, 1991).

Castelli, Elizabeth, *Imitating Paul: A Discourse of Power* (Louisville: Westminster John Knox Press, 1991).

Cate, Robert L., *One Untimely Born: The Life and Ministry of the Apostle Paul* (Macon: Mercer University Press, 2006).

Chabwera, Elinettie Kwanjana, 'Madness and Spirituality in Bessie Head's *A Question of Power*', *African Studies Bulletin*, Vol. 71 (Winter 2009/10), 59–70.

Chappell, Anne Louise, 'Still Out in the Cold: People with Learning Difficulties and the Social Model of Disability', in Tom Shakespeare (ed.), *The Disability Reader: Social Science Perspectives* (London: Continuum, 1998), 211–20.

Charlesworth, James H., 'Should Specialists in Jesus Research Include Psychobiography?', in James H. Charlesworth, Brian Rhea and Petr Pokorn (eds), *Jesus Research: New Methodologies and Perceptions* (Grand Rapids: Eerdmans Publishing Company, 2014), 436–67.

Charry, Ellen, *God and the Art of Happiness* (Grand Rapids: William Eerdmans Publishing Company, 2010).

Chew, Kristina, 'Odysseus and "the Fools": Applying Concepts of Neurodiversity to the Ancient World', in Alexandra Perry and Chris Herrara (eds), *Ethics and Neurodiversity* (Newcastle: Cambridge Scholars Publishing, 2013), 276–85.

Choi, Jin Young, *Postcolonial Discipleship of Embodiment: An Asian and Asian American Feminist Reading of the Gospel of Mark* (New York: Springer, 2015).

Clark, Hilary, *Depression and Narrative: Telling the Dark* (New York: SUNY Press, 2008).

Clegg, Sue, 'The Space of Academia: Privilege, Agency and the Erasure of Affect', in C. Maxwell and P. Aggleton, *Privilege, Agency and Affect: Understanding the Production and Effects of Action* (New York: Palgrave Macmillan, 2013).

Clements, E. Anne, *Mothers on the Margin?: The Significance of the Women in Matthew's Genealogy* (Oregon: Pickwick Publications, 2014).

Clifton, Jeremy, 'Book Review, The Eudaimonic Turn: Well-Being in Literary Studies', *Journal of Psychology in Africa*, Vol. 24 (2014), 123–4.

Cloete, Nettie, 'Psychological Afflictions as Expressed in Bessie Head's *A Question of Power* and Tsitsi Dangarembga's *Nervous Conditions*', *Uterator*, Vol. 21, No. 1 (2000), 37–52.

Cohen, Bruce, *Psychiatric Hegemony: A Marxist Theory of Mental Illness* (Basingstoke: Palgrave Macmillan, 2016).

Collins, Adela Yarbro, 'Paul's Disability: The Thorn in His Flesh', in C. Moss and J. Schipper (eds), *Disability Studies and Biblical Literature* (Waco: Baylor University Press, 2006), 169–80.

Colson, Robert, 'The Performance of Madness as Resistance in Nuruddin Farah's Close Sesame', *Ariel: A Review of International English Literature*, Vol. 46, No. 4 (2015), 1–35.

Cook, Christopher, 'The Prophet Samuel, Hypnagogic Hallucinations and the Voice of God – Psychiatry and Sacred Texts', *British Journal of Psychiatry*, Vol. 203 (2013), 380–80.

Cook, Christopher, 'Psychiatry in Scripture: Sacred Texts and Psychopathology', *The Psychiatrist*, Vol. 36 (2012), 225–9.

Cooper, Michael, 'The Transformational Leadership of the Apostle Paul: A Contextual and Biblical Leadership for Contemporary Ministry', *Christian Education Journal*, Vol. 2, No. 1 (2005), 48–61.

Corbeill, Anthony, *Nature Embodied: Gesture in Ancient Rome* (Princeton: Princeton University Press, 2006).

Corker, Marian (ed.), *Disability Discourse* (Buckingham: Open University Press, 1999).

Costa, Lucy, 'Mad Studies – What It Is and Why You Should Care', Blog post. Available online at: https://madstudies2014.wordpress.com/2014/10/15/mad-studies-what-it-is-and-why-you-should-care-2/.

Couch, Mal (ed.), *A Bible Handbook to the Acts of the Apostles* (Grand Rapids: Kregal Publications, 1999).

Couser, G. Thomas, *Signifying Bodies: Disability in Contemporary Life Writing* (Michigan: University of Michigan Press, 2009).

Craig Evans, *Luke* (Understanding the Bible Commentary Series) (Grand Rapids: Baker Books, 2011).

Cross, Simon, 'Bedlam in Mind: Seeing and Reading Historical Images of Madness', *European Journal of Cultural Studies*, Vol. 15, No. 1 (2012), 19–34.

Cross, Simon, *Mediating Madness: Mental Distress and Cultural Representation* (London: Palgrave Macmillan, 2010).

Crossley James, *Jesus in an Age of Neoliberalism: Quests, Scholarship and Ideology* (Durham: Acumen Press, 2012).

Cuneo, Terence, 'Liturgy and the Moral Life', in Christian B. Miller, R. Michael Furr, Angela Knobel and William Fleeson, *Character: New Directions from Philosophy, Psychology, and Theology* (Oxford: Oxford University Press, 2015), 572–89.

Cushman, Philip, *Constructing the Self, Constructing America: A Cultural History of Psychotherapy* (Reading, MA: Addison-Wesley, 1995).

Dalke, Anne and Mullaney, Clare, 'On Being Transminded: Disabling Achievement, Enabling Exchange', *Disability Studies Quarterly*, Vol. 34 (2014), no pages. Available online at: http://dsq-sds.org/article/view/4247/3599.

Davidson, Joyce and Smith, Mick, 'Autistic Autobiographies and More-Than-Human Emotional Geographies', *Society and Space*, Vol. 27 (2009), 898–916.

Davis, Lennard, *The End of Normal: Identity in a Biocultural Era* (Michigan: University of Michigan Press, 2013).

de Vries, Manfred F. R. Kets, *Lessons on Leadership by Terror: Finding Shaka Zulu in the Attic* (Edward Elgar Publishing, 2004).

de Vries, Manfred F. R. Kets, 'The Spirit of Despotism: Understanding the Tyrant within Human Relations', *Human Relations*, Vol. 59, No. 2 (2006), 195–220.

Debling, Heather, '"How Will They Ever Heal …?" Bearing Witness to Abuse and the Importance of Female Community in Sarah Daniels's *Beside Herself, Head-Rot Holiday*, and *The Madness of Esme and Shaz*', *Modern Drama*, Vol. 51, No. 2 (2008), 259–73.

Dent, Shirley, 'Don't Diagnose Fictional Characters', Guardian Book Blog (2007). Available online at: http://www.theguardian.com/books/booksblog/2007/apr/04/dontdiagnosefi ctionalcharacters.

Diamond, Shaindl, 'What Makes Us a Community? Reflections on Building Solidarity in Anti-sanist Praxis', in Brenda LeFrançois et al. (eds), *Mad Matters* (Ontario: Canadian Scholars Press, 2013), 64–78.

Dillon, Jacqui and Longden, Eleanor, 'Hearing Voices Group: Creating Safe Spaces to Share Taboo Experiences', in Marius Romme and Sandra Escher (eds), *Psychosis as a Personal Crisis: An Experience-Based Approach* (London: Routledge, 2011), chapter 12, digital version.

Dingwall-Jones, Christopher, 'Antic Dispositions: The Representation of Madness in Modern British Theatre' PhD Thesis, University of Kent (2014). Available online at: https://kar.kent.ac.uk/48042/1/130C%20D J%20Final%20(Amendments,%20 Redacted).pdf.

Dodd, C. H., 'The Mind of Paul: I', *New Testament Studies* (1953), 67–82.

Donaldson, Laura, 'Gospel Hauntings: The Postcolonial Demons of New Testament Criticism', in Fernando Segovia and Stephen Moore (eds), *Postcolonial Biblical Criticism: Interdisciplinary Intersections* (London: T&T Clark, 2007), 97–113.

Donnelly, Taylor, 'Vogue Diagnosis: The Function of Madness in Twentieth Century American Literature', Doctoral dissertation (2012). Retrieved from University of Oregon Graduate Dissertations and Theses. Available online at: https://www.google.co.uk/url?url=https://scholarsbank.uoregon.edu/xmlui/bitstream/handle/1794/12366/Donnelly_oregon_0171A_10353.pdf%3Bsequence%3D1&rct=j&frm=1&q=&esrc=s&sa=U&ved=0ahUKEwiB7sGQpL7VAhXiCsAKHW6qCGIQFggUMAA&usg=AFQjCNGMwY228bevkvzBN6CTNPDGznaDGg.

Dormandy, Richard, *The Madness of St Paul* (Alton: Redemptorist Publications, 2011).

Douglas, Susan, *Understanding Actions, States, and Events: Verb Learning in Children with Autism* (Berlin: Walter de Gruyter, 2012).

Dube, Musa, *Postcolonial Feminist Interpretation of the Bible* (St Louis: Chalice Press, 2000).

Dunn, James D. G., *The Theology of Paul the Apostle* (Grand Rapids: William Eerdmans, 2006).

Dunn, Leslie, *Embodied Voices: Representing Female Vocality in Western Culture* (Cambridge: Cambridge University Press, 1996).

Dykstra, Laurel and Myers, Ched (eds), *Liberating Biblical Study: Scholarship, Art, and Action in Honor of the Center and Library for the Bible and Social Justice* (Oregon: Wipf and Stock, 2011).

Elliott, Carl, 'The Tyranny of Happiness', in Erik Parens (ed.), *Enhancing Human Traits: Ethical and Social Implications* (Washington: Georgetown University Press, 1998), 177–88.

Eyer, Shane, 'The Strange Case of the Secret Gospel According to Mark', *Alexandria: The Journal of the Western Cosmological Traditions*, Vol. 2 (1995), 103–29.

Fabris, Erik, 'Experiences Labelled Psychotic: A Settler's Autoethnography beyond Psychosic Narrative', PhD Thesis, University of Toronto (2012). Available online at: https://tspace.library.utoronto.ca/bitstream/1807/33990/1/Fabris_Erick_P_201211_PhD_thesis.pdf.

Fabris, Erick, *Tranquil Prisons: Chemical Incarceration under Community Treatment Orders* (Toronto: University of Toronto Press, 2011).

Fanon, Frantz, *Black Skin, White Masks*, trans. Charles Lam Markmann (New York: Grove, 1967 [original French 1952]).

Fee, Dwight, 'The Broken Dialogue: Mental Illness as Discourse and Experience', in Dwight Fee (ed.), *Pathology and the Postmodern: Mental Illness as Discourse and Experience* (London: Sage Publications, 2000), 1–17.

Feinstein, Adam, *A History of Autism: Conversations with the Pioneers* (Chichester: Wiley Blackwell, 2010).

Finkelstein, Marvin, 'The Ivory Tower in a Flat World: The University and Applied Sociology in the Global Economy', *Journal of Applied Social Science*, Vol. 1, No. 1 (2007), 16–22.

Fiorenza, Elisabeth Schüssler, *Democratizing Biblical Studies: Toward an Emancipatory Educational Space* (Louisville: Westminster John Knox Press, 2009).

Fiorenza, Elisabeth Schüssler, 'Introduction', in Elisabeth Schüssler Fiorenza and Kent Harold Richards (eds), *Transforming Graduate Biblical Education: Ethos and Discipline* (Atlanta: SBL, 2010), 1–18.

Fiorenza, Elisabeth Schüssler, *Wisdom Ways: Introducing Feminist Biblical Interpretation* (New York: Orbis Books, 2001).

Fisher, Evelyn, 'Autism in Literature the Negotiation between Syndrome and Silent Wisdom' (2010). Available online at: http://aladinrc.wrlc.org/bitstream/handle/1961/9279/Fisher,%20Evelyn%20%20Spring%20'10%20(P).pdf?sequence=1.

Fortinash, Katherine M. and Worret, Patricia A. Holoday, *Psychiatric Mental Health Nursing* (St Louis: Mosby Incorporated, 1996).

Foucault, Michel, *History of Madness*, trans. Jonathan Murphy and Jean Khalfa (London: Routledge, 2006).

Foucault, Michel, *Madness and Civilisation: A History of Insanity in the Age of Reason* (New York: Vintage, 1962).

Fox, Ann and Lipkin, Joan, 'Res(Crip)ting Feminist Theater Through Disability Theater: Selections from the DisAbility Project', *NWSA Journal*, Vol. 14, No. 3 (2002), 77–98.

Fox, Matthew, 'Review of Maurizio Bettini, *Voci: Antropologia sonora del mondo antico. Saggi, 892*. Torino: Einaudi, 2008', *Bryn Mawr Classical Review* (2008). Available online at: http://bmcr.brynmawr.edu/2008/2008-12-09.html.

Frawley, Ashley, 'Happiness Research: A Review of Critiques', *Sociology Compass*, Vol. 9, No. 1 (2015), 62–77.

Frith, Uta, *Autism: Explaining the Enigma* (Oxford: Blackwell, 2003).

Frosh, Stephen, *Feelings* (Oxford: Taylor and Francis, 2011).

Fulford, K. W. M., Davies, Martin, Gipps, Richard, Graham, George, Sadler, John and Thornton, Tim (eds), *The Oxford Handbook of Philosophy and Psychiatry* (Oxford: Oxford University Press, 2013).

Fullerton, Susannah, *Happily Ever After: Celebrating Jane Austen's Pride and Prejudice* (London: Frances Lincoln, 2013).

Garland, David E., *Second Corinthians* (Nashville: Broadman and Holman, 1999).

Garrett, Susan R., *The Temptations of Jesus in Mark's Gospel* (Grand Rapids: Eerdmans Publishing, 1998).

Ghaemi, Nassir, 'Depression in Command: In Times of Crisis, Mentally Ill Leaders Can See What Others Don't', *Wallstreet Journal* (2011), no pages. Available online at: http://www.wsj.com/articles/SB10001424053111904800304576474451102761640.

Ghaemi, Nassir, *A First-Rate Madness: Uncovering the Links between Leadership and Mental Illness* (London: Penguin, 2011).

Gillis, Alex, 'The Rise of Mad Studies: A New Academic Discipline Challenges Our Ideas of What It Means to Be "Sane"'. Available online at: http://www.universityaffairs.ca/features/feature-article/mad-studies/.

Gilman, Sander L., 'Book review: Media Madness: Public Images of Mental Illness by O. F. Wahl (1995). New Brunswick, New Jersey: Rutgers University Press', *Psychiatric Services*, Vol. 48, No. 2 (1997).

Gilman, Sander L., *Difference and Pathology: Stereotypes of Sexuality, Race, and Madness* (New York: Cornell University Press, 1985).

Glezerman, Tatyana B., *Autism and the Brain: Neurophenomenological Interpretation* (New York: Springer, 2013).

Goffman, Erving, *Asylums: Essays on the Social Situation of Mental Patients and Other Inmates* (Chicago: Aldine, 1961).

Gold, Joel and Gold, Ian, *Suspicious Minds: How Culture Shapes Madness* (New York: Free Press, 2015).

Good, Byron J., Good, Mary-Jo DelVecchio, Hyde, Sandra Teresa, and Pinto, Sarah, 'Introduction: Postcolonial Disorders: Reflections on Subjectivity in the Contemporary World', in Mary-Jo DelVecchio Good, Sandra Teresa Hyde, Sarah Pinto and Byron J. Good (eds), *Postcolonial Disorders* (California: University of California Press, 2008), 1–40.

Goodley, Dan, *Dis/ability Studies: Theorising Disablism and Ableism* (New York: Routledge, 2014).

Goodley, Dan, Lawthom, Rebecca and Runswick Cole, Katherine, 'Posthuman Disability Studies', *Subjectivity*, Vol. 7 (2014), 342–361.

Goodman, Lizbeth, *Literature and Gender* (Hove: Psychology Press, 1996).

Gorman, Rachel, 'Mad Nation? Thinking through Race, Class and Mad Identity Politics', in Brenda LeFrançois et al. (eds), *Mad Matters* (Ontario: Canadian Scholars Press, 2013), 269–80.

Goulder, Michael, 'Nicodemus', *Scottish Journal Theology* 44 (1991), 153–68.

Graby, Steve, 'Neurodiversity: Bridging the Gap between the Disabled People's Movement and the Mental Health System Survivor's Movement?' in H. Spandler et al. (eds), *Madness, Distress and the Politics of Disablement* (Bristol: Policy Press, 2015), 231–43.

Grandin, Temple with Scariano, Margaret, *Emergence: Labeled Autistic* (Florida: Costello, 1986).

Green, Barbara, *Jeremiah and God's Plan of Wellbeing* (Columbia: University of South Carolina Press, 2013).

Green, Joel, 'We Had to Celebrate and Rejoice! Happiness in the Topsy-Turvy World of Luke-Acts', in Brent Strawn (ed.), *The Bible and the Pursuit of Happiness: What the Old and New Testaments Teach Us about the Good Life* (Oxford: Oxford University Press, 2012), 169–86.

Green, Mark, 'DSM-5: Rewriting the Bible', *Progress in Neurology and Psychiatry* (2013), 24–6.

Haddon, Mark, *The Curious Incident of the Dog in the Night-Time* (New York: Doubleday, 2003).

Hall, Kim Q., 'Cripping Sustainability, Realizing Food Justice', in Sarah Jaquette Ray and Jay Sibara (eds), *Disability Studies and the Environmental Humanities: Toward an Eco-Crip Theory* (Nebraska: University of Nebraska Press, 2017), Chapter 15.

Halberstam, Judith, *In a Queer Time and Place: Transgender Bodies, Subcultural Lives* (New York: New York University Press, 2005).

Halperin, David, *Seeking Ezekiel: Text and Psychology* (Pennsylvania: Pennsylvania State University Press, 1993).

Halperin, Laura, *Intersections of Harm: Narratives of Latina Deviance and Defiance* (New Jersey: Rutgers University Press, 2013).

Halpern, Richard, *Norman Rockwell: The Underside of Innocence* (Chicago: University of Chicago Press, 2006).

Halvor Moxnes, *Putting Jesus in His Place: A Radical Vision of Household and Kingdom* (Louisville: Westminster John Knox, 2003).

Handel, Michael I. and Walling, Karl-Friedrich, *Strategic Logic and Political Rationality: Essays in Honor of Michael I. Handel* (Hove: Psychology Press, 2003).

Happé, Francesca and Frith, Uta, *Autism and Talent* (Oxford: Oxford University Press, 2010).

Harjunen, Hannele, *Neoliberal Bodies and the Gendered Fat Body* (London: Routledge, 2016).

Harner, Michael, *The Way of the Shaman* (San Francisco: Harper, 1980).

Harnick, Douglas, *Paul among the Post-Liberals: Pauline Theology beyond Christendom and Modernity* (Grand Rapids: Brazos Press, 2003).

Harper, Stephen, *Madness, Power and the Media: Class, Gender and Race in Popular Presentations of Mental Illness* (Basingstoke: Palgrave Macmillan, 2009).

Harpin, Anna and Foster, Juliet, 'Introduction: Locating Madness and Performance', in Anna Harpin and Juliet Foster (eds), *Performance, Madness and Psychiatry: Isolated Acts* (Basingstoke: Palgrave Macmillan, 2014), 1–18.

Harvey, D., *A Brief History of Neoliberalism* (Oxford: Oxford University Press, 2005).

Hauerwas, Stanley, 'Community and Diversity: The Tyranny of Normality', in John Swinton (ed.), *Critical Reflections on Stanley Hauerwas' Theology of Disability* (New York: Haworth Pastoral Press, 2004), 37–43.

Head, Bessie, *A Question of Power* (South Africa: Heinemann, 1974).

Heighton, Luke, 'Reason Dazzled: Klimt, Krakauer and the Eyes of Medusa', in Gemma Blackshaw and Sabine Wieber (eds), *Journeys into Madness: Mapping Mental Illness in the Austro-Hungarian Empire* (Oxford: Berghahn Books, 2012), 145–60.

Heinämaa, Sara, *European Rationality in the Break from Modernity: Studies in Phenomenology and Hermeneutics*, Project website: http://www.helsinki.fi/erbm/description/index.html.

Herrstrom, David Sten, *The Book of Unknowing: A Poet's Response to the Gospel of John* (Oregon: Wipf and Stock, 2012).

Hisey, Alan and Beck, James S. P., 'Paul's "Thorn in the Flesh": A Paragnosis', *Journal of Bible and Religion*, Vol. 29, No. 2 (1961), 125–9.

Hock, Dee, 'The Art of Chaordic Leadership'. Available online at: http://www.meadowlark.co/the_art_of_chaordic_leadership_hock.pdf.

Hollenbach, Paul W., 'Jesus, Demoniacs, and Public Authorities: A Socio-historical Study', *Journal of the American Academy of Religion*, Vol. 49, No. 4 (1981), 567–88.

Homans, Peter, *Jung in Context: Modernity and the Making of a Psychology* (Chicago: University of Chicago Press, 1979).

Horsley, Richard, *Jesus and the Powers: Conflict, Covenant and the Hope of the Poor* (Minneapolis: Augsburg Fortress, 2011).

Howell, Alison, *Madness in International Relations: Psychology, Security, and the Global Governance of Mental Health* (London: Routledge, 2011).

Hubert, Susan, *Questions of Power: The Politics of Women's Madness Narratives* (Newark: University of Delaware, 2002).

Hübner, Sabine R. and Ratzan, David M., 'Fatherless Antiquity? Perspectives on Fatherlessness in the Ancient Mediterranean', in Sabine R. Hübner and David M. Ratzan (eds), *Growing Up Fatherless in Antiquity* (Cambridge: Cambridge University Press, 2009), 3–28.

Hudon, Mark, 'Norman Rockwell: Lost America Captured in Kitsch', *The Telegraph*, 2 December 2010. Available online at: http://www.telegraph.co.uk/culture/art/art-features/8177324/Norman-Rockwell-lost-America-captured-in-Kitsch.html.

Hughes, Richard, 'The Cain Complex and the Apostle Paul', *Soundings: An Interdisciplinary Journal*, Vol. 65, No. 1 (1982), 5–22.

Hughes, Virginia, 'Shades of Grief: When Does Mourning Become a Mental Illness?', *Scientific American*, 1 June 2011. Available online at: https://www.scientificamerican.com/article/shades-of-grief/.

Huntsman, Alonzo, 'Authoring Authority: The Apostle Paul and the Prophet Joseph Smith – A Critical Comparison of Texts and Power in the Generation of Religious Community', *CGU Theses & Dissertations* Paper 28 (2012). Available online at: http://scholarship.claremont.edu/cgu_etd/28.

Hyer, O. Q., 'On the Mental Health of Jesus Christ', *Journal of Psychology and Theology*, Vol. 5 (1977), 3–12.

Ingram, Richard, 'Doing Mad Studies: Making (Non)Sense Together', *Intersectionalities: A Global Journal of Social Work Analysis, Research, Polity, and Practice*, Vol. 5, No. 3 (2006), 11–17.

Ingram, Richard, 'From Mad Movement to Mad Studies'. Available online at: http://www.academia.edu/15986428/From_the_Mad_movement_to_Mad_studies.

Inkson, Kerr, *Understanding Careers: The Metaphors of Working Lives* (Thousand Oaks: Sage Publications, 2006).

Jay, Mike, *Bedlam: The Asylum and Beyond* (2016). Available online at https://wellcomecollection.org/press/bedlam-asylum-and-beyond-opens-wellcome-collection.

Jay, Mike, *This Way Madness Lies: The Asylum and Beyond* (Wellcome Collection, Thames and Hudson, 2016).

Jeffrey, Peter, 'Frequently Asked Questions about Morton Smith, the Secret Gospel of Mark, and My Book, *The Secret Gospel of Mark Unveiled*', Interview. Available online at: http://music2.princeton.edu/jeffery/smithfaq.html.

Jeffrey, Peter, *The Secret Gospel of Mark Unveiled: Imagined Rituals of Sex, Death, and Madness in a Biblical Forgery* (New Haven: Yale University Press, 2007).

Jeffrey, Peter, 'The Secret Gospel of Mark Unveiled: Reply to Scott G. Brown' (2008). Available online at: http://music2.princeton.edu/jeffery/Review%20of%20Biblical%20LiteratureJeffery%20reply%20to%20Brown.pdf.

Jensen, Robert, *Baptismal Imagery in Early Christianity: Ritual, Visual, and Theological Dimensions* (Michigan: Grand Rapids, 2012).

Jeory, Ted, 'Jesus Christ May Have Suffered Mental Health Problems', *Daily Express*, 28 August 2012. Available online at: http://www.express.co.uk/news/uk/341926/Jesus-Christ-may-have-suffered-from-mental-health-problems-claims-Church-of-England.

Jewett, Robert, *Paul the Apostle to America: Cultural Trends and Pauline Scholarship* (Louisville: Westminster John Knox Press, 1994).

Jones, Larry Paul, *The Symbol of Water in the Gospel of John* (Sheffield: Sheffield Academic Press, 1997).

Joseph, Ameil J., 'The Necessity of an Attention to Eurocentrism and Colonial Technologies: An Addition to Critical Mental Health Literature', *Disability & Society*, Vol. 30, No. 7 (2015), 1021–41.

Jurecic, Ann, 'Neurodiversity', *College English*, Vol. 69, No. 5 (2007), 421–42.

Kafai, Shayda, 'The Mad Border Body: A Political In-betweeness', *Disability Studies Quarterly*, Vol. 33 (2013). Available online at: http://dsq-sds.org/article/view/3438.

Kafer, Alison, *Feminist, Queer, Crip* (Bloomington: Indiana University Press, 2013).

Kahn, Jack, 'Racing toward Uncertainty: An Ethico-Aesthetics of Imagination'. Pomona College, Claremont, California. Available online at: http://consideringdisability.com/wp-content/uploads/2015/04/Considering-Disability-Journal.97 101.pdf.

Kalinowski, C. and Risser, P., *Identifying and Overcoming Mentalism*, InforMed Health Publishing & Training (2005). Available online at: http://www.newmediaexplorer.org/sepp/Mentalism.pdf.

Kamionkowski, S. Tamar, *Gender Reversal and Cosmic Chaos: A Study in the Book of Ezekiel* (London: Bloomsbury, 2003).

Kapstein, Helen, 'A Peculiar Shuttling Movement: Madness, Passing and Trespassing in Bessie Head's A Question of Power', in Helen Kapstein and Maxine Sample (eds), *Critical Essays on Bessie Head* (Westport, CT; London: Praeger Publishers, 2003), Contributions in Afro-American and African Studies, No. 205, 71–98.

Karlen, Arno, *Napoleon's Glands and Other Ventures in Biohistory* (New York: Grand Central Publishing, 1985).

Kartzow, Marianne Bjelland, *Destabilizing the Margins: An Intersectional Approach to Early Christian Memory* (Oregon: Wipf and Stock, 2012).

Kasher, Aryeh and Witztum, Eliezer, *King Herod: A Persecuted Persecutor: A Case Study in Psychohistory and Psychobiography* (Berlin: De Gruyter, 2008).

Kaufman, James C. (ed.), *Creativity and Mental Illness* (Cambridge: Cambridge University Press, 2014).

Kelley, Nicole, 'Review of Jeffrey's The Secret Gospel of Mark Unveiled', *Magic, Ritual, and Witchcraft*, Vol. 4 (2009), 114–17.

Keskinen, Mikko, 'Her Mistress's Voice: Gynophonocentrism in Feminist Discourses', *Journal of International Women's Studies*, Vol. 2, No. 1 (2000), 1–15.

Klauck, Hans-Josef, *Magic and Paganism in Early Christianity: The World of the Acts of the Apostles* (Edinburgh: T&T Clark, 2000).

Knowles, Caroline, *Bedlam on the Streets* (London: Routledge, 2000).

Koester, Craig, 'Theological Complexity and Characterization of Nicodemus in John's Gospel', in Christopher W. Skinner (ed.), *Characters and Characterization in the Gospel of John* (New York: Bloomsbury, 2013), 165–81.

Köstenberger, Andreas J., *John* (Grand Rapids: Baker Academic, 2004).

Kotrosits, Mai and Taussig, Hal, *Re-reading the Gospel of Mark amidst Loss and Trauma* (New York: Palgrave Macmillan, 2013).

Kroncke, Anna P., Willard, Marcy, Huckabee, Helena, *Assessment of Autism Spectrum Disorder: Critical Issues in Clinical, Forensic and School Settings* (New York: Springer, 2016).

Kruse, Colin G., *The Gospel According to John: An Introduction and Commentary* (Grand Rapids: Wm. B. Eerdmans Publishing, 2004).

Kunsthaus Baselland, 'Javier Tellez'. Available online at: https://artmap.com/baselland/exhibition/javier-te-llez-2009.

Kuppers, Petra, 'Dancing Autism: The Curious Incident of the Dog in the Nighttime and Bedlam', *Text and Performance Quarterly*, Vol. 28 (2008), 192–205.

Kuppers, Petra, *Disability and Contemporary Performance: Bodies on the Edge* (London: Routledge, 2003).

Kwok-Pui-lan, 'Reading the Christian New Testament in the Contemporary World', in Margaret Aymer, Cynthia Briggs Kittredge and David Arthur Sánchez (eds), *Fortress Commentary on the Bible: The New Testament* (Minneapolis: Fortress Press, 2014), 5–30.

Kyaga, Simon, *Creativity and Mental Illness: The Mad Genius in Question* (London: Palgrave Macmillan, 2015),

Lakes, Richard, 'Unemployed Youth and Vocational Pathways: Opportunity Structures in the New Economy', in Liv Mjelde and Richard Daly (eds), *Working Knowledge in a Globalizing World: From Work to Learning, from Learning to Work* (Bern: Peter Lang, 2006), 255–66.

Lavis, Anna, '"La Muse Malade", "The Fool's Perceptions" & "Il Furore dell'Arte": An Examination of the Socio-cultural Construction of Genius through Madness', *Anthropology & Medicine*, Vol. 12, No. 2 (2005), 151–63.

Lawrence, Louise, *Sense and Stigma in the Gospels: Depictions of Sensory-Disabled Characters* (Oxford: Oxford University Press, 2013).

Lawrence, Louise, 'Transcript of Conversations with Bridge Collective', 7 May 2015.

Le Donne, Anthony, *The Wife of Jesus: Ancient Texts and Modern Scandals* (London: Oneworld Publications, 2013).

Lear, Jonathan, *Catharsis* (Blackwell Reference). Available online at: http://www.blackwellreference.com/public/tocnode?id=g9781405141703_chunk_g978140514170313.

LeBlanc, Stephanie and Kinsella, Elizabeth Anne, 'Toward Epistemic Justice: A Critically Reflexive Examination of "Sanism" and Implications for Knowledge Generation', *Studies in Social Justice*, Vol. 10, No. 1 (2016), 59–78.

LeFrançois, Brenda, et al., 'Glossary of Terms, Madness', in Brenda LeFrançois et al. (eds), *Mad Matters* (Ontario: Canadian Scholars Press, 2013), 334–40.

LeFrançois, Brenda, et al. (eds), *Mad Matters* (Ontario: Canadian Scholars Press, 2013).

LeFrançois, Brenda, Menzies, Robert and Reaume, Geoffrey, 'Introducing Mad Studies', in Brenda LeFrançois et al. (eds), *Mad Matters* (Ontario: Canadian Scholars Press, 2013), 1–22.

Lentz, John Clayton, *Luke's Portrait of Paul* (Cambridge: Cambridge University Press, 1993).

Levin, Len and Gildea, Ruthann, 'Bibliotherapy: Tracing the Roots of a Moral Therapy Movement in the United States from the Early Nineteenth Century to the Present', *Medical Library Association*, Vol. 101, No. 2 (2013), 89–91. Available online at: http://www.ncbi.nlm.nih.gov/pmc/articles/PMC3634391/.

Levinson, Daniel, *The Seasons of a Man's Life* (New York: Ballantine Books, 1978).

Lewis, C. S., *Mere Christianity* (New York: MacMillan, 1952, revised edition).

Liegghio, Maria, 'A Denial of Being: Psychiatrization as Epistemic Violence', in Brenda LeFrançois et al. (eds), *Mad Matters* (Ontario: Canadian Scholars Press, 2013), 122–9.

Link, Bruce and Phelan, Jo, 'Conceptualising Stigma', *Annual Review of Sociology*, Vol. 27 (2001), 363–85.

Livermore, Abiel Abbot, *The Acts of the Apostles: With a Commentary* (Boston: James Munroe and Company, 1844).

Lockyer, Herbert, *All the Women of the Bible* (Grand Rapids: Zondervan, 1967).

Loubser, J. A. (Bobby), 'Media Criticism and the Myth of Paul: The Creative Genius and His Forgotten Co-workers', *Neotestamentica*, Vol. 34, No. 2 (2000), 329–45.

Love, Stuart L., *Jesus and Marginal Women: The Gospel of Matthew in Social-Scientific Perspective* (Cambridge: Clarke, 2009).

Lutz, Catherine A., 'Engendered Emotion: Gender, Power, and the Rhetoric of Emotional Control in American Discourse', in R. Harre and W. G. Parrot (eds), *The Emotions* (Thousand Oaks, CA: Sage, 1996), 152–70. Available online at: http://www.brown.uk.com/brownlibrary/EMOT.htm.

Maahs, Kenneth H., *The John You Never Knew: Decoding the Fourth Gospel* (Bern: Peter Lang Publishing, 2006).

MacDonald, Michael, *Mystical Bedlam: Madness, Anxiety and Healing in Seventeenth-Century England* (Cambridge: Cambridge University Press, 1983).

Macdonald, Nathan, 'Is There Happiness in the Torah?', in Brent Strawn (ed.), *The Bible and the Pursuit of Happiness: What the Old and New Testaments Teach Us about the Good Life* (Oxford: Oxford University Press, 2012), 57–74.

Mainwaring, Simon, *Mark, Mutuality and Mental Health* (Atlanta: SBL Press, 2014).

Malina, Bruce and Neyrey, Jerome, *Portraits of Paul: An Archaeology of Ancient Personality* (Louisville: Westminster John Knox, 1996).

Manisty, Dinah and يتسينام ةيناد, 'Madness as Textual Strategy in the Narratives of Three Egyptian Women Writers'/ثالث دنع درسلا يف ةيصن ةيجيتارتسإك نونجلا تايرصم تابتاك', *Alif: Journal of Comparative Poetics*, Vol. 14 (1994), 152–74.

Marais, Nadia, 'Happy? A Critical Analysis of Salvation in Ellen Charry That Portrays Human Flourishing as Healing, Beauty and Pleasure', *Verbum et Ecclesia*, Vol. 36, No. 1 (2015). Available online at: http://dx.doi.org/10.4102/ve.v36i1.1359.

Marlowe, Jonathan, 'Spiritual Autism' (2005). Available online at: http://theivybush.blogspot.co.uk/2005/02/spiritual-autism.html.

Marshall, George N. and Poling, David, *Schweitzer: A Biography* (Maryland: John Hopkins University Press, 2000).

Marshall, Mary, 'Becoming "Another": Nicodemus and His Relationships in the Fourth Gospel', in Ulrich Schmiedel and James Matarazzo (eds), *Dynamics of Difference: Christianity and Alterity: A Festschrift for Werner Jeanrond* (London: Bloomsbury, 2015), 33–40.

Mathew, Stephen and Pandian, Jeyaraj, 'Newer Insights to the Neurological Diseases among Biblical Characters of Old Testament', *Annals of Indian Academy of Neurology*, Vol. 13, No. 3 (2010), 164–6.

Mattila, Talvikki, *Citizens of the Kingdom: Followers in Matthew from a Feminist Perspective* (Helsinki: Finnish Exegetical Society, 2002).

Maxwell, Claire and Aggleton, Peter, 'Introduction', in Claire Maxwell and Peter Aggleton (eds), *Privilege, Agency and Affect: Understanding the Production and Effects of Action* (Basingstoke: Palgrave Macmillan, 2013) 1–11.

McDaniel, Jacqueline, *'Madness' in Exile Literature: Insanity as a Byproduct of Subjugation and Manipulation in Bessie Head's A Question of Power*, Seton Hall University Dissertations and Theses (ETDs). (2011).

McGeer, Victoria, 'The Thought and Talk of Individuals with Autism: Reflections on Ian Hacking', *Metaphilosophy*, Vol. 40, No. 3-4 (2009), 26–1068.

McGinty, Emma, 'Mental Illness and the Media', in Samuel J. Rosenberg, *Community Mental Health: Challenges for the 21st Century* (New York: Routledge, 2018), 178–99.

McGrath, James, 'Autistic Criticism: An Autistic Reading of BBC1's The Syndicate (2015) and the Cultural State of Asperger Syndrome'. Available online at: http://www.rowmaninternational.com/cultural-studies/autistic-criticism-an-autistic-reading-of-bbc1s-the-syndicate-2015-and-the-cultural-state-of-asperger-syndrome.

McGrath, James, 'Independent Scholars' Patheos.com (2014). Available online at: http://www.patheos.com/blogs/religionprof/2014/12/independent-scholars.html.

McGuire, Anne, 'Representing Autism: A Sociological Examination of Autism Advocacy', *Atlantis*, Vol. 35, No. 2 (2011), 62–71, 62. Available online at http://journals.msvu.ca/index.php/atlantis/article/viewFile/918/9143.

McLean, B. H., *Biblical Interpretation and Philosophical Hermeneutics* (Cambridge: Cambridge University Press, 2012).

McManus, Robert M. and Perruci, Gamaliel, *Understanding Leadership: An Arts and Humanities Perspective* (London: Routledge, 2015).

McNabb, Jonathan, 'I Dont Want to Be a Pioneer I Just Want to Be Me'. Available online at: http://archive.autistics.org/library/nopioneer.html.

Mcruer, Robert, *Crip Theory: Cultural Signs of Queerness and Disability* (New York: New York University Press, 2006).

McWade, Brigit, Milton, Damian and Beresford, Peter, 'Mad Studies and Neurodiversity: A Dialogue', *Disability & Society*, Vol. 30, No. 2 (2015), 305–309. Available online at: http://dx.doi.org/10.1080/09687599.2014.1000512.

Meeks, Wayne, 'The Man from Heaven in Johannine Sectarianism', *Journal of Biblical Literature*, Vol. 41 (1972), 44–72.

Meerai, Sonia, Abdilllahi, Idil and Poole, Jennifer, 'An Introduction to Anti-Black Sanism', *Intersectionalities*, Vol. 5 (2016), 18–35.

Meggitt, Justin, 'The Historical Jesus and Healing: Jesus' Miracles in Psychosocial Context', in Fraser Watts (ed.), *Spiritual Healing: Scientific and Religious Perspectives* (Cambridge: Cambridge University Press, 2011), 17–43.

Meggitt, Justin J., 'The Madness of King Jesus: Why Was Jesus Put to Death, but His Followers Were Not?', *JSNT*, Vol. 29, No. 4 (2007), 379–413.

Memmot, Ann, 'Enabling Church 2014 – Presentation Slides', Torch Trust. Available online at: http://churchesforall.org.uk/wp-content/uploads/2014/04/Enabling-Church-presentations-handout-17pt.pdf.

Menachel, Sophia, 'Dogs: God's Worst Enemies?' *Society and Animals*, Vol. 5, No. 1 (1997), 23–44.

Meyerding, J., 'Thoughts on Finding Myself Differently Brained' (1998), No pages. Available online at: http://mjane.zolaweb.com/diff.html.

Mieszkowski, Sylvia, Smith, Joy and de Valck, Marijke, 'Sonic Interventions', *Journal of International Women's Studies*, Vol. 2 (2000), 11–12.

Miller, John, *Jesus at Thirty: A Psychological and Historical Portrait* (Minneapolis: Fortress Press, 1997).

Mills, James, *Madness, Cannabis and Colonialism: The Native Only Lunatic Asylums of British India 1857–1900* (London: Palgrave Macmillan, 2000).

Mitchell, David and Snyder, Sharon, *Narrative Prosthetics: Disability and the Dependencies of Discourse* (Michigan: University of Michigan Press, 2000).

Mitchell, Don, *Cultural Geography: A Critical Introduction* (Oxford: Blackwell Publishing, 2000).

Mitchell, Margaret Mary, *The Heavenly Trumpet: John Chrysostom and the Art of Pauline Interpretation* (Louisville: Westminster John Knox, 2002).

Moncrieff, Joanna, 'Neoliberalism and Psychiatry: A Marriage of Convenience', in Carl I. Cohen and Sami Timimi (eds), *Liberatory Psychiatry: Philosophy, Politics and Mental Health* (Cambridge: Cambridge University Press, 2008), 235–55.

Monroe, Russell R., *Creative Brainstorms: The Relationship between Madness and Genius* (New Hampshire: Irvington Publishers, 2002).

Moore, Stephen, *God's Gym: Divine Male Bodies of the Bible* (New York: Routledge, 1996).

Moosavinia, Sayyed Rahim, 'Janus-Faced Madness in Bessie Head's *A Question of Power*', *Journal of Research in Applied Linguistics*, Vol. 7, No. 2 (2012), 135–50.

Morgan, Alastair, Felton, Anne, Fulford, Bill, Kalathil, Jayasree and Stacey, Gemma, *Values and Ethics in Mental Health: An Exploration for Practice* (London: Palgrave, 2015).

Morrison, Blake, 'The Reading Cure', *Guardian*, 5 January 2008. Available online at: http://www.theguardian.com/books/2008/jan/05/fiction.scienceandnature.

Moss, Candida and Schipper, Jeremy (eds), *Disability Studies and Biblical Literature* (New York: Palgrave Macmillan, 2011).

Muhammed, Louwai, 'A Retrospective Diagnosis of Epilepsy in Three Historical Figures: St Paul, Joan of Arc and Socrates', *Journal of Medical Biography*, Vol. 21, No. 4 (2013), 208–11.

Mukhopadhyay, Tito Rajarshi, *The Mind Tree* (New York: Arcade Publishing, 2003).

Mullins, Terence Y., 'Paul's Thorn in the Flesh', *Journal of Biblical Literature*, Vol. 76, No. 4 (1957), 299–303.

Murray, Evan D., Cunningham, Miles G. and Price, Bruce H., 'The Role of Psychotic Disorders in Religious History Considered', *Journal of Neuropsychiatry Clinical Neuroscience*, Vol. 24, No. 4 (2012). Available online at: http://neuro.psychiatryonline.org.

Murray, Stuart, 'Autism and the Contemporary Sentimental: Fiction and the Narrative Fascination of the Present', *Literature and Medicine*, Vol. 25, No. 1 (2006), 24–45.

Murray, Stuart, 'Autism Functions/The Function of Autism', in *Disability Studies Quarterly*, Vol. 30, No. 1 (2010), no pages. Available online at: http://dsq-sds.org/article/view/1048.

Murray, Stuart, *Representing Autism: Culture, Narrative, Fascination* (Liverpool: Liverpool University Press, 2008).

Nanos, Mark, 'Paul's Reversal of Jews Calling Gentiles "Dogs" (Philippians 3:2): 1600 Years of an Ideological Tale Wagging an Exegetical Dog?', Blog Post (2007). Available online at: http://www.marknanos.com/Phil3Dogs-Reverse-6-27-07.pdf.

Nelavala, Surekha, *Liberation beyond Borders: Dalit Feminist Hermeneutics and Four Gospel Women* (Lambert Academic Publishing, 2009).

Neufeld, Dietmar, *Mockery and Secretism in the Social World of Mark's Gospel* (London: Bloomsbury T&T Clark, 2014).

Neyrey, Jerome H., *An Ideology of Revolt: John's Christology in Social-Science Perspective* (Oregon: Wipf & Stock Publishing, 2007).

Nishida, Akemi, 'Neoliberal Academia and a Critique from Disability Studies', in Pamela Block, Devva Kasnitz, Akemi Nishida and Nick Pollard (eds), *Occupying Disability: Critical Approaches to Community, Justice, and Decolonising Disability* (New York: Springer, 2016), 159–74.

Oikkonen, Venla, 'Mad Embodiments: Female Corporeality and Insanity in Janet Frame's *Faces in the Water* and Sylvia Plath's *The Bell Jar*', *The Electronic Journal of the Department of English at the University of Helsinki*, Vol. 3 (2004). Available online at: http://blogs.helsinki.fi/hes-eng/volumes/volume-3-special-issue-on-literary-studies/mad-embodiments-female-corporeality-and-insanity-in-janet-frames-faces-in-the-water-and-sylvia-plaths-the-bell-jar-venla-oikkonen/.

Olaogun, Modupe, 'Slavery and Etiological Discourse in the Writing of Ama Ata Aidoo, Bessie Head, and Buchi Emecheta', *Research in African Literatures*, Vol. 33, No. 2 (2002), 171–93.

Olson, Karin, Young, Richard A. and Schultz, Izabela Z. (eds), *Handbook of Qualitative Health Research for Evidence-Based Practice* (New York: Springer, 2016).

Olyan, Saul, *Disability in the Hebrew Bible: Interpreting Mental and Physical Differences* (Cambridge: Cambridge University Press, 2008).

O'Rourke, Michael (ed.), *The Ashgate Research Companion to Queer Theory* (Farnham: Ashgate, 2009).

Ortega, Francisco, 'The Cerebral Subject and the Challenge of Neurodiversity', *BioSocieties*, Vol. 4 (2009), 425–45.

Osteen, Mark (ed.), *Autism and Representation* (New York: Routledge, 2008).

Osteen, Mark, 'Autism and Representation: A Comprehensive Introduction', in Mark Osteen (ed.), *Autism and Representation* (London: Routledge, 2010), 1–48.

Oyebode, Femi, *Sims' Symptoms in the Mind: An Introduction to Descriptive Psychopathology* (Exeter: Elsevier Limited, 2008).

Padilla, Raymond V. and Chaivez, Rudolfo Chdivez, *The Leaning Ivory Tower: Latino Professors in American Universities* (Albany: State University of New York Press, 1995).

Palmer, Earl F., *Integrity: A Commentary on the Book of Philippians* (Vancouver: Regent College Publishing, 1992).

Papacostas, Savvas, *Madness and Leadership: From Antiquity to the New Common Era* (Northampton: Edward Elgar Publishing, 2015).

Park, Bert Edward, *Ailing, Aging, Addicted: Studies of Compromised Leadership* (Kentucky: University of Kentucky Press, 1993).

Park, Young-Ho, *Paul's Ekklesia as a Civic Assembly: Understanding the People of God in their Politico-Social World* (WUNT II, 393. Tübingen: Mohr Siebeck, 2015).

Parker, Ian, 'Psychology Politics Resistance: Theoretical Practice in Manchester', in Bonnie Bursto et al. (eds), *Psychiatry Disrupted* (Montreal: McGill-Queen's University Press, 2014), 52–64.

Parker, Ian, et al., *Deconstructing Psychopathology* (London: Sage Publications, 1995).

Parry, John and Drogin, Eric, *Criminal Mental Health and Disability Law, Evidence and Testimony* (Chicago: American Bar Association, 2007).

Parry, Robin, *Lamentations* (THOTC) (Cambridge: William Eerdmans Publishing Company, 2010).

Parsons, Mikeal C., *Acts: Paideia Commentaries on the New Testament* (Grand Rapids: Baker Academic, 2008).

Patton, Cheryl, 'Asoka and Paul: Transformations That Led to Effective Transformational Leadership', *Leadership and the Humanities* (2015), 133–44.

Pawelski, James and Moores, D. J., 'What Is the Eudaimonic Turn?', in James Pawelski and D. J. Moores (eds), *The Eudaimonic Turn: Well-Being in Literary Studies* (Madison: Fairleigh Dickinson University Press, 2013), 1–63.

Pawelski, James O., 'Today, Tomorrow, and the Day After Tomorrow: A Case Study for the Theology of Joy Project'. Available online at: http://faith.yale.edu/sites/default/files/pawelski_today_tomorrow_and_the_day_after_tomorrow.pdf.

Pearse, Adetokunbo, 'Apartheid and Madness: Bessie Head's, A Question of Power', *Kunapipi*, Vol. 5, No. 2 (1983), 81–98, 83. Available online at: http://ro.uow.edu.au/kunapipi/vol5/iss2/9.

Perlin, Michael, 'You Have Discussed Lepers and Crooks: Sanism in Clinical Teaching', *Clinical Law Review*, Vol. 9 (2003), 683–704.

Peters, Theo and Gillberg, Chris, *Autism: Medical and Educational Aspects* (New Jersey: Wiley, 1999).

Peterson, David, *The Acts of the Apostles* (Grand Rapids: Eerdmans, 2009).

Phillips, Maggi, 'Storytellers, Shamans and Clowns: Postcolonial Engagement with the Supra-human in the Novels of R. K. Narayan, Nuriddin Farah, Bessie Head, Ben Okri and Salman Rushdie', PhD Thesis, Northern Territory University (1996).

Pierer, Heinrich V. and Oetinger, Bolko V., *A Passion for Ideas: How Innovators Create the New and Shape Our World* (Indiana: Purdue University Press, 2001).

Pilch, John, *Healing in the New Testament: Insights from Medical Anthropology* (Minneapolis: Fortress Press, 2000).

Pilgrim, David, *Understanding Mental Health: A Critical Realist Exploration* (London: Routledge, 2014).

Pinsent, Andrew, 'Wisdom and Evil', in Paul K. Moser and Michael T. Mcfall (eds), *The Wisdom of the Christian Faith* (Cambridge: Cambridge University Press, 2013), 99–120.

Pitts, Victoria, *In the Flesh: The Cultural Politics of Body Modification* (New York: Palgrave Macmillan Press, 2003).

Pollock, Sheldon, *The Language of the Gods in the World of Men: Sanskrit, Culture, and Power in Premodern India* (California: University of California Press, 2009).

Poole, Jennifer M., Jivraj, Tania, Arslanian, Araxi, Bellows, Kristen, Chiasson, Sheila, Hakimy, Husnia, Pasini, Jessica and Reid, Jenna, 'Sanism: Mental Health and Social Work/Education', *Intersectionalities: A Global Journal of Social Work Analysis, Research, Polity, and Practice*, Vol. 1 (2012). Available online at: http://journals.library.mun.ca/ojs/index.php/IJ/article/view/348.

Poole, Jennifer and Ward, Jennifer, 'Breaking Open the Bone: Storying, Sanism and Mad Grief', in Brenda LeFrançois et al. (eds), *Mad Matters* (Ontario: Canadian Scholars Press, 2013), 94–104.

Potkay, Adam, 'Foreword', in James Pawelski and D. J. Moores (eds), *The Eudaimonic Turn: Well-Being in Literary Studies* (Madison: Fairleigh Dickinson University Press, 2013), xi–xiv.

Price, Margaret, 'Assaults on the Ivory Tower', Lecture at Leeds University (2008). Available online at: http://pf7d7vi404s1dxh27mla5569.wpengine.netdna-cdn.com/files/library/price-Leeds-talk.pdf.

Price, Margaret, *Mad at School: Rhetorics of Mental Disability in Academic Life* (Michigan: University of Michigan Press, 2011).

Prince-Hughes, Dawn, *Songs of the Gorilla Nation: My Journey through Autism* (New York: Three Rivers, 2004).

Prothero, Stephen, *American Jesus: How the Son of God Became a National Icon* (New York: Farrar, Straus and Giroux, 2003).

Pryal, Katie Rose Guest, 'The Creativity Mystique and the Rhetoric of Mood Disorders', *Disability Studies Quarterly*, Vol. 31, No. 3 (2011), no pages. Available online at: http://dsq-sds.org/article/view/1671/1600.

Puar, Jasbir, 'Queer Times, Queer Assemblages', *Social Text*, Vol. 23 (2005), 121–39.

Puar, Jasbir, 'Rethinking Homonationalism', *International Journal of Middle East Studies*, Vol. 45 (2013), 336–9.

Rappolt, Mark, 'Eva Kot'átková', *Art Review Asia*. Available online at: http://artreview.com/features/april_2016_feature_eva_kotatkova/, no pages.

Read, John, 'A History of Madness', in John Read, Loren R. Mosher and Richard P. Bentall (eds), *Models of Madness: Psychological, Social and Biological Approaches to Schizophrenia* (Hove: Psychology Press, 2004), 9–20.

Renz, Gabi, 'Nicodemus: An Ambiguous Disciple? A Narrative Sensitive Investigation', in John Lierman (ed.), *Challenging Perspectives on the Gospel of John* (Tübingen: Mohr Siebeck, 2006), 255–82.

Revsbech, Rasmus, Mortensen, Erik Lykke, Owen, Gareth, Nordgaard, Julie, Jansson, Lennart, Sæbye, Ditte, Flensborg-Madsen, Trine and Parnas, Josef, 'Exploring Rationality in Schizophrenia', *British Journal of Psychiatry* (2015), 98–103.

Reyes, Pedro, 'Bomb: Artists in Conversation Javier Téllez' (2010). Available online at: http://bombmagazine.org/article/3379/javier-t-llez.

Richter, Amy, *Enoch and the Gospel of Matthew* (Oregon: Pickwick Publications, 2012).

Robbins, Vernon K., *The Invention of Christian Discourse: From Wisdom to Apocalyptic* (Blandford Forum: Deo Publishing, 2008).

Robinson, Andrew, *Genius and Madness: A Very Short Introduction* (Oxford: Oxford University Press, 2011).

Rockenbach, Barbara and Mendina, Tom (eds), *Ethics and Electronic Information: A Festschrift for Stephen Almagno* (North Carolina: McFarland and Co, 2002).

Rollins, Wayne, *Soul and Psyche: The Bible in Psychological Perspective* (Minneapolis: Fortress Press, 1999).

Rose, Irene, 'Review of Stuart Murray, Autism and the Contemporary Sentimental: Fiction and the Narrative Fascination of the Present', *Disability Studies Quarterly*, Vol. 30, No. 1 (2010). Available online at: http://dsqsds.org/article/view/1072/1251.

Rosenthal, Seth A. and Pittinsky, Todd L., 'Narcissistic Leadership', *The Leadership Quarterly*, Vol. 17 (2006), 617–33.

Rowe, Dorothy, *Depression: The Way Out of Your Prison* (New York: Routledge, 2003).

Rudd, Betty, *Introducing Psychopathology* (London: Sage, 2014).

Rudd, Steve, 'Bedlam: A Madhouse by Any Other Name Is Still a Jail!' Available online at: http://www.bible.ca/psychiatry/psychiatry-history-bedlam-bethlem-bethlehem.htm.

Russell, Ronald, 'Redemptive Suffering and Paul's Thorn in the Flesh', *JETS*, Vol. 39, No. 4 (1996), 559–70. Available online at: http://www.etsjets.org/files/JETS-PDFs/39/39-4/39-4-pp559-570_JETS.pdf.

Russo, Jasna and Beresford, Peter, 'Between Exclusion and Colonisation: Seeking a Place for Mad People's Knowledge in Academia', *Disability and Society*, Vol. 30 (2015), 153–7.

Rutis, Mari, *The Ethics of Opting Out: Queer Theory's Defiant Subjects* (New York: Columbia University Press, 2017).

Ryan, R. M. and Deci, E. L., 'On Happiness and Human Potentials: A Review of Research on Hedonic and Eudaimonic Well-Being', *Annual Review of Psychology*, Vol. 52 (2001), 141–66.

Ryken, Leland, Wilhoit, James C. and Longman III, Tremper, 'Madness', in Leland Ryken, James C. Wilhoit and Tremper Longman III (eds), *Dictionary of Biblical Imagery* (Downers Grove, IL: IVP, 1998), 524.

Ryland, Howard, 'New Wellcome Exhibition Invites You Into Bedlam'. Available online at: http://londonist.com/2016/09/bedlam-the-inside-story.

Ryskamp, Dani Alexis, '"Neurodiversity's Lingua Franca?": *The Wild Iris*, *Autobiography of Red*, and the Breakdown of Cognitive Barriers through Poetic Language', *The Hilltop Review*, Vol. 7 (2014). Available online at: http://scholarworks.wmich.edu/hilltopreview/vol7/iss1/5 2014.

Sacks, Oliver, *Anthropologist on Mars* (New York: Vintage Books, 1995).

Sadler, Philip, *Leadership* (London: Kogan Page Publishers, 2003).

Sanchez-Blake, Elvira and Kanost, Laura, *Latin American Women and the Literature of Madness: Narratives at the Crossroads of Gender, Politics and the Mind* (North Carolina: McFarland and Co, 2015).

Sanders, J. Oswald, *Dynamic Spiritual Leadership: Leading Like Paul* (Grand Rapids: Discovery House Publishers, 1999).

Sass, Louis, 'Civilized Madness: Schizophrenia, Self-Consciousness and the Modern Mind', *History of the Human Sciences*, Vol. 7 (1994), 83–120.

Sassower, Raphael, *A Sanctuary of Their Own: Intellectual Refugees in the Academy* (Lanham: Rowman and Littlefield, 2000).

Savarese, Ralph, 'More Than a Thing to Ignore: An Interview with Tito Rajarshi Mukhopadhyay', *Disability Studies Quarterly*, Vol. 30 (2010), no pages. Available online at: http://dsqsds.org/article/view/1056/1235.

Savarese, Ralph, 'Parent & Sibling Roundtable: Neurodiversity and Caregiving', *Disability Studies Quarterly*, Vol. 30, No. 1 (2010), no pages. Available online at http://dsq-sds.org/article/view/1061/1236.

Savarese, Ralph, 'Toward a Postcolonial Neurology: Autism, Tito Mukhopadhyay, and a New Geo-poetics of the Body', *Journal of Literary & Cultural Disability Studies*, Vol. 4 (2010), 273–89.

Savarese, Ralph, 'What Some Autistics Can Teach Us about Poetry: A Neurocosmopolitan Approach', in Lisa Zunshine (ed.), *The Oxford Handbook of Cognitive Literary Studies* (Oxford: Oxford University Press, 2015), 393–417.

Savarese, Ralph and Savarese, Emily, '"The Superior Half of Speaking": An Introduction', *Disability Studies Quarterly*, Vol. 30 (2010). Available online at: http://dsq-sds.org/article/view/1062/1230.

Savarese, Ralph and Zunshine, Lisa, 'The Critic as Neurocosmopolite; Or, What Cognitive Approaches to Literature Can Learn from Disability Studies: Lisa Zunshine in Conversation with Ralph James Savarese', *Narrative*, Vol. 22 (2014), 17–44.

Sawyer, Keith, 'The Western Cultural Model of Creativity: It's Influence on Intellectual Property Law', *Notre Dame Law Review* (2011), 2053–54.

Schenk, Joshua Wolf, *Lincoln's Melancholy: How Depression Challenged a President and Fueled His Greatness* (Boston: Mariner Books, 2006).

Scheper-Hughes, N., *Death without Weeping: The Violence of Everyday Life in Brazil* (Berkeley: University of California Press, 1992).

Scheslinger, Judith, *The Insanity Hoax: Exposing the Myth of the Mad Genius* (New York: Shrinktunes Media, 2012).

Schlichter, Annette, 'Do Voices Matter? Vocality, Materiality, Gender Performativity', *Body & Society*, Vol. 17, No. 1 (2011), 31–52.

Schlimm, Matthew Richard, 'From Fratricide to Forgiveness: The Ethics of Anger in Genesis', PhD Thesis, Duke University (2008). Available online at: http://dukespace.lib.duke.edu/dspace/bitstream/handle/10161/890/D_Schlimm_Matthew_a_200812.pdf?sequence=1.

Schumm, Darla, 'A Review of Jesus the Village Psychiatrist', *Journal of Religion, Disability and Health*, Vol. 14 (2010), 419–21.

Schutz, William Todd, *Handbook of Psychobiography* (Oxford: Oxford University Press, 2005).
Schweitzer, Albert, *The Psychiatric Study of Jesus: Exposition and Criticism* (Whitefish: Literary Licensing, 2011 [German original 1913]).
Schweitzer, Albert, *The Quest of the Historical Jesus*, trans. W. Montgomery (Mineola: Dover Publications, 2005 [German original 1906]).
Scott, Ian W., *Paul's Way of Knowing: Story, Experience, and the Spirit* (Grand Rapids: Baker Academic, 2008).
Scull, Andrew, *The Insanity of Place/The Place of Insanity* (London: Routledge, 2006).
Scull, Andrew, *Museums of Madness* (London: Allen Lane, 1979).
Segeral, Nathalie, 'Reclaimed Experience: Gendering Trauma in Slavery, Holocaust, and Madness Narratives', UCLA Electronic Theses and Dissertations, PhD, French & Francophone Studies (2012). Available online at: http://escholarship.org/uc/item/3xw6t98t.
Seligman M. and Csikszentmihalyi, M., 'Positive Psychology: An Introduction', *American Psychologist*, Vol. 55 (2000), 5–14.
Senior, Donald, *The Passion of Jesus in the Gospel of Luke* (Collegeville: Liturgical Press, 1989).
Shantz, Colleen, '"I Have Learned to be Content?" Happiness According to St Paul', in Brent Strawn (ed.), *The Bible and the Pursuit of Happiness: What the Old and New Testaments Teach Us about the Good Life* (Oxford: Oxford University Press, 2012), 187–202.
Shantz, Colleen, *Paul in Ecstasy: The Neurobiology of Paul's Life and Thought* (Cambridge: Cambridge University Press, 2009).
Shapin, Steven, 'The Ivory Tower: The History of a Figure of Speech and Its Cultural Uses', *British Journal for the History of Science*, Vol. 45 (2012), 1–27.
Shaughnessy, Nicola, 'Imagining Otherwise: Autism, Neuroaesthetics and Contemporary Performance', *Interdisciplinary Science Reviews*, Vol. 38, No. 4 (2013), 321–34.
Sheppard, Beth M., *The Craft of History and the Study of the New Testament* RBS 60 (Atlanta: Society of Biblical Literature, 2012).
Shillington, V. George, *An Introduction to the Study of Luke-Acts* (London: T&T Clark, 2006).
Shoemaker, Pamela J. and Vos, Timothy, *Gatekeeping Theory* (New York: Routledge, 2009).
Simonton, Dean Keith, *Genius, Creativity, and Leadership: Historiometric Inquiries* (Cambridge: Harvard University Press, 2013).
Singh, Anita, 'Mark Haddon – Don't Use Curious Incident as an Autism Textbook', *The Telegraph*, 1 June 2015. Available online at: http://www.telegraph.co.uk/culture/culturenews/9311242/Mark-Haddon-dont-use-Curious-Incident…as-an-autism-textbook.html.
Skinner, Christopher, *John and Thomas: Gospels in Conflict? A Study in Johannine Characterization* (Oregon: Pickwick Publications, 2009).
Skinner, Christopher, *Reading John* (Oregon: Cascade Books, 2015).
Slattery, Dennis Patrick, *The Wounded Body: Remembering the Markings of Flesh* (New York: SUNY Press, 1999).
Smith, Mitzi J., *The Literary Construction of the Other in the Acts of the Apostles: Charismatics, the Jews and Women* (Cambridge: James Clarke, 2012).
Smith, Morton, 'Psychiatric Practice and Christian Dogma', *Journal of Pastoral Care*, Vol. 3 (1949), 12–20.
Smith, R. C., *Society and Social Pathology: A Framework for Progress* (New York: Springer International Publishing, 2017).

Smith, Rachel Greenwald, *Affect and American Literature in the Age of Neoliberalism* (Cambridge: Cambridge University Press, 2015).
Soja, Edward, *Thirdspace: Journeys to Los Angeles and Other Real-and-Imagined Places* (Oxford: Oxford University Press, 1996).
Sorensen, Eric, *Possession and Exorcism in the New Testament and Early Christianity* (Tubingen: Mohr Siebeck, 2002).
Spadler, Helen and Anderson, Jill, 'Unreasonable Adjustments? Applying Disability Policy to Madness and Distress', in Helen Spadler, Jill Anderson and Bob Sapey (eds), *Madness, Distress and the Politics of Disablement* (Bristol: Policy Press, 2015), 13–25.
Spandler, Helen and Barker, Meg-John, 'Mad and Queer Studies: Interconnections and Tensions', a guest blog post. Available online at: https://madstudies2014.wordpress.com/.
Spencer, F. Scott, 'Out of Mind, Out of Voice: Slave Girls and Prophetic Daughters in Luke-Acts', *Biblical Interpretation*, Vol. 7, No. 2 (1999), 133–55.
Spencer, Richard, 'Madness', in David Noel Freedman and Allen C. Myers (eds), *Eerdmans Dictionary of the Bible* (Grand Rapids: William Eerdmans, 2000), 843.
Squire, Michael, *Image and Text in Graeco-Roman Antiquity* (Cambridge: Cambridge University Press, 2009).
Starkman, Mel, 'The Movement', in Brenda LeFrançois et al. (eds), *Mad Matters* (Ontario: Canadian Scholars Press, 2013), 27–37.
Stecker, Christian, 'Jesus and the Demoniacs', in Wolfgang Stegemann, Bruce Malina and Gerd Theissen (eds), *The Social Setting of Jesus and the Gospels* (Minneapolis: Fortress Press, 2002), 117–34.
Stockdill, Brett and Danico, Mary Yu (eds), *Transforming the Ivory Tower: Challenging Racism, Sexism, and Homophobia in the Academy* (Hawaii: University of Hawaii Press, 2012).
Storr, Anthony, *Churchill's Black Dog* (New York City: Harper Collins, 2011).
Straus, Joseph, 'Autism as Culture', in Lennard J. Davis (ed.), *The Disability Studies Reader* (New York: Routledge, 2013), 460–84.
Straus, Joseph, 'Autism and Postwar Serialism as Neurodiverse Forms of Cultural Modernism', in Blake Howe, Stephanie Jensen-Moulton, Neil Lerner, Joseph Straus (eds), *The Oxford Handbook of Music and Disability Studies* (Oxford: Oxford University Press, 2016), 684–706.
Strawn, Brent (ed.), *The Bible and the Pursuit of Happiness: What the Old and New Testaments Teach Us about the Good Life* (Oxford: Oxford University Press, 2012).
Strawn, Brent, 'The Triumph of Life: Towards a Biblical Theology of Happiness', in Brent Strawn (ed.), *The Bible and the Pursuit of Happiness: What the Old and New Testaments Teach Us about the Good Life* (Oxford: Oxford University Press, 2012), 287–322.
Stumm, Sophie von and Furnham, Adrian, *The Wiley-Blackwell Handbook of Individual Differences* (New Jersey: Wiley Blackwell, 2011).
Sussman, Adrienne, 'Mental Illness and Creativity: A Neurological View of the "Tortured Artist"', *Stanford Journal of Neuroscience*, Vol. 1 (2007), 21–4.
Sweat, Laura, *The Theological Role of Paradox in the Gospel of Mark* (London: Bloomsbury T&T Clark, 2013).
Swinton, John, 'What Does Autistic Love Look Like? Reflections on Autistic Love', in Hans S. Reinders (ed.), *Authenticity and Community: Essays in Honor of Herman P. Meininger* (Antwerpen: Garant, 2011), 141–56.

Szasz, Thomas, *The Manufacture of Madness: A Comparative Study of the Inquisition and the Mental Health Movement* (Syracuse: Syracuse University Press, 1970).
Tam, Louise, 'Whither Indigenizing the Mad Movement? Theorizing the Social Relations of Race and Madness Through Conviviality', in Brenda LeFrançois et al. (eds), *Mad Matters* (Ontario: Canadian Scholars Press, 2013), 281–97.
Tang, Lynn, *Recovery, Mental Health and Inequality* (London: Routledge, 2017).
Tantam, Digby, *Autism Spectrum Disorders through the Life Span* (London: Jessica Kingsley Publishers, 2011).
Teather, Elizabeth Kenworthy, *Embodied Geographies* (London: Routledge, 1999).
Thibault, Ronnie, 'A Performative Space for Autistic Embodiment Autistic Aesthetic in Disability Theater' (2012). Available online at: https://sites.google.com/a/uw.edu/thibault-academic-portfolio/bculst501-cultural-studies-as-collaboration-winter-2013/collapsing-boundaries-of-autistic-embodiment-rsvp-cycles-and-the-social-sphere/a-space-for-autistic-embodiment-in-disability-theater.
Thiemann, Anna and Kern-Stahler, Annette, 'Metaphor and (Dis)Embodiment: Inside the Autistic Mind', *REAL: Yearbook of Research in English and American Literature* 24 (2008): 215–31.
Thomas, John Christopher, *The Devil, Disease and Deliverance: Origins of Illness in New Testament Thought* (Sheffield: Sheffield Academic Press, 1998).
Thrall, Margaret, *ICC Commentary, II Corinthians 8–13* (London: T&T Clark, 2000).
Tierney, Katrina Kathleen, 'Resilience and the Neoliberal Project: Discourses, Critiques, Practices', *American Behavioural Scientist*, Vol. 59, No. 10 (2015), 1327–42.
Toensing, Holly, 'Living among the Tombs: Society Mental Illness and Self-Destruction in Mark 5:1–20', in Hector Avalos, Sarah Melcher and Jeremy Schipper (eds), *This Abled Body: Rethinking Disabilities in Biblical Studies* (Atlanta: Society of Biblical Literature, 2007), 131–43.
Tofighi, Fatima, *Paul's Letters and the Construction of the European Self* (New York: Bloomsbury T&T Clark, 2017).
Tucker, Margaret E., '"A Nice-Time Girl" Strikes Back: An Essay on Bessie Head's "A Question of Power"', *Research in African Literatures*, Vol. 19, No. 2 (1988), 170–81.
Tuell, Steven Shawn, 'Should Ezekiel go to Rehab?: The Method to Ezekiel's "Madness"', *Perspectives in Religious Studies*, Vol. 36 (2009), 289–302.
Twelftree, Graham, *In the Name of Jesus: Exorcism among Early Christians* (Grand Rapids: Baker Academic, 2007).
Twelftree, Graham, *Jesus the Miracle Worker: A Historical and Theological Study* (Downers Grove, IL: Intervarsity Press, 1999).
Ussher, Jane, *The Madness of Women: Myth and Experience* (London: Routledge, 2011).
Ussher, Jane, *Women's Madness: Misogony or Mental Illness?* (Amherst: University of Massachusetts Press, 1992).
van Aarde, Andries, 'Fatherlessness in First-Century Mediterranean Culture: The Historical Jesus Seen from the Perspective of Cross-Cultural Anthropology and Cultural Psychology', *HTS*, Vol. 55, No. 1(1999), 97–119, 97. Available online at: http://www.hts.org.za/index.php/HTS/article/viewFile/1526/2819.
van Aarde, Andries, *Fatherless in Galilee: Jesus as Child of God* (Atlanta: Trinity Press International, 2001).
Van Os, Bas, *Psychological Analysis and the Historical Jesus* (London: T&T Clark, 2011).
Venturino, Steven J., *The Complete Idiot's Guide to Literary Theory and Criticism* (USA: Alpha, 2013).

Village, Andrew, 'Psychological Type Functions and Biblical Scholarship: An Empirical Enquiry among Members of the Society of Biblical Literature', *Mental Health, Religion & Culture*, Vol. 18, No. 7 (2015), 605–21.

Viusenco, Anca-Luisa, 'The Madness Narrative: Between the Literary, Therapeutic and the Political', *Romanian Journal of English Studies*, Vol. 10, No. 1 (2013). Available online at: http://www.degruyter.com/dg/viewarticle.fullcontentlink:pdfeventlink/$002fj$002frjes.2013.10.issue-1$002frjes-2013-0030$002frjes-2013-0030.pdf?t:ac=j$002frjes.2013.10.issue-1$002frjes-2013-0030$002frjes-2013-0030.xml.

Voronka, Jijian, 'Turning Mad Knowledge into Affective Labor: The Case of the Peer Support Worker', *American Quarterly*, Vol. 69 (2017), 333–8.

Wacquant, Loïc, *Punishing the Poor: The Neoliberal Government of Social Insecurity* (Durham: Duke University Press, 2009).

Wahl, Otto, *Media Madness: Public Images of Mental Illness* (New Brunswick: Rutgers University Press, 1995).

Walaskay, Paul, *Acts* (Louisville: Westminster John Knox, 1998).

Wald, C., *Hysteria, Trauma and Melancholia: Performative Maladies in Contemporary Anglophone Drama* (London: Palgrave Macmillan, 2007).

Walker, Nick, 'Neurocosmopolitanism'. Available online at: http://neurocosmopolitanism.com/neurodiversity-some-basic-terms-definitions/.

Waller, Alexis, 'Violent Spectacles and Public Feelings: Trauma and Affect in The Gospel of Mark and The Thunder: Perfect Mind', *Biblical Interpretation*, Vol. 22 (2014), 473–502.

Waltz, Mitzi, 'Metaphors of Autism, and Autism as Metaphor: An Exploration of Representation', Paper presented at the *Making Sense of Health and Disease, 2nd Global Conference*. Available online at: http://www.persons.org.uk/mso/hid/hid2/hid03s11a.htm.

Wang, Hui Kuan, 'Sense Perception and Testimony in the Gospel According to John', PhD Thesis, Durham University (2014). Available online at: http://etheses.dur.ac.uk/10844/1/Finall_Thesis_20141115.pdf?DDD32+.

Way, Niobe, *Every Day Courage: The Lives and Stories of Urban Teenagers* (New York: New York University Press, 1998).

Welborn, Laurence L., *Paul, the Fool of Christ: A Study in 1 Corinthians 1–4* (New York: Bloomsbury, 2005).

Wenzel, Marita, 'An Approach to Power Relations: Bessie Head and Luisa Valenzuela', *Literator*, Vol. 19, No. 1 (1998), 51–64.

White, Kimberly and Pike, Ryan, 'The Making and Marketing of Mental Health Literacy in Canada', in Brenda LeFrançois et al. (eds), *Mad Matters* (Ontario: Canadian Scholars Press, 2013), 239–64.

Whittington, Lee, et al., 'Legacy Leadership: The Leadership Wisdom of the Apostle Paul', *The Leadership Quarterly*, Vol. 16, No. 5 (2005), 749–70.

Williams, Jennifer, 'Re-membering Madness in Africana Women's Literature', Dissertation, Department of African and African American Studies (1998). Available online at: http://digitalcommons.auctr.edu/cgi/viewcontent.cgi?article=2195&context=dissertations.

Williams, Kathy, 'At the Expense of Women: Humor (?) in Acts 16: 14–40', in Athalya Brenner (ed.), *Are We Amused?: Humour about Women in the Biblical World* (London: T&T Clark, 2003).

Wolframe, PhebeAnn, 'The Madwoman in the Academy, or, Revealing the Invisible Straightjacket: Theorizing and Teaching Saneism and Sane Privilege', *Disability Studies*

Quarterly, Vol. 33, No. 1 (2013). Available online at: http://dsq-sds.org/article/view/3425/3200.

Wolframe, PhebeAnn, 'Reading through Madness: Counter-psychiatric Epistemologies and the Biopolitics of (In)sanity in Post-World War II Anglo- Atlantic Narratives', PhD Thesis, Mcmaster University (2014). Available online at: https://macsphere.mcmaster.ca/bitstream/11375/13900/1/fulltext.pdf.

Yacobi, Tamar, 'Fictive Beholders: How Ekphrasis Dramatizes Visual Perception', in Ellen Spolsky (ed.), *Iconotropism: Turning toward Pictures* (Pennsylvania: Bucknell University Press, 2004), 69–88.

Yla-Kapee, Annina, 'Telling Madness: Narrative, Diagnosis, Power and Literary Theory', PhD Thesis, University of Tampere (2014). Available online at: https://tampub.uta.fi/bitstream/handle/10024/96148/978-951-44-9557-1.pdf?sequence=1.

Yong, Amos, *Theology and Down Syndrome: Reimagining Disability in Late Modernity* (Waco: Baylor University Press, 2007).

Zinato, Susanna and Pes, Annalisa, 'Introduction', in Susanna Zinato and Annalisa Pes (eds), *Ex-centric Writing: Essays on Madness in Postcolonial Fiction* (Cambridge: Cambridge Scholars Publishing, 2013), 1–24.

Zunshine, Lisa, *Why We Read Fiction: Theory of Mind and the Novel* (Columbus: Ohio State University Press, 2006).

INDEX